Cambodia

a Lonely Planet travel survival kit

Chris Taylor   Tony Wheeler
Daniel Robinson

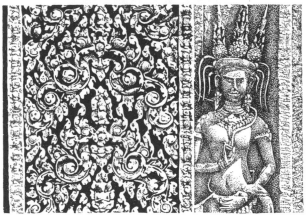

Cambodia

2nd edition

Published by
Lonely Planet Publications
Head Office: PO Box 617, Hawthorn, Vic 3122, Australia
Branches: 155 Filbert St, Suite 251, Oakland, CA 94607, USA
10 Barley Mow Passage, Chiswick, London W4 4PH, UK
71 bis rue du Cardinal Lemoine, 75005 Paris, France

Printed by
SNP Printing Pte Ltd, Singapore

Script Typeset by
Jason Roberts

Photographs by
Glenn Beanland
Mick Elmore
Chris Taylor
Tony Wheeler

Front cover: Monks in the galleries at Angkor Wat (Mick Elmore)

First Published
September 1992

This Edition
November 1996

National Library of Australia Cataloguing in Publication Data

Taylor, Chris
Cambodia

2nd ed.
Includes index.
ISBN 0 86442 447 7.

Cambodia - Guidebooks. I. Taylor, Chris. Cambodia.
II. Title (Series : Lonely Planet travel survival kit).

915.96044

text & maps © Lonely Planet 1996
photos © photographers as indicated 1996

Chris Taylor

Chris Taylor grew up in England and Australia. After stints in Tokyo and London punctuated by bouts of Asian travel, he settled down to a degree in English literature. Somewhere betweens Dickens and Conrad he fell under the spell of Chinese and ended up joining Lonely Planet to edit our phrasebook series. Chris has written or co-written guides to *Tibet, China, Japan, Malaysia* and *Tokyo*, and also wrote Lonely Planet's *Mandarin phrasebook*. He occasionally finds the time to write for anyone else who will publish his musings.

Tony Wheeler

Tony Wheeler was born in England but spent most of his youth overseas. He returned to England to do a university degree in engineering, worked as an automotive design engineer, returned to university to complete an MBA, then dropped out on the Asian overland trail with his wife Maureen. They've been travelling, writing and publishing guidebooks ever since, having set up Lonely Planet Publications in the mid-70s. Travel for the Wheelers is now considerably enlivened by their daughter Tashi and their son Kieran.

Daniel Robinson

Daniel was raised in the USA and Israel. He graduated from Princeton University with a BA in Near Eastern Studies. Daniel has travelled extensively in the Middle East and South, South-East and East Asia. He has also written a guide to Vietnam and chapters on France and Andorra for Lonely Planet.

From Chris Taylor

Lots of people ended up helping out on the Cambodia research trip. In Hong Kong, as always, Christine Jones of Phoenix Services organised my flights and Patrick Horgan put me up in his Happy Valley flat at short notice.

In Phnom Penh I have so many people to thank that I'm bound to miss a few. Advance apologies to anyone who's forgotten. First and foremost a big thank you to Khourn Meng Kry, who accompanied me as interpreter and guide on trips to Kompong Cham, Kompong Chhnang, Udong, Takeo and Sihanoukville, but who most of all took the hard work out of researching Phnom Penh.

Anthony and Kelly of the Phnom Penh FCC were helpful in introducing me to people and providing tips on dining out around town.

Thanks to everyone at the *Phnom Penh Post*, in particular Matthew Grainger for information on Battambang. Maja Wallengren of Reuters provided useful information on Rattanakiri, as did Claudia from the *Cambodia Daily*.

Martin Wall of the Australian embassy was helpful on issues of travel security in Cambodia, and also intervened to save me being evicted from a party at the ambassador's residence. Charles and Anthony Ainsworth, Craig Martin and Paul gave me the lowdown on nightlife in Phnom Penh and provided endless tips on things to do and restaurants to eat at. Bert of Bert's Books & Guesthouse was never at a loss for advice (all of it sound), and long-term resident of Bert's, Mark Lioi, pitched in with information on Kratie.

In Sihanoukville, thanks to Victor of Sam's Guesthouse and to Claude of Claude's Restaurant. In Siem Reap, Brian of the Landmine Studio was generous with insider's tips.

This book received no assistance from the Cambodian tourism authorities.

This Book

As researcher and writer for this book, Chris Taylor scrubbed the lichen off the first edition of Cambodia and provided an extensive update of the original work by Tony Wheeler and Daniel Robinson.

From the Publisher

This edition was pointed in the right direction by Greg Alford. Mic Looby was responsible for the indexing, editing and proofing, along with Christine Niven. Glenn Beanland was in charge of design, illustration and mapping. Thanks to Trudi Canavan for providing the fresh batch of illustrations, Jason Roberts for the Khmer language section and Sarah Langlet on work experience. Simon Bracken did the front cover design and Adam McCrow handled the back.

Thanks

Many thanks to the following travellers who cared enough to write and tell us about their experiences in Cambodia:

Martha Barkunstey, Felicity Beatty, David Boyall, Kai Broeer, Mary Buchalter, D Buck, Virginia Caldwell, Richard Cohan, A Crouch, Michele Delgado, Geoff Finch, Werner Funk, Bob Gibbons, P Groenendyh, E Halasz, Roland Hemming, Kenneth Jademo, Britt Jademo, Jeffrey Kaye, Jerry Kilker, Jeanne Kolb, Ilse Lamphere, Bavo Lauwaert, G Lorentzen, Jane Lowery, Phill Miller, M Maggot, Mark Moore, John Murphey, Alan Myren, Christoph Oelke, Karin Persson, Joona Pietarila, Mike Raship, Simon Robins, Jean Robinson, Laurence Rosoff, Ronald Rotunda, Rolf Schenker, Dr Gavin Scott, Richard Sterling, Anna St Helens, Laurent Tognazzi, Edward Tsuei, Thom van Every, Hugh Waters and Alexander Winter.

Warning & Request

Things change, prices go up, schedules change, good places go bad and bad ones go bankrupt – nothing stays the same. So if you find things better or worse, recently opened or long since closed, please write and tell us and help make the next edition better!

Your letters will be used to help update future editions and, where possible, important changes will also be included as an Update section in reprints.

All information is greatly appreciated, and the best letters will receive a free copy of the next edition, or any other Lonely Planet book of your choice.

Contents

Map Legend

BOUNDARIES

	International Boundary
	Regional Boundary

ROUTES

	Freeway
	Highway
	Major Road
	Unsealed Road or Track
	City Road
	City Street
	Railway
	Underground Railway
	Tram
	Walking Track
	Walking Tour
	Ferry Route
	Cable Car or Chairlift

AREA FEATURES

	Parks
	Built-Up Area
	Pedestrian Mall
	Market
	Cemetery
	Reef
	Beach or Desert
	Rocks

HYDROGRAPHIC FEATURES

	Coastline
	River, Creek
	Intermittent River or Creek
	Rapids, Waterfalls
	Lake, Intermittent Lake
	Canal
	Swamp

SYMBOLS

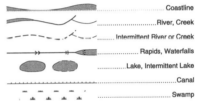

✪ CAPITAL		National Capital
◉ Capital		Regional Capital
CITY		Major City
● City		City
● Town		Town
● Village		Village
■ ▼		Place to Stay, Place to Eat
		Cafe, Pub or Bar
✉ ☎		Post Office, Telephone
❶ ⑤		Tourist Information, Bank
⊖ ℗		Transport, Parking
🏛 ⚑		Museum, Youth Hostel
Å		Caravan Park, Camping Ground
➕		Church, Cathedral
◙		Mosque, Synagogue
卍		Buddhist Temple, Hindu Temple
✪ ★		Hospital, Police Station

⊘ ℗		Embassy, Petrol Station
✈ ✝		Airport, Airfield
✿		Swimming Pool, Gardens
❖ 🐘		Shopping Centre, Zoo
🏞		Winery or Vineyard, Picnic Site
← A25		One Way Street, Route Number
🏛 👤		Stately Home, Monument
■		Castle, Tomb
⌂		Cave, Hut or Chalet
▲ ☼		Mountain or Hill, Lookout
🌴		Lighthouse, Shipwreck
)(◉		Pass, Spring
		Beach, Surf Beach
∴		Archaeological Site or Ruins
		Ancient or City Wall
		Cliff or Escarpment, Tunnel
		Railway Station

Introduction

For two decades, war and a vast communist-inspired 'experiment' removed Cambodia from the traveller's map. The very word Cambodia came to be associated with atrocities, poverty and refugees. The tragedy of it all belongs to the Cambodians themselves. But it has also been a great loss to travellers in Asia.

Cambodia lies at the heart of Indochina, bordered by Thailand to the west, Laos to the north and Vietnam to the east. It is a fascinating place that, despite its tiny size and its large, powerful neighbours, has managed to remain uniquely Khmer. Its cultural traditions predate those of Thailand, and unlike Vietnam, which was always influenced by China, its dominant influences stem from the Indian subcontinent.

Modern-day Cambodia is the successor-state of the mighty Khmer Empire, which during the Angkorian period (9th to 14th centuries) was the cultural heartland of South-East Asia. It ruled over much of what is now Vietnam, Laos and Thailand, and its legacy is one of the wonders of the world. The ruins of Angkor are in a category of their own. There is no other historical site in South-East Asia that matches the grandeur of Angkor. The traveller's first glimpse of Angkor Wat, which represents the full flowering of Khmer genius, is a breathtaking experience, matched only by sights such as the Potala Palace of Lhasa or the Forbidden City of Beijing.

The bad news is that the Cambodian civil war still limps along with no end in sight. The Khmer Rouge, whose brutal rule in the mid to late 1970s claimed some two to three million lives, have spurned political settlement and have retreated into the forests and hills. In recent years, the war has claimed the lives of seven foreign travellers.

The question on everyone's mind when visiting Cambodia is, not surprisingly, how safe is it? The answer depends on what you plan to do and where you plan to go. A visit

to Phnom Penh, its surrounding attractions and to Angkor need be no more dangerous than a trip to any of the countries surrounding Cambodia. Adventurous travel, on the other hand, is irresponsible. Those who attempt to travel by train, who take roads that are designated as having security risks, and who blaze new trails in Cambodia, put their own lives at risk and in doing so threaten Cambodia's slowly recovering tourist industry.

Cambodia has enormous potential as a travel destination, and already investors (largely Malaysian) are moving in with an eye to the day when the country's internal security problems are solved. There are unspoiled beaches and islands along the south-west coast of the country. The meandering Mekong

River holds the promise of boat trips through Cambodia, Laos and even into China. Access to Angkor, Cambodia's greatest tourist attraction, will hopefully soon be safely navigated via the vast Tonlé Sap Lake. In the north-east of the country are unexplored minority regions.

Finally there are the people. Cambodians have weathered years of bloodshed, poverty and political instability. Somehow they have come through the experience with smiles still intact. Admittedly Cambodia needs the money that tourism brings, but there is an air of genuine enthusiasm and warmth towards foreign visitors. Nobody comes away from Cambodia without a measure of admiration and affection for the inhabitants of this beautiful yet troubled country.

Facts about the Country

HISTORY
Early Beginnings
Cambodia came into being, so the legend goes, through the union of a princess and a foreigner. The foreigner was an Indian Brahman named Kaudinya. The princess was the daughter of a dragon king, or *naga*, who ruled over a watery place, as befitted a naga. One day, as Kaudinya sailed by, the princess paddled out in a boat to greet him. Kaudinya shot an arrow from his magic bow into her boat, causing the princess to fearfully agree to marriage. As a dowry, her father drank up the waters of his land and presented them to Kaudinya to rule over. The new kingdom was named Kambuja.

Like many legends, this one is historically opaque. But it does say something about the cultural forces that brought Cambodia into existence; in particular its relationship with its great subcontinental neighbour, India. Cambodia's religious, royal and written traditions stemmed from India and began to coalesce as a cultural tradition in their own right from around the 1st century AD.

Very little is known about prehistoric Cambodia. Evidence of cave dwellers has been found in the north-west of Cambodia. Carbon dating on pots found there show they were made around 4200 BC. But it is difficult to say whether there is a direct relationship between these cave-dwelling pot-makers and contemporary Khmers. Examinations of bones dating back to around 1500 BC, however, suggest that the people living in Cambodia at that time resembled Cambodians of today.

Archaeological evidence shows that Cambodians prior to 1000 BC lived in houses on stilts (as they still do today), and subsisted on a diet that included large quantities of fish and cultivated rice. Early Chinese records report that the Cambodians were 'ugly' and 'dark' and went about naked; a pinch of culturally chauvinistic salt is always required when reading the reports of imperial China concerning its 'barbarian' neighbours.

Indianisation & Funan
The early Indianisation of Cambodia probably occurred via trading settlements that sprang up from the 1st century AD on the coastline of what is now southern Vietnam. Such settlements served as ports of call for boats following the trading route from the Bay of Bengal to the southern provinces of China. The largest of these was known as Funan, close to contemporary Oc-Eo in Kien Giang Province of southern Vietnam.

Funan is a Chinese name, and it may be a transliteration of the ancient Khmer name for mountain: *bnam*. It is unknown what the local name was. This is telling. Although very little is known about Funan, much has been made of its importance as an early South-East Asian centre of power despite there being little evidence to support this.

It is most likely that between the 1st and 8th centuries Cambodia was a collection of small states, each with its own elites that sometimes strategically intermarried and sometimes went to war with each other. Funan was no doubt one of these states, and as a major sea port was undoubtedly pivotal in the transmission of Indian culture into the interior of Cambodia.

What historians do know about Funan, they have mostly gleaned from Chinese sources. These report that Funan period Cambodia (1st-6th centuries AD) embraced the worship of Shiva and Vishnu and at the same time Buddhism. The *lingam*, a phallic totem, appears to have been the focus of ritual and an emblem of kingly might, a feature that was to evolve further in the Angkorian cult of the god king. The people practised primitive irrigation which enabled the cultivation of rice, and they traded raw commodities such as spices with China and India.

Chenla
From the 6th century Funan's importance as a port declined, and Cambodia's population

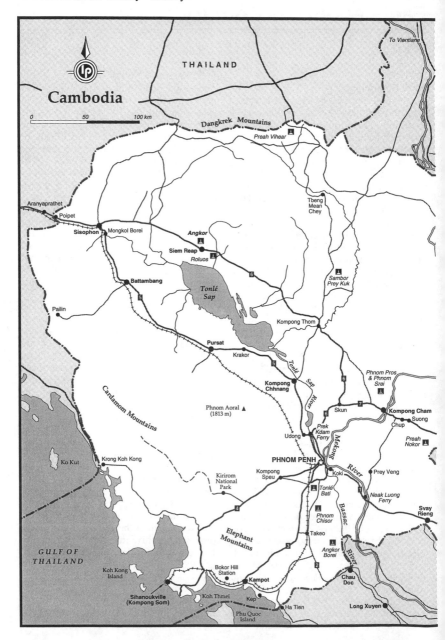

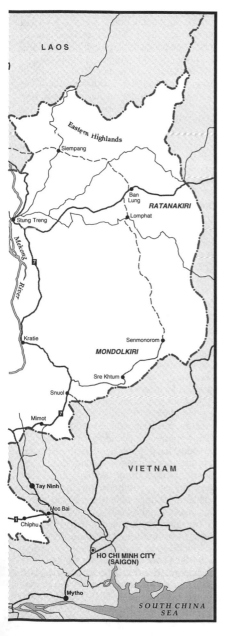

gradually concentrated along the Mekong and Tonlé Sap rivers (as is the case today). The move may be related to the development of wet-rice agriculture. From the 6th to the 8th centuries Cambodia was probably a collection of competing kingdoms, ruled by autocratic kings who legitimised their absolute rule through hierarchical social concepts borrowed from India.

This period is generally referred to as the Chenla. Again, as is the case with Funan, it is a Chinese term and there is little to support the idea that the Chenla was a unified kingdom that held sway over all Cambodia. Indeed, the Chinese themselves referred to the 'water Chenla' and the 'land Chenla', the former probably located in the Mekong Delta, the latter in the upper reaches of the Mekong River.

Still, the people of Cambodia were known at least to the Chinese, and gradually the country was becoming more cohesive. Before long the fractured kingdoms of Cambodia would merge to become the greatest kingdom of South-East Asia.

Angkorian Period

An inscription at Kulen, to the north of Angkor, reads that in the year 802 Jayavarman II participated in a ritual that proclaimed him a 'universal monarch', or a 'god king'. Who was Jayavarman II and what was he doing before this? It is thought he may have resided in the Shailendras court in Java as a young man. One of the first things he did when he returned to Cambodia was to hold a ritual that made it impossible for Java to control the lands of Cambodia. From this point, he brought the lands of Cambodia under his control through alliances, proclaiming himself king in the process.

Jayavarman II was the first of a long succession of kings who presided over the rise and fall of the South-East Asian empire that was to leave behind the stunning legacy of Angkor. The first records of the massive irrigation works that supported the population of Angkor begin in the reign of Indravarman (reigned 877-889). His rule also marks the beginning of Angkorian art with the building of temples in the Roluos area, notably the Bakong. His son, Yasovarman I (reigned 889-910), moved the royal court to Angkor proper, establishing a temple mountain on Phnom Bakheng.

By the turn of the 11th century, the kingdom of Angkor was losing control of its territories. Suryavarman I (1002-1049), a usurper, moved into the power vacuum and, like Jayavarman two centuries before, reunified the kingdom through war and alliances. He annexed the kingdom of Lopburi in Thailand and extended his control of Cambodia. A pattern was beginning to emerge which can be seen throughout the Angkor period: dislocation and turmoil, followed by reunification and further expansion under a powerful king. The most productive periods architecturally occurred after periods of turmoil, indicating that newly incumbent monarchs felt the need to celebrate and perhaps legitimise their rule with massive building projects.

From around 1066, Angkor was once again riven by conflict, becoming the focus of rival bids for power. It was not to be until 1112, with the accession of Suryavarman II that the kingdom was once again unified. Suryavarman embarked on another phase of expansion, waging wars in Vietnam and the region of southern Vietnam known as Champa. He also established links with China. But Suryavarman will mostly be remembered as the king who, in his devotion to the Hindu deity Vishnu, commissioned Angkor Wat.

Suryavarman II had brought Champa to heel and reduced it to vassal status. In 1177, however, the Chams struck back in a naval expedition up the Mekong and into the Tonlé Sap Lake. They took the city of Angkor by surprise and put its king to death. A year later a cousin of Suryavarman gathered forces about him and defeated the Chams in another naval battle. The new leader was crowned in 1181 as Jayavarman VII.

A devout follower of Mahayana Buddhism, Jayavarman VII built the city of Angkor Thom and many other monuments. Indeed most of the monuments visited by tourists in Angkor today were constructed during Jayavarman VII's reign. He also commissioned a vast array of public works. But as David Chandler points out in his *History of Cambodia*, Jayavarman VII is a figure of many contradictions. The bas reliefs of the Bayon, for example, depict him presiding over battles of terrible ferocity, while statues of the king show him in a meditative otherworldly aspect. His programme of temple construction and other public works were carried out in great haste, no doubt bringing enormous hardship to the labourers who provided the muscle.

Decline & Fall

Some scholars maintain that decline was hovering in the wings at the time Angkor Wat was built, when the Angkorian Empire was at the height of its remarkable productivity. There are indications that the irrigation network was overworked, and massive construction projects such as Angkor Wat and Angkor Thom no doubt put an enormous strain on the royal coffers and on the common people who subsidised them all in taxes and hard work. Certainly, after the reign of Jayavarman VII, temple construction effectively came to a halt, in large part because Jayavarman VII's public works quarried local sandstone into oblivion.

Another important aspect of this period was the decline of Cambodian political influence on the peripheries of its empire. The Thai kingdom of Ayudhya (Ayuthaya), on the other hand, grew in strength and made repeated incursions into Angkor, sacking the city in 1431. During this period, perhaps drawn by the opportunities for sea trade with China, the Khmer elite began to migrate to the area of Phnom Penh.

The next century and a half of Khmer history was dominated by confusing dynastic rivalries and almost continuous warfare with the Thais. Although the Khmers once pushed westward all the way to the Thai capital of Ayudhya (only to find it occupied by the Burmese), the Thais recovered and dealt a crushing blow to the Khmers by capturing their capital in 1594.

Shortly before the Khmer defeat of 1594, the Cambodian king, Satha, requested the assistance of the Spanish and Portuguese, who had recently become active in the region. In 1596 a Spanish expedition arrived in Cambodia to assist Satha only to find that he had been deposed by a usurper, Chung Prei. After a series of disagreements and the sacking of the Chinese quarter of Phnom Penh by the Spanish forces, the Spanish attacked the palace and killed Chung Prei. The Spanish then decided to return to Manila, but while marching through Laos, they changed their minds and returned to Phnom Penh, installing one of Satha's sons on the throne. Resentment of the power wielded by the Spanish grew among court officials until 1599, when the Spanish garrison at Phnom Penh was massacred. Shortly thereafter, Satha's brother ascended the throne with the help of the Thais.

From about 1600 until the arrival of the French in 1863, Cambodia was ruled by a series of weak kings who, because of continual challenges by dissident members of the royal family, were forced to seek the protection – granted, of course, at a price – of either Thailand or Vietnam. In the 17th century, assistance from the Nguyen Lords of southern Vietnam was given on the condition that Vietnamese be allowed to settle in what is now the southern region of Vietnam, at that time part of Cambodia, and today still referred to by the Khmers as 'Lower Cambodia'. In the west, the Thais established dominion over the provinces of Battambang and Siem Reap; by the late 18th century they had firm control of the Cambodian royal family. Indeed, one king was crowned in Bangkok and placed on the throne at Udong with the help of the Thai army. That Cambodia survived through the 18th century as a distinct entity is due to the preoccupations of its neighbours: while the Thais were expending their energy and resources in fighting the Burmese, the Vietnamese were wholly absorbed by internal strife, including the rivalry between the Trinh Lords and the Nguyen Lords, and the Tay Son Rebellion.

French Rule

Cambodia's dual Thai and Vietnamese suzerainty ended in 1864, when French gunboats intimidated King Norodom (reigned 1860 to 1904) into signing a treaty of protectorate. French control of Cambodia, which developed as an adjunct to French colonial interests in Vietnam, at first involved relatively little direct interference in Cambodia's affairs of state. However, the French presence did prevent Cambodia's expansionist neighbours from annexing any more Khmer territory and helped keep Norodom on the throne despite the ambitions of his rebellious half-brothers.

By the 1870s, French officials in Cambodia began pressing for greater control over internal affairs. In 1884, Norodom was forced to sign a treaty turning his country into a virtual colony, sparking a two-year rebellion that constituted the only major anti-French movement in Cambodia until after WWII. This uprising ended when the king was persuaded to call upon rebel fighters to lay down their weapons in exchange for a return to the pre-treaty arrangement.

During the next two decades, senior Cambodian officials, who saw certain advantages in acquiescing to French power, opened the door to direct French control over the day-to-day administration of the country. At the same time, the French maintained Norodom's court in a splendour probably unequalled since the Angkorian period, thereby greatly enhancing the symbolic position of the monarchy. The king's increased stature served to legitimise the Cambodian state, thereby pre-empting the growth of any sort of broad-based nationalist movement; a situation in marked contrast to that in Vietnam. Indeed, the only large-scale popular protest of any kind between the 1880s and the 1940s was an essentially peaceful peasant uprising in 1916 which ended when the king agreed to consider their grievances.

King Norodom was succeeded by King Sisowath (reigned 1904 to 1927), who was followed on the throne by King Monivong (reigned 1927 to 1941). Upon the death of King Monivong, the French governor general of

Japanese-occupied Indochina, Admiral Jean Decoux, placed 19-year-old Prince Norodom Sihanouk on the Cambodian throne. The choice was based on the assumption that Sihanouk would prove pleasingly pliable; this proved to be a major miscalculation.

After WWII, the French returned, making Cambodia an 'autonomous state within the French Union' but retaining de facto control. The years after 1945 were marked by strife among the country's various political groupings, a situation made more unstable by the Franco-Viet Minh War then raging in Vietnam and Laos.

Independence

In January 1953, King Sihanouk, who had been at odds with the dominant Democratic Party, took decisive action, dissolving the parliament, declaring martial law and embarking on what became known as the Royal Crusade: his campaign to drum up international support for his country's independence.

Independence was proclaimed on 9 November 1953 and recognised by the Geneva Conference of May 1954, which ended French control of Indochina. However, internal political turmoil continued, much of it the result of conflicts between Sihanouk and his domestic opponents. In March 1955, Sihanouk abdicated in favour of his father, Norodom Suramarit, in order to pursue a career as a politician. His newly established party, the People's Socialist Community (Sangkum Reastr Niyum), won every seat in parliament in the September 1955 elections. Sihanouk dominated Cambodian politics for the next 15 years, serving as prime minister until his father's death in 1960, when no new king was named and he became chief of state.

Although he feared the Vietnamese communists, during the early 1960s Sihanouk considered South Vietnam and Thailand, both allies of the USA (which he mistrusted), the greatest threats to Cambodia's security and even survival. In an attempt to fend off these many dangers, he declared Cambodia neutral in international affairs. In May 1965, Sihanouk, convinced that the USA had been

plotting against him and his family, broke diplomatic relations with Washington and tilted towards North Vietnam, the Viet Cong and China. In addition, he accepted that the North Vietnamese army and the Viet Cong would use Cambodian territory in their battle against South Vietnam and the Americans.

These moves and his socialist economic policies alienated right-leaning elements in Cambodian society, including the officer corps of the army and the urban elite. At the same time, left-wing Cambodians, many of them educated abroad, deeply resented his internal policies, which did not allow for political dissent. Compounding Sihanouk's problems was the fact that all classes were fed up with the pervasive corruption. Although most peasants – the vast majority of the population – revered Sihanouk as a semi-divine figure, a rural-based rebellion broke out in 1967, leading him to conclude that the greatest threat to his regime now came from the left. Bowing to pressure from the army, he implemented a policy of harsh repression against left-wingers.

In 1969 the USA began a secret programme of bombing suspected communist base camps in Cambodia. For the next four years, until bombing was halted by the US Congress in August 1973, huge areas of the eastern half of the country were carpet bombed by US B-52s, killing uncounted thousands of civilians and turning hundreds of thousands more into refugees.

Lon Nol Regime

By 1969 the conflict between the army and leftist rebels had become more serious and Sihanouk's political position had greatly deteriorated. In March 1970, while Sihanouk was on a trip to France, General Lon Nol and Prince Sisowath Matak, Sihanouk's cousin, deposed him as chief of state, apparently with US support. Pogroms against ethnic Vietnamese living in Cambodia soon broke out, prompting many ethnic Vietnamese inhabitants of the country to flee. Sihanouk took up residence in Beijing, where he set up a government-in-exile nominally in control of an indigenous Cambodian revolutionary

MICK ELMORE

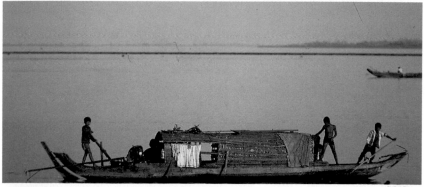

CHRIS TAYLOR

CHRIS TAYLOR

Cambodia
Top: Stone faces lining the entrance to the South Gate at Angkor Thom.
Middle: Boats plying the Mekong River near Phnom Penh.
Bottom: The causeway leading to the awe-inspiring Angkor Wat.

CHRIS TAYLOR

CHRIS TAYLOR

MICK ELMORE

People & Culture
Top: A Khmer woman on a boat near Siem Reap.
Left: A musician playing the flute.
Right: Classical dancers performing at Angkor Wat.

movement that Sihanouk himself had nick-named the Khmer Rouge (French for Red Khmer).

On 30 April 1970, US and South Vietnamese forces invaded Cambodia in an effort to rout some 40,000 Viet Cong and North Vietnamese troops who were using bases inside Cambodia in their war to overthrow the South Vietnamese government. As a result of the invasion, the Vietnamese communists withdrew deeper into Cambodia, thus posing an even greater threat to the Lon Nol government. At the same time, the new government was becoming very unpopular as a result of the unprecedented greed and corruption of its leaders. Savage fighting quickly engulfed the entire country, bringing misery to millions of Cambodians, many of whom fled rural areas for the relative safety of Phnom Penh and provincial capitals. Between 1970 and 1975, several hundred thousand people died in the fighting.

During the next few years, the Khmer Rouge came to play a dominant role in trying to overthrow the Lon Nol regime. The leaders of the Khmer Rouge, including Paris-educated Pol Pot (formerly Saloth Sar) and Khieu Samphan, had fled into the country-side in the 1960s to escape the summary justice then being meted out to suspected leftists by Sihanouk's security forces.

Despite massive US military and economic aid, Lon Nol never succeeded in gaining the initiative against the Khmer Rouge, which pursued a strategy of attrition. Large parts of the countryside fell to the rebels, and many provincial capitals were cut off from Phnom Penh. On 17 April 1975 – two weeks before the fall of Saigon – Phnom Penh surrendered to the Khmer Rouge.

Khmer Rouge Regime

Upon taking Phnom Penh, the Khmer Rouge implemented one of the most radical and brutal restructurings of a society ever attempted; its goal was to transform Cambodia into a Maoist, peasant-dominated agrarian cooperative. Within two weeks of coming to power, the entire population of the capital and provincial towns, including everyone in

the hospitals, were force-marched out to the countryside and placed in mobile work teams to do slave labour – preparing the fields, digging irrigation canals – for 12 to 15 hours a day. Disobedience of any sort often brought immediate execution. The advent of Khmer Rouge rule was proclaimed 'Year Zero'. Currency was abolished and postal services were halted. Except for one fortnightly flight to Beijing (China was providing aid and advisers to the Khmer Rouge), the country was completely cut off from the outside world.

It is still not known how many Cambodians died at the hands of the Khmer Rouge over the next four years. The Vietnamese claimed three million deaths, while foreign experts long considered the number closer to one million. Ongoing investigations by Yale University researchers concluded in early 1996, however, that the figure is at least two million, and may even end up being higher than this.

Sihanouk returned to Phnom Penh in September 1975 as titular chief of state but resigned three months later. He remained in Phnom Penh, imprisoned in his palace and kept alive only at the insistence of the Chinese, who considered him useful. During the Vietnamese invasion of Cambodia in December 1978, Sihanouk was flown to Beijing to prevent his falling into the hands of the new government.

Vietnamese Intervention

Between 1976 and 1978, the xenophobic government in Phnom Penh instigated a series of border clashes with Vietnam, whose southern region – once part of the Khmer Empire – it claimed. Khmer Rouge incursions into Vietnamese border provinces left hundreds of Vietnamese civilians dead. On 25 December 1978, Vietnam launched a full-scale invasion of Cambodia, toppling the Pol Pot government two weeks later (on 7 January 1979). As Vietnamese tanks neared Phnom Penh, the Khmer Rouge fled westward with as many civilians as they could seize, taking refuge in the jungles and mountains on both sides of the border with

King Sihanouk

Norodom Sihanouk has been a constant presence in the topsy-turvy world of Cambodian politics. A colourful man of many enthusiasms and shifting political positions, his amatory exploits tended to dominate his early reputation. Later he became the prince who stage-managed the close of French colonialism, autocratically led an independent Cambodia, was imprisoned by the Khmer Rouge and, from privileged exile, finally returned triumphant as king. If nothing else, he is a survivor.

Sihanouk was born in 1922, the only son of Prince Norodom Suramarit, grandson of King Norodom (1860-1904), and Princess Sisowath Kossamak, daughter of King Sisowath Monivong (1927-41). He was not an obvious contender for the throne. The French saw the young prince as a pliant monarch. He was crowned in 1941, just 19 years old, his education incomplete. And in the four years before the Japanese arrived and presented Cambodia briefly with the gift of liberation, he was all the French had hoped he would be.

With the French colonial masters removed, however, Sihanouk promptly abolished two French laws: the first was the compulsory romanisation of the Khmer alphabet; the second was the enforcement of the Gregorian calendar over the traditional lunar one. This was, it must be said, his only act of defiance in five months of de facto independence, but it marks the cautious beginning of Sihanouk's involvement in politics.

Sihanouk acquiesced quietly to the return of French rule in August 1945. But by 1952 he had embarked on his self-styled 'royal crusade' for independence. He began it by dismissing an elected government and appointing himself prime minister, announcing that within three years Cambodia would be independent. He embarked on a lobbying and publicity campaign in France and the USA, a brief defiant exile in Thailand, and sponsored a civil militia that attracted some 100,000 volunteers. The French backed out of Cambodia in late 1953.

A year after achieving independence, Sihanouk made one of his characteristically unpredictable decisions: he would abdicate. Thwarted in his attempts to revise the constitution and provide the throne with far-reaching political powers, he was probably afraid of being marginalised to the pomp of royal ceremony. The 'royal crusader' became 'citizen Sihanouk'. He vowed never again to return to the throne. Meanwhile his father became king. It was a masterstroke that offered Sihanouk both royal authority and supreme political power.

Thailand. The Vietnamese installed a new government led by two former Khmer Rouge officers, Hun Sen, who had defected to Vietnam in 1977, and Heng Samrin, who had done the same in 1978. The official version of events is that the Heng Samrin government came to power in a revolutionary uprising against the Pol Pot regime.

The social and economic dislocation that accompanied the Vietnamese invasion – along with the destruction of rice stocks and unharvested fields by both sides (to prevent their use by the enemy) – resulted in a vastly reduced rice harvest in early 1979. The chaotic situation led to very little rice being planted in the summer of 1979. By the middle of that year, the country was on the verge of widespread famine. As hundreds of thousands of Cambodians fled to Thailand, a massive international famine relief effort, sponsored by the UN, was launched.

In June 1982, Sihanouk agreed, under pressure from China, to head a military and political front opposed to the Phnom Penh government and the 170,000 Vietnamese troops defending it. The Sihanouk-led resistance coalition brought together – on paper, at least – FUNCINPEC (the French acronym

Elections were held in 1955. They were marred by intimidatory violence and voting fraud. Sihanouk's People's Socialist Community party won 83% of the vote. By this time he was in full political swing, and had discovered a passion for rhetoric. On one occasion, in 1957, he summoned his political opposition to a palace debate before a huge audience and demolished them in three hours of impassioned oratory. They were beaten by the palace guards as they slunk away.

By the mid-1960s Sihanouk had been supreme commander of Cambodia for a decade. After innumerable love affairs, he had finally settled on Monique Izzi, the daughter of a Franco-Italian father and a Cambodian mother, as his consort. As war raged in Vietnam and leftist discontent with right-wing politics blossomed at home, Sihanouk launched his movie career. Between 1966 and 1969 he directed, produced and starred in nine movies.

It seems that Sihanouk himself had come to believe the conventional wisdom that 'Sihanouk is Cambodia' and probably felt his leadership was unassailable. But as the cinema took more and more of his time, Cambodia was being drawn inexorably into the Vietnam War. Government troops battled with a leftist insurgency in the countryside; the economy was in tatters; and Sihanouk came to be regarded as a liability. His involvement in cinema and his announcements that Cambodia was 'an oasis of peace' suggested a man who had not only abdicated from the throne but who had abdicated from reality too.

In early 1970, with forces gathering against him, Sihanouk briefly flirted with the idea of reclaiming the throne. Instead, he departed for France. On 18 March the National Assembly voted to remove Sihanouk from office. Not long after, Cambodia was declared a republic and Sihanouk was sentenced to death *in absentia*.

Sihanouk went into exile in Beijing and threw in his lot with the communists. It was a practical step. The communists aimed to topple the Lon Nol government, and this suited Sihanouk. In 1973, he and Monique joined Pol Pot and other communist leaders on a trip to Khmer Rouge-controlled Angkor. Photographs and film record the royal couple sightseeing in the black peasant garb preferred by the Khmer Rouge. When the Khmer Rouge marched into Phnom Penh on 17 April 1975, Sihanouk issued a statement in Beijing heralding the event as a great victory against imperialism.

In a deserted Phnom Penh, Sihanouk was confined to the Royal Palace as a prisoner of the Khmer Rouge. He remained there until early 1979, when, on the eve of the Vietnamese invasion, he was put on a plane and sent to Beijing. The Khmer Rouge killed most of Sihanouk's children, grandchildren and relatives, but curiously they spared the patriarch's life.

It was to be a decade before Sihanouk finally returned to Cambodia. Meanwhile, against all odds, he was back at centre stage again, calling the shots, forming alliances with the Khmer Rouge, breaking them off. When the UNTAC forces moved into Cambodia in 1992, Sihanouk briefly cut off his support for them. After the May 1993 elections, Sihanouk suddenly announced that he was forming a coalition government with himself starring as president, prime minister and military leader. He failed.

Sihanouk has never quite given up wanting to be everything for Cambodia: international statesman, general, president, film director, man of the people. On 24 September 1993, after 38 years in politics, he settled once again for the role of king. ■

---

for the National United Front for an Independent, Neutral, Peaceful and Cooperative Cambodia), which comprised a royalist group loyal to Sihanouk; the Khmer People's National Liberation Front, a non-communist grouping formed by former prime minister and banker Son Sann; and the Khmer Rouge, officially known as the Party of Democratic Kampuchea and by far the largest and most powerful of the three. Although Pol Pot officially retired in 1985, and rumours abound about his failing health, the figurehead of the Khmer Rouge is still out there.

By the late 1980s, the weak royalist group,

the Armée Nationale Sihanoukiste, had 12,000 troops; Son Sann's faction, plagued by internal divisions, could field some 8000 soldiers; and the Khmer Rouge's National Army of Democratic Kampuchea was believed to have 40,000 troops. The army of the Phnom Penh government, the Kampuchean People's Revolutionary Armed Forces, had 50,000 regular soldiers and another 100,000 men and women serving in local militia forces.

In 1985, the Vietnamese overran all the major rebel camps inside Cambodia, forcing the Khmer Rouge and their allies to retreat into Thailand. Since that time, the Khmer Rouge – and, to a much more limited extent, the other two factions – has engaged in guerrilla warfare aimed at demoralising its opponents. Tactics used by the Khmer Rouge include shelling government-controlled garrison towns, planting thousands of mines along roads and in rice fields, attacking road transport, blowing up bridges, kidnapping village chiefs and killing local administrators and school teachers. The Khmer Rouge has also forced thousands of men, women and children living in the refugee camps it controls to work as porters, ferrying ammunition and other supplies into Cambodia across heavily mined sections of the border.

Throughout the 1980s, Thailand actively supported the Khmer Rouge and the other resistance factions, seeing them as a counterweight to Vietnamese power in the region. In fact, in 1979 Thailand demanded that as a condition for allowing international food aid for Cambodia to pass through its territory, food had to be supplied to the Khmer Rouge forces encamped in the Thai border region as well. Along with weaponry supplied by China (and delivered by the Thai army), this international assistance was essential in enabling the Khmer Rouge to rebuild its military strength. At the same time, Malaysia and Singapore supplied weapons to the two smaller factions of the coalition. As part of its campaign to harass and isolate Hanoi (capital of Vietnam), the USA gave more than US$15 million a year in aid to the non-communist factions of the Khmer Rouge-dominated coalition and helped it to retain its UN seat.

UNTAC at the Helm

In September 1989 Vietnam, suffering from economic woes and eager to reduce its international isolation, announced that it had withdrawn all of its troops from Cambodia; however, evidence suggests that Vietnamese soldiers wearing Cambodian uniforms remained in the country well into 1990. With most of the Vietnamese gone, the opposition coalition, still dominated by the Khmer Rouge, launched a series of offensives,

bringing the number of refugees inside the country to over 150,000 by the autumn of 1990. In the first eight months of 1990, over 2000 Cambodians lost their lives in the fighting.

Diplomatic efforts to end the civil war began to bear fruit in September 1990, when a plan agreed upon by the five permanent members of the UN Security Council (the USA, the former USSR, China, France and Britain) was accepted by both the Phnom Penh government and the three factions of the resistance coalition.

According to the plan, the Supreme National Council (SNC), a coalition of all factions, was formed under the presidency of Sihanouk. Meanwhile the United Nations Transitional Authority in Cambodia (UNTAC) was to supervise the administration of the country and to create an atmosphere in which free elections could take place.

UNTAC was successful in achieving SNC agreement to most international human rights covenants; a large number of NGOs were established in Cambodia; and most importantly on 25 May 1993 elections were held with a 89.6% turnout. The results were far from decisive, however, with FUNCINPEC, led by Prince Norodom Ranariddh, taking 58 seats in the National Assembly, the Cambodian People's Party (CPP), which represented the previous communist government, taking 51 seats, and the Buddhist Liberal Democratic Party (BLDP) taking 10 seats. As a result, Cambodia ended up with two prime ministers: Norodom Ranariddh as first prime minister, and Hun Sen as second prime minister. Control of the various ministries was also spread among the three contending parties.

Within months of the elections taking place, local diplomats and reporters were complaining that the diffusion of central authority had led to a situation where real power lay in the hands of provincial leaders, whose loyalties lay with the CPP and communist-style power structures.

Dealing with the Khmer Rouge

When the Vietnamese toppled the Pol Pot

government in 1979, the Khmer Rouge disappeared into the jungle. Nearly two decades later, despite UN brokered free elections, they are still there and remain a significant threat to the security of the country. The Khmer Rouge boycotted the 1993 elections and rejected peace talks aimed at bringing about a ceasefire. Although they were signatories to the Paris peace accords, the alliance came apart over the role the CPP should play in the political process.

Defections of some 2000 troops from the Khmer Rouge army in the months following the elections offered some hope that the long-running insurrection would fizzle out. Government-sponsored amnesty programmes, however, initially turned out to be ill-conceived: reconscripting Khmer Rouge troops and turning them back to fight their former comrades with poor pay and conditions provided little in the way of an incentive to desert.

In April 1994, in response to a government offensive, the Khmer Rouge recaptured Pailin near the Thai border and caused havoc around Battambang, creating 40,000 refugees. The dry season offensive (which was to become an annual event), far short of decimating the Khmer Rouge, actually allowed them to extend their influence wider than it had been since the Vietnamese overran Cambodia in the late 1970s.

The problem was not just the poorly equipped and frequently unpaid Cambodian army. Evidence points to high level military cooperation with the Khmer Rouge. Leaked Khmer Rouge documents in mid-1994 revealed that large quantities of arms were sold to them by the Cambodian military leadership, and that such arms sales were continuing even as the very same officers conducting the sales were attacking Khmer Rouge positions.

Some insiders responded by saying aloud that a military solution to the Khmer Rouge insurgency was no solution at all. After all, Malaysia's communist rebels had successfully been drawn out of the jungle through rising standards of living and increasing marginalisation. Nevertheless, in July 1994,

the Cambodian government went ahead and outlawed the Khmer Rouge, sticking with the military option.

The dry season offensive of 1995 saw further defections from Khmer Rouge ranks, though observers note that probably only around 25% of the defectors were trained soldiers. The Thai government, a long-time supporter of the rebels, finally began to clamp down on Khmer Rouge border movements, an act that theoretically severed the Khmer Rouge lines of revenue: gems and timber transported into Thailand for sale. At the same time, defectors maintained that the Khmer Rouge leadership was divided and floundering ideologically. Still, Pol Pot and his followers have survived in the jungle since 1960.

Cross-border sales of timber with Thailand are reported to be continuing, generating as much as US$10 million per month for the Khmer Rouge. It is unlikely that it will be brought to heel in the near future. In 1996, the dry season offensive once again went about the now routine task of recapturing positions by the Khmer Rouge during the wet season. Cambodia looks to be set for a long drawn-out struggle with its former persecutors.

Cambodia Today

Both politically and economically, Cambodia is in a shaky position. Many observers are pessimistic about the prospects for democracy in the country, while rampant corruption has blighted Cambodia's economic development.

In 1995 there were two major political incidents which boded ill for democratic politics. The first of these was the ouster of Sam Rainsy, a Paris-educated accountant, from FUNCINPEC. Rainsy lost his position as finance minister in mid-1994, a job he had excelled at, largely it was surmised because of his outspoken criticisms concerning corruption and government policy. In May 1995, his party membership was rescinded and one month later he was sacked from the National Assembly. Rainsy responded in November of the same year by announcing

But What's it Really Called?

Cambodia has changed its name so many times over the last few decades that there are understandable grounds for confusion. For the Cambodians themselves, their country is Kampuchea. The name is derived from the word *Kambu-ja*, meaning 'those born of Kambu', the mythical founder of the country. It dates back as far as the 10th century. The Portuguese 'Camboxa' and the French 'Cambodge', from which the English name 'Cambodia' is derived, are adaptations of 'Kambu-ja'.

Since gaining independence in 1953, the country has been known in English as many things before coming, full circle, back to where it started.

* The Kingdom of Cambodia (in French, Le Royaume du Cambodge).
* The Khmer Republic (under Lon Nol, who ruled from 1970 to 1975).
* Democratic Kampuchea (under the Khmer Rouge, the Communist Party which controlled the country from 1975 to 1979).
* The People's Republic of Kampuchea (under the Vietnamese-backed Phnom Penh government from 1979 to 1989).
* The State of Cambodia (in French, L'État du Cambodge; in Khmer, Roët Kampuchea) from mid-1989.
* The Kingdom of Cambodia (from the May 1993 elections)

It was the Khmer Rouge who insisted that the outside world use the name Kampuchea. Changing the country's official English name back to Cambodia (which has been used by the US State Department all along) was intended as a symbolic move to distance the present government in Phnom Penh from the bitter connotations of the name Kampuchea, which westerners and overseas Khmer alike associate with the murderous Khmer Rouge regime. ■

the formation of the Khmer Nation Party (KNP). Although the launching of his party was attended by over 1000 people, some of them prominent diplomats, the KNP was declared illegal by the government until new electoral laws were drawn up, a process which was expected to take a year.

The other political headliner of 1995 was the arrest and exile of Prince Norodom Sirivudh, half-brother of King Sihanouk, secretary general of FUNCINPEC and former foreign minister. He had allegedly plotted to kill Hun Sen. Prince Sirivudh has been described as a good-humoured man, always quick with an off-the-cuff joke. If his quip about assassinating Hun Sen was indeed a joke, the only one laughing is Hun Sen, who found himself with the perfect excuse to clear another political adversary from his path.

The local media have fared badly in recent times too. In July 1995 the National Assembly approved the Press Law, creating the spectre of jail terms for unruly journalists. The law was enacted against a background of clampdowns on local newspapers and the acquittal of a military officer accused of murdering a prominent Phnom Penh Khmer journalist. The controversial *New Liberty News* was the target of frequent attacks during 1995; a grenade was tossed into its office at one point and on another occasion its office was ransacked by three truckloads of 'protesters'.

Recent developments have seen King Sihanouk, who is aged and ailing from cancer, largely sidelined. Calls by the BLDP in January 1995 for the king to intervene for national reconciliation (to mediate in the Khmer Rouge standoff) were roundly denounced by the two prime ministers, Hun Sen and Prince Ranariddh. And for his part Sihanouk has repeatedly denied rumours that he plans to abdicate and re-enter politics. Nevertheless, the king remains the wild card in Cambodian politics. Insiders and voters disillusioned with the Ranariddh/Hun Sen alliance and the Khmer Rouge impasse look to the king as a source of solutions. With elections slated for 1998, many conjecture that the king might give a royal endorsement of Rainsy's Khmer Nation Party, an act that would be of considerable consequence to its fortunes.

Meanwhile, Hun Sen continues to gain in power, silencing critical voices wherever possible. Prince Sirivudh, a cautious supporter of 'Sihanoukism' has been sent into exile. As for Rainsy, unceremoniously stripped of his rank and booted from FUNCINPEC, Prince Ranariddh was famously heard to remark in early 1995 that foremost among the prospects for Rainsy's wife was widowhood. It is unlikely that King Sihanouk will sit quietly through the maelstrom of Cambodian politics. The question is whether anyone will be brave enough to second him.

GEOGRAPHY

Cambodia covers a land area of 181,035 sq km, which is the size of Missouri and a bit over half the size of Italy or Vietnam. The country's maximum extent is about 580 km from east to west and 450 km from north to south. Cambodia is bounded on the west by Thailand, on the north by Thailand and Laos, on the east and south-east by Vietnam and on the south by the Gulf of Thailand.

Cambodia's two dominant topographical features are the Mekong River, which is almost five km wide in places, and the Tonlé Sap (Great Lake). The Mekong, which rises in Tibet, flows about 315 km through Cambodia before continuing on, via southern Vietnam, to the South China Sea. At Phnom Penh, it splits into its two major branches: the Upper River (called simply the Mekong or, in Vietnamese, the Tien Giang) and the Lower River (the Bassac River; in Vietnamese, the Hau Giang). The rich sediment deposited during the Mekong's annual wet-season flooding has made for very fertile agricultural land. Most of Cambodia's streams and rivers flow into the Mekong-Tonlé Sap basin.

The Tonlé Sap is linked to the Mekong at Phnom Penh by a 100-km-long channel which is named after the lake it flows into and from (depending on the season): the Tonlé Sap River. From mid-May to early October (the rainy season), the level of the Mekong rises, backing up the Tonlé Sap River and causing it to flow north-westward into the Tonlé Sap Lake. During this period, the Tonlé Sap swells from 3000 sq km to over 7500 sq km; its maximum depth increases from about 2.2m to more than 10m. As the water level of the Mekong falls during the dry season, the Tonlé Sap River reverses its flow, draining the waters of the lake back into the Mekong. This extraordinary process makes the Tonlé Sap one of the world's richest sources of freshwater fish.

In the centre of Cambodia, around the Tonlé Sap and the upper Mekong Delta, is a low-lying alluvial plain where the vast majority of Cambodia's people live. Extending outward from this plain are thinly forested transitional plains with elevations of no more than about 100m above sea level.

In the south-west, much of the area between the Gulf of Thailand and the Tonlé Sap is covered by a highland region formed by two distinct upland blocks: the Cardamom Mountains (Chuor Phnom Kravanh) in south-western Battambang Province and Pursat Province, and the Elephant Mountains (Chuor Phnom Damrei) in the provinces of Kompong Speu, Koh Kong and Kampot. Along the southern coast is a heavily forested lowland strip isolated from the rest of the country by the mountains to the north. Cambodia's highest peak, Phnom Aoral (1813m), is on the eastern part of the border, between the provinces of Kompong Chhnang and Kompong Speu.

Along Cambodia's northern border with Thailand, the plains abut an east-west oriented sandstone escarpment, over 300 km long and 180 to 550m in height, that marks the southern limit of the Dangkrek Mountains (Chuor Phnom Dangkrek). In the north-eastern corner of the country (the provinces of Ratanakiri and Mondulkiri), the transitional plains give way to the Eastern Highlands, a remote region of densely forested mountains and high plateaus that extends eastward into Vietnam's Central Highlands and northward into Laos.

CLIMATE

The climate of Cambodia is governed by two monsoons, which set the rhythm of rural life. The cool, dry, north-eastern monsoon, which carries little rain, blows from about November to March. From May to early October, the south-western monsoon brings strong winds, high humidity and heavy rains. Between these seasons, the weather is transitional. Even during the wet season, it rarely rains in the morning: most precipitation comes in the afternoon, and even then only sporadically.

Maximum daily temperatures range from 35°C in April, the hottest month, to the high 20s during January, the coolest month. Daily minimum temperatures are usually about 8°C to 11°C below the maximums.

Annual rainfall varies considerably from area to area. Whereas the seaward slopes of the south-western highlands receive more than 5000 mm of precipitation per annum, the central lowlands average only about 1400 mm. Between 70% and 80% of the annual rainfall is brought by the south-western monsoon.

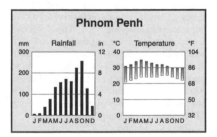

ECOLOGY & ENVIRONMENT
Logging

The biggest threat to the environment in Cambodia is logging. In the mid-1960s, Cambodia was reckoned to have around 75% rainforest coverage. Surveys carried out in mid-1993 concluded this had been reduced to 49%, around half of which was primary forest. Worse still, reports also concluded that the shift from a command economy to a market economy had led to an asset-stripping bonanza by the cash-strapped government, and that virtually all of Cambodia's primary resources were under some kind of unaccountable foreign control.

The problem is not just the parlous state of the Cambodian economy but the international demand for timber and the fact that neighbouring countries like Thailand and Laos enforce much tougher logging regulations. It's small wonder then that foreign logging companies have been flocking to Cambodia. By late 1995, 27 companies had licences or applications to log Cambodia's rainforests. The Malaysian Samling Group was granted a 60-year licence to log 800,000 hectares in late 1994, before a brief ban on logging was put into force from 30 December 1995. By July it was business as usual, with the Malaysian Grand Atlantic Group signing a deal for 500,000 hectares, and just a month later the Indonesian Macro Pannin Group grabbing 1.5 million hectares. The total land area of these deals alone amounts to around 12% of Cambodia's national territory.

Deals like these are controversial for many reasons. They were made by the prime ministers without reference to forestry officials; the sums changing hands in exchange for the contracts are not public knowledge; and stipulations on how the logging should be carried out are hazy.

In December 1995 the government seemed to pause again in its cavalier logging programme. It announced that contracts already signed by Samling, Grand Atlantic, Macro Pannin and the Japanese group Shinwa, would be honoured but most others would be cancelled. The reason provided was that the government had no more forests left to give.

Damming the Mekong

With a meandering length of around 4200 km, the Mekong is the longest river in South-East Asia, and some 50 million people depend on it for their livelihoods. In terms of fish biodiversity, the Mekong is second only to the Amazon. But with energy needs ever spiralling in Thailand and Vietnam, it is very tempting for a poor country like Cambodia to dam the river and make money from hydroelectric power. Even more tempting for Cambodia is the fact that the United Nations Development Programme (UNDP) and the Asia Development Bank would pay for much of the construction costs. Environmental groups are already calling foul.

Overseeing development plans for the river is the Mekong River Commission (MRC), formed by the UNDP and comprising Cambodia, Thailand, Laos and Vietnam. The odd one out is China, which has around 20% of the Mekong but calls it the Lancang and feels it can do what it wants with the river without reference to its neighbours. China is already at work on a number of dam projects on the upper reaches of the Mekong, and many environmentalists fear that such projects will have an adverse affect on the down-river flow.

China's dam projects are shrouded in secrecy, but there are thought to be 15 of them planned, three of these operational by the year 2009. Meanwhile, the MRC plans 11 dams for the Mekong in Laos and Cambodia.

Environmental concerns focus on a number of issues. For a start, even though the MRC dams planned for the Mekong will be small, it is thought they will still flood some 1900 sq km and displace around 60,000 people. Secondly, there are worries about how the dams will affect fish migration – some environmentalists claim that the dams might halve the fish population of the Mekong and perhaps even the Tonlé Sap Lake. And finally, and perhaps of most concern, is the importance of the annual monsoon flooding of the Mekong in depositing nutrient-rich silt across vast tracts of land used for agriculture. Even, say environmentalists, a drop of one metre in Mekong water levels would result in around 2000 sq km less flood area around the Tonlé Sap Lake, a result with potentially disastrous consequences for Cambodia's farmers.

The Mekong is a huge untapped resource. It is probably inevitable that it be harnessed

to make much needed power for the region. Local environmentalists hope that this can be done in the context of open discussion and with foresight. Many fear, however, that long-term interests will be scrapped in favour of short-term profits.

Meanwhile, Down on the Shrimp Farm

Thai shrimp farmers have descended on Cambodia, mainly in the coastal areas of Koh Kong Province. Mangroves make ideal grounds for the commercial farming of the tiger prawn, a seafood with phenomenal money-making powers throughout Asia. In order to farm tiger prawns, however, you need to clear the mangroves and create artificial ponds. Fertilisers and chemical feeds are required, and it is also necessary to pump out polluted water and replenish it with clean water, creating damage to the surrounding environment. Within two or three years the pool will have to be abandoned and the farming relocated to another area, leaving a trail of environmental destruction.

There's very little in it for Cambodia. Generally shrimp farms are established with big-business bucks, unskilled Khmer labour is used for the menial work, and 90% of the product produced is shipped off to Thailand. The pity of it is that mangroves are remarkably diverse ecosystems and have an integral relationship with oceanic fish populations, serving as spawning grounds for many varieties of fish that are commercially fished. The government is looking at ways to regulate commercial shrimp farming in its mangroves, but underfunding and ignorance on the part of locals living in mangrove areas is making the job very difficult.

FLORA & FAUNA
Flora
The central lowland consists of rice paddies, fields of dry crops such as corn and tobacco, tracts of reeds and tall grass, and thinly wooded areas. The transitional plains are mostly covered with savanna grasses, which grow to a height of 1.5m.

In the south-west, there are virgin rainforests growing to heights of 50m or more on the rainy seaward slopes of the mountains. Nearby, higher elevations support pine forests. Vegetation in the coastal strip includes both evergreen and mangrove forests. In the northern mountains there are broadleaf evergreen forests with trees soaring 30m above the thick undergrowth of vines, bamboos, palms and assorted woody and herbaceous ground plants. The Eastern Highlands are covered with grassland and deciduous forest. Forested upland areas support many varieties of orchid.

In the past two decades, a great deal of deforestation has taken place, and the pace has been quickening over the past five years. Both the Malaysians and the Indonesians have bought major timber concessions.

The symbol of Cambodia is the sugar palm tree, which is used in construction (for roofs and walls) and to make medicine, wine and vinegar. Because of the way sugar palms grow (over the years, the tree keeps getting taller but the trunk, which lacks a normal bark, does not grow thicker), their trunks retain shrapnel marks from every battle that ever raged around them. Some sugar palms survive despite having been shot clear through the trunk.

Fauna

Cambodia's larger wild animals include bears, elephants, rhinoceroses, leopards, tigers and wild oxen. The lion, although often incorporated into Angkorian heraldic devices, has never been seen here. Among the country's more common birds are cormorants, cranes, egrets, grouse, herons, pelicans, pheasants and wild ducks. There is also a great variety of butterflies. Four types of snake are especially dangerous: the cobra, the king cobra, the banded krait and Russell's viper.

In 1995 the World Wildlife Fund (WWF) announced a fundraising campaign to save the tigers of Indochina. There are thought to be tigers in the recently established Kirirom National Park, but reports indicate that they are threatened by poachers. Magical powers of potency (sexual, mainly) are ascribed to tiger parts throughout Asia, but mostly by the Chinese.

Given that much of the country has been off limits for such a long time, there is conjecture that Cambodia harbours animals that have become extinct elsewhere in the region. Sightings of rare storks last seen in Laos in 1993 were reported in early 1995. Meanwhile, the kouprey (wild ox), adopted by Sihanouk as the national animal in 1963, is thought to linger on in very small numbers in the north-east of Cambodia.

National Parks

With the country still beset by security problems and tourism at a low ebb, Cambodia has

Cambodia's ecosystem supports a number of larger animals including bears.

not yet embarked on a programme of protecting its environment and establishing national parks. Still, a start was made in November 1993, when the Kirirom – Preah Soramriddh Koh Somak National Park (usually referred to as Kirirom) – was set up.

GOVERNMENT

As of the May 1993 elections, Cambodia became a constitutional monarchy. Prince Sihanouk, who abdicated in 1955, accepted the crown and rules as king. The constitution of September 1993 theoretically allows for separation of powers between the executive, legislative and judicial branches of government. In practice it rarely works this way, however. Decades of war and one-party rule have made Cambodia's administrative and legal structures slow to respond to the challenge of neutrality.

Although elections are scheduled for 1998, there are many ominous signs that the current coalition government of Cambodia, headed by two prime ministers, Prince Norodom Ranariddh and Hun Sen, is entrenching itself and has its sights set on long-lasting one-party rule. While the form of the Paris peace accords is being followed more or less, the substance of the agreement is under threat. Sam Rainsy's dismissal from the political process and the obstructions to his attempts to re-enter it via his own party are bad signs. The Buddhist Liberal Democratic Party (BLDP), which gained 10 seats in the 1993 elections, was denied authorisation to hold its annual party congress. When it went ahead and held it all the same, the proceedings were interrupted by the unannounced arrival of two grenades – 39 people were injured. The culprits were never caught.

With the BLDP crippled and Rainsy's Khmer Nation Party (KNB) hobbled by red tape, military interference and even death threats, this leaves the two major winners of the 1993 elections, the Cambodian People's Party (CPP), headed by Hun Sen, and FUNCINPEC (the French acronym for the National United Front for an Independent, Neutral, Peaceful and Cooperative Cambodia). But the exile of FUNCINPEC's general secretary, Prince Norodom Sirivudh, due to allegations of a death threat against Hun Sen, and the withdrawal of support by King Sihanouk has left this party considerably weakened. Most commentators see Hun Sen's CPP, the former communist government of Cambodia, tightening its grip on the government.

The 1998 elections will be the litmus test for democratic politics in Cambodia. At the time of writing, there was little cause for optimism.

ECONOMY

Badly shaken by decades of internal conflict, Cambodia's economy is gradually improving but is still in very poor shape. For a long time rubber was Cambodia's primary export. This has been eclipsed in recent years by timber exports, which in 1994 accounted for US$194 million, nearly half the country's export earnings. Such figures, of course, disguise illegal exports of timber such as those carried out by the Khmer Rouge.

Curiously, Cambodia's second biggest export earner is the transshipment of gold and cigarettes. These come from Singapore, Malaysia and China. Cambodia has low import tariffs, and imports can thus be lucratively shipped on to more restrictive regional markets such as Vietnam.

Cambodia's economic statistics are low by international standards, and they look worse when you consider that Cambodia's principal sources of foreign exchange are unsustainable: foreign aid and timber sales. Foreign aid has far and away been Cambodia's chief money-spinner over recent years. It accounts for most of the signs of affluence that the visitor sees in Phnom Penh – foreign cars, European restaurants, cellular phones etc. Out in the countryside, however, Cambodia remains a very poor place where most people's livelihoods are agriculturally based and reliant on the vagaries of the annual monsoon. A shortage of rain resulted in two successive bad harvests in 1994 and 1995. International relief efforts and government assistance only narrowly staved off famine in some areas.

The challenge for Cambodia is creating an environment in which sustainable economic development can take place. At present, the signs indicate that the government is all too willing to encourage foreign investment in projects that generate short-term wealth for a few but offer few long-term benefits for the many. The denuding of the country's forests is one such development, while Malaysian investment in casinos (which are said to make certain local politicians a great deal of quick money) is another.

POPULATION & PEOPLE

As of July 1995, Cambodia's total population was 10.4 million. It is estimated that it will reach 12 million by the year 2000. Infant mortality rates, however, are the highest in the region at 120 per 1000. Due to poverty, poor sanitation and disease, it is estimated that nearly one child in five dies before the age of five. The much discussed imbalance of women to men is not as serious as is sometimes made out, but is still significant. Women account for 54% of the population. Approximately 50% of the population is under the age of 17.

Ethnic Khmers

According to official statistics, around 96% of the people who live in Cambodia are ethnic Khmers (ethnic Cambodians), making the country the most homogeneous in South-East Asia. In reality, though, there are probably much higher numbers of Vietnamese than such statistics account for.

The Khmers have inhabited Cambodia since the beginning of recorded history (around the 2nd century AD), many centuries before the Thais and Vietnamese migrated to the region. During the next six centuries, Khmer culture and religion were Indianised by contact with the civilisations of India and Java. Over the centuries, the Khmers have mixed with other groups resident in Cambodia, including the Javanese (8th century), Thai (10th to 15th centuries), Vietnamese (from the early 17th century) and Chinese (since the 18th century).

Ethnic Vietnamese

The Vietnamese are the largest non-Khmer ethnic group in Cambodia. According to figures published in March 1995, the government reckons Cambodia is host to around

Khmer Krom

The Khmer Krom of southern Vietnam are ethnic Khmer separated from Cambodia by historical deals and Vietnamese encroachment on what was once Cambodian territory. Nobody is sure just how many of them there are – estimates vary from one million to seven million, depending on who is doing the counting. But, however many Khmer Krom there are, the issue of their treatment in Vietnam is gaining increasing attention. Local representatives of these displaced Khmer point to Bosnia as an example of how ethnic frustration can erupt into violence if left to simmer for too long.

The history of Vietnamese expansionism into Khmer territory has long been a staple of Khmer schoolbooks. King Chey Chetha II of Cambodia, in keeping with the wishes of his Vietnamese queen, first allowed Vietnamese to settle in the Cambodian town of Prey Nokor in 1620. It was obviously the thin edge of the wedge. Prey Nokor is now better known as Ho Chi Minh City (Saigon).

Representatives of the Khmer Krom claim that although they dress as Vietnamese and carry Vietnamese identity cards, they remain culturally Khmer. Vietnamese attempts to quash Khmer Krom language and religion (the Khmer are Hinayanan Buddhists, while the Vietnamese practise Mahayanan Buddhism), have for the most part failed. Even assimilation through intermarriage has failed to take place on a large scale.

Many Khmer Krom would like to see Cambodia act as a mediator in the quest for greater autonomy and ethnic representation in Vietnam. The Cambodian government for its part is more concerned with the vast numbers of illegal Vietnamese inside its borders, as well as reports of encroachments by the Vietnamese into the west of Cambodia. ■

100,000 Vietnamese. Non-official observers claim that the real figure may be as high as one million. The official Khmer Rouge position is that there are four million Vietnamese in Cambodia. The truth is, no-one knows.

There is a great deal of mutual dislike and distrust between the Cambodians and the Vietnamese, even those who have been living in Cambodia for generations. While the Khmers refer to the Vietnamese as *yuon*, a derogatory term that means 'barbarians', the Vietnamese look down on the Khmers and consider them lazy for not farming every available bit of land, an absolute necessity in densely populated Vietnam. Historic antagonisms between the Vietnamese and the Khmers are exacerbated by the prominence of ethnic Vietnamese among shopowners.

For the Khmers, who rarely discriminate against the Thais in the same way, the mistrust of Vietnamese has an historical basis. The Vietnamese appropriated the lands of the Mekong Delta from the Khmers in the 16th and 17th centuries and now govern the people and area known as Kampuchea Krom. With Vietnamese encroachments on Cambodian territory continuing to be a major concern in Cambodia, it is unlikely that such prejudice will disappear in the near future.

Ethnic Chinese

Officially, the government claims there are around 50,000 ethnic Chinese in Cambodia. This is another disputed figure. Other observers say there may be as many as 400,000 of them.

Until 1975 the ethnic Chinese controlled the country's economic life. In recent years they have re-emerged as a powerful economic force, mainly due to investment by overseas Chinese from other parts of Asia. Although intermarriage with the Khmers is not infrequent, the Chinese have managed to retain a significant degree of cultural distinctiveness.

Cham Muslims

Cambodia's Cham Muslims (known locally as the Khmer Islam) officially number around 203,000. Unofficial counts put the figure at around half a million. They live in villages on the banks of the Mekong and the Tonlé Sap rivers, mostly in Kompong Cham and Kompong Chhnang provinces. The Cham Muslims suffered particularly vicious persecution between 1975 and 1979, when a large part of their community was exterminated. Many Cham mosques that were destroyed under the Khmer Rouge are now being rebuilt.

Ethno-Linguistic Minorities

Cambodia's diverse ethno-linguistic minorities (hill tribes), who live in the country's mountainous regions, probably number between 60,000 to 70,000. Collectively, they are known as *Khmer loeu*, literally the 'upper Khmer'.

The majority of the hill tribes are in the north-east of Cambodia, in the provinces of Ratanakiri, Mondulkiri, Stung Treng and Kratie. The largest group is known as the Tumpoun (many other spellings are used), who number around 15,000. Other groups include the Krung, Kra Chok, Kavet, Brao and Jorai.

The hill tribes of Cambodia have long been isolated from mainstream Khmer society and there is little in the way of mutual understanding. They practise shifting cultivation, rarely staying in one place for more than four or five years. Finding a new location for a village requires the mediation of a village elder with the spirit world.

Little research has been done on Cambodia's hill tribes, and tourism in the north-east is still in its infancy. A seminar held in 1995 entitled 'Ethnic Communities and Sustainable Development in North-East Cambodia' was given over almost entirely to reports on the fate of hill tribes in Thailand and Laos. Given the plight of the Thai hill tribes, the seminar found much to be concerned about regarding the impact of tourism, development and logging on Cambodia's even more isolated hill tribes.

Repatriation Programmes

Since 1992, the United Nations High Commissioner for Refugees (UNHCR) has repatriated more than 370,000 Cambodians, most of whom had sought refuge in Thailand. The first returnees crossed the border at Poipet (Poay Pet) on 30 March 1992. The following year, hundreds of thousands more were resettled and able to take part in their country's elections. Dozens of non-government aid agencies provided support for the programme, one of the largest and most complex ever undertaken.

EDUCATION
King Sihanouk took a lively interest in education early in his reign. Between 1953 and 1968, the number of primary students rocketed from 300,000 to one million. Even more spectacularly, secondary students increased from 5000 to around one million. Nine universities were also established in this period. Unfortunately, for all its good intentions, the programme has been widely criticised for creating uniformly poor educational levels and unrealistic employment expectations – there were not enough highly-skilled jobs to go around.

The Pol Pot regime of the 1970s put a stop to educational development. Indeed, as far as the Khmer Rouge was concerned, education was an evil. Many qualified teachers perished at this time, so that by 1979 Cambodia had only around 3000 qualified secondary teachers left.

Through the 1980s and 1990s, the situation has been gradually improving. Adult literacy rates vary from 30% to 70%, depending on who is doing the counting, but it is generally thought that overall education standards are higher than they have ever been. Four technical institutions and two universities have been established. In Phnom Penh and in regional centres, private schools have also blossomed, offering courses in English, French, computer literacy and accounting, among other subjects.

ARTS
The Khmer Rouge assault on the past and on artists and intellectuals was a terrible blow to Cambodian culture. Indeed for many years the common consensus among many Khmers was that their culture had been irrevocably lost. The Khmer Rouge not only did away

with living bearers of Khmer culture, they also destroyed cultural artefacts, statues, musical instruments, books, anything that served as a reminder of a past they wished to efface. Despite this, Cambodia today is witnessing a resurgence of traditional arts and a limited amount of experimentation in modern arts. A trip to the School of Fine Arts in Phnom Penh is evidence of the extent to which Khmer culture has kicked back.

Dance & Theatre
Cambodia's royal ballet is more than any of the other traditional arts a link with the glory of Angkor. Early in his reign, King Sihanouk released the traditional harem of royal *apsaras* (heavenly nymphs) that went with the crown. Nevertheless, prior to the Pol Pot regime, classical ballet was still taught at the palace. Its traditions stretched long into the past, when the art of the apsaras redounded to the glory of the divine king.

Cambodian court dance is related to the dance of Thailand, Java and India. They all share the same cultural sources, and many of the dances enact scenes from the Hindu *Ramayana*.

Dance fared particularly badly during the Pol Pot years. Very few dancers and teachers survived, and only one old woman survived who knew how to make the elaborate costumes that are sewn piece by piece onto the dancers before a performance. In 1981, with a handful of teachers, the School of Fine Arts was reopened and the training of dance students resumed. For the first intake of students, preference was given to orphans.

At a performance of royal dance, you will see much that resembles Thai dance (unless you are expert in such things): the same stylised hand movements; the same sequined, lamé costumes; the same opulent stupa-like head gear. But many popular dances staged nowadays also mix elements of more lively folk dance into the performance. Where traditionally royal dance was an all-female affair (with the exception of the role of the monkey), there are now often more male dancers featured.

Another interesting dance tradition is *lkhaon khaol*, Cambodia's masked theatre.

Traditionally all roles are played by men, like *kabuki* in Japan and some regional opera styles in China. In times past it was a popular form of entertainment, with troupes touring the country presenting performances of the *Ramayana* over several evenings. A narrator presides over the performance, providing dialogue and instructions to the small accompanying orchestra. Short performances of masked theatre are sometimes included in shows for foreign tourists.

Music

The bas reliefs on some of the monuments of Angkor depict musicians and apsaras holding instruments. The instruments shown are similar to the traditional Khmer instruments of today, suggesting that Cambodia has a long musical tradition all its own.

Traditionally the music of Cambodia was an accompaniment to a ritual or performance that had religious significance. Musicologists have identified six types of musical ensemble, each used in different settings. The most traditional of these is the *areak ka*, an ensemble that makes music for weddings. The instruments used include a three-stringed fiddle *(tro khmae)*, a singled-stringed bowed instrument *(khsae muoy)* and drums *(skor areak)*, among others.

Instruments used in performances of dance are naturally more percussive. If you see a dance performance in Cambodia, you will probably see a reduced ensemble of musicians performing, though sometimes the dances are performed to taped music. The instruments generally include at least one stringed instrument, a xylophone *(roneat)*, and sets of drums and cymbals.

Much of Cambodia's traditional music was lost during the Pol Pot era. During this time many Khmers settled in the USA, where a lively Khmer pop industry developed. Influenced by local American music and later exported back to Cambodia, it has been enormously popular. Phnom Penh too has a burgeoning pop industry nowadays.

Sculpture

Even in the pre-Angkor era, in the periods generally referred to as Funan and Chenla, the people of Cambodia were producing masterfully sensuous sculpture that was no simple copy of the Indian forms it was modelled on. Some scholars maintain that the Cambodian forms are unrivalled in India itself.

The earliest surviving Cambodian sculpture dates from the 6th century. Most of it depicts Vishnu with four or eight arms. Generally Vishnu has acquired Indochinese facial characteristics and his muscles are more pronounced than similar Indian sculpture, in which divinities tend towards rounded flabbiness. A large eight-armed Vishnu from this period is displayed at the National Museum in Phnom Penh.

Also on display at the National Museum is a statue of Harihara, a divinity who combines aspects of both Vishnu and Krishna.

The 11th century sculpture *Vishnu Reclining on the Serpent Ananta* on display in the National Museum in Phnom Penh.

The statue dates from the end of the 7th century, and the sensuous plasticity of the musculature prefigures the technical accomplishment of Angkor era art.

The sculpture of the pre-Angkor period is not restricted to the depiction of Hindu deities, but also features much Buddhist-inspired sculpture, mainly in the form of bodhisattvas. By the 9th century and the beginning of the Angkor era proper, however, the sculptures become exclusively Hindu-inspired.

Innovations of the early Angkor era include free-standing sculpture that dispenses with the stone aureole that earlier supported the multiple arms of Hindu deities. The faces assume an air of tranquillity, and the overall effect is less animated. In the National Museum, look for the statue of Shiva from the Bakong, Roluos, for an example of early Angkorian sculpture: the sculpture depicts a stocky frame and a smiling face that is characteristic of this period.

The Banteay Srei style of the late 10th century is commonly regarded as a high point in the evolution of South-East Asian art. The National Museum has a splendid piece from this period: a sandstone statue of Shiva holding his wife, Uma, on his knee. The Baphuon style of the 11th century was inspired to a certain extent by the sculpture of Banteay Srei, producing some of the finest works to have survived into the 20th century. In the National Museum, look for the life-size *Vishnu Reclining* which is featured in the bronze display hall. Only the head, shoulders and two right arms have survived; it was once inlaid with precious metal and gems that would have brought the statue to life.

The statuary of the Angkor Wat period is felt to be conservative and stilted, lacking the grace of much earlier work. The genius of this period manifests itself more clearly in the architecture and fabulous bas reliefs of Angkor Wat itself.

The final high point in Angkorian sculpture is the Bayon period from the end of the 12th century to the beginning of the 13th. In the National Museum, look for the superb representation of Jayavarman VII, an image that simultaneously projects great power and sublime tranquillity. Also represented from this period is the simple image of Jayarajadevi from Preah Khan in central Cambodia.

Sculpture in Cambodia went into decline from the end of the Angkor era.

Architecture

Khmer architecture reached its period of greatest magnificence during the Angkorian era (the 9th to 14th centuries). Some of the finest examples of architecture from this period are Angkor Wat and the structures of Angkor Thom. See the Angkor chapter for more information on the architectural styles of the Angkor era.

Today, most Cambodian houses in rural areas are built on high wood pilings (if the family can afford it) and have thatch roofs, walls made of palm mats and floors of woven bamboo strips resting on bamboo joists. The shady space underneath is used for storage and for people to relax at midday.

Cinema

Cambodians complain that their film industry is all but dead. In 1989, some 200 film companies were registered with the Cinema Department. By mid-1995 only six were left. Local directors point to low cinema audience numbers and the popularity of foreign videos as the main problem. Even second Prime Minister Hun Sen has weighed in on the issue, claiming that local scriptwriters should 'write more happy endings' if they want to revive Cambodian film.

At least one Cambodian director has had success in recent years, though. Rithy Panh's *People of the Rice Fields* was nominated for the Palme d'Or at the Cannes Film Festival in May 1995. The film touches only fleetingly on the Khmer Rouge, depicting the lives of a family eking out an arduous existence in the rice fields. Rithy Panh has been active in encouraging other young Cambodians to take up film making, holding screenwriting seminars in Phnom Penh. He has plans to make another feature film.

Sihanouk & the Silver Screen

Between 1966 and 1969, Sihanouk wrote, directed and produced nine feature films, a figure that would put the average workaholic Hollywood director to shame. As had been the case with previous interests (horse riding and magazine publishing among them), Sihanouk took the business of making films very seriously indeed. Family and officials were called upon to do their bit – the minister of foreign affairs played the male lead in Sihanouk's first feature, *Apsara*. When, in the same movie, a show of military hardware was required, the airforce was brought into action, as was the army's fleet of helicopters.

The meandering plot of *Apsara* explores the conflict between personal love and the love of one's country. It features opulent sets and expensive cars – a far cry from the reality of Cambodia in the 1960s. The world premiere was something of a flop, the foreign community failing to patronise the movie. Although, as Milton Osbourne says in his biography *Sihanouk – Prince of Light, Prince of Darkness*, the Chinese Embassy staff did at least have the good manners to excuse themselves on the pretext of pressing business elsewhere – 'because of the Cultural Revolution'.

Not that this put the royal film maker off. On the contrary, Sihanouk continued to make movies, often taking on the leading role himself. Notable performances saw him as a spirit of the forest and as a victorious general. Perhaps it was no surprise, given the king's apparent addiction to the world of celluloid dreams, that Cambodia should challenge Cannes and Berlin with its Phnom Penh International Film Festival. The festival was held twice, in 1968 and 1969. Sihanouk won the grand prize on both occasions. ■

SOCIETY & CONDUCT

Greetings

Like the Thais, who have their *wai*, the Cambodians traditionally greet each other with the *sompiah*, which involves pressing the hands together in prayer and bowing. In general the higher the hands and the lower the bow the more respect is shown. In recent decades, this custom has been partially replaced by the western practice of shaking hands. But, although men tend to shake hands with each other, women usually use the traditional greeting with both men and women. It is considered acceptable (or perhaps excusable) for foreigners to shake hands with Cambodians of both sexes.

Visiting Khmers

As is the case throughout Asia, a small token of gratitude in the form of a gift is always appreciated when you visit someone. Gifts should always be offered with the right hand. If you want to be particularly polite, support your right elbow with the fingers of your left hand as you do so. Before entering a Khmer home, always remove your shoes.

Dress

Both men and women often wear sarongs (made of cotton, a cotton-synthetic blend or silk), especially at home. Men who can afford it usually prefer silk sarongs. Most urban Khmer men dress in trousers these days, and many women dress western style.

On formal occasions such as religious festivals and family celebrations, women often wear *hols* (type of shirt) during the daytime. At night, they change into single-colour silk dresses called *phamuongs*, which are decorated along the hems. The colours of such garments are stipulated by the day of the week on which the wedding is held.

Modesty

The women of Cambodia are very modest in their dress – much more so than the Vietnamese. When eating at home, they sit on floor mats with their feet to the side rather than in the lotus position, as do the men. As in Thailand, nude bathing is unacceptable.

Visiting Pagodas

The Khmer are a tolerant people and may choose not to point out improper behaviour to their foreign guests, but you should dress and act with the utmost respect when visiting wats or other religious sites (such as some of the temples of Angkor). This is all the more important given the vital role Buddhist beliefs and institutions have played in the lives of many Cambodians in the aftermath of the Khmer Rouge holocaust. Proper etiquette in pagodas is mostly a matter of common sense.

Unlike Thailand, a woman may accept something from a monk, but she should be careful not to touch him as she does so.

A few other tips:

- Don't wear shorts or tank tops.
- Take off your hat when entering the grounds of the wat.
- Take off your shoes before going into the *vihara* (sanctuary).
- If you sit down in front of the dais (the platform on which the Buddhas are placed), sit with your feet to the side rather than in the lotus position.
- Never point your finger – or, heaven forbid, the soles of your feet – towards a person or a figure of the Buddha.

Dos & Don'ts

There are some rules that are worth remembering while you are in the country.

- Getting angry and showing it by shouting or becoming abusive is both impolite and a poor reflection on you; in addition, it is unlikely to accomplish much. If things aren't being done as they should, remember that there is a critical shortage of trained people in the country because the vast majority of educated Cambodians either fled the country or were killed between 1975 and 1979.
- As in Thailand, it is improper to pat children on the head.
- If you would like someone to come over to you, motion with your whole hand held palm down – signalling with your index finger and your palm pointed skyward may be interpreted as being sexually suggestive.
- When picking your teeth with a toothpick after a meal, it is considered polite to hold the toothpick in one hand and to cover your open mouth with the other.

RELIGION
Hinduism

Hinduism flourished alongside Buddhism from the 1st century until the 14th century. In Funan and during the pre-Angkorian period, Hinduism was represented by the worship of Harihara (Shiva and Vishnu embodied in a single deity). During the time of Angkor, Shiva was the deity most in favour with the royal family, although in the 12th century he seems to have been superseded by Vishnu.

Buddhism

The majority of the people of Cambodia are followers of Theravada, or Hinayana, Buddhism. Buddhism was introduced to Cambodia between the 13th and 14th centuries and was the state religion until 1975.

The Theravada (Teaching of the Elders) school of Buddhism is an earlier and, according to its followers, less corrupted form of Buddhism than the Mahayana schools found in East Asia or in the Himalayan lands. The Theravada school is also called the 'Southern' school since it took the southern route from India, its place of origin, through South-East Asia (Burma/Myanmar, Thailand, Laos and Cambodia in this case), while the 'Northern' school proceeded north into Nepal, Tibet, China, Korea, Mongolia, Vietnam and Japan. Because the Southern school tried to preserve or limit the Buddhist doctrines to only those canons codified in the early Buddhist era, the northern school gave Theravada Buddhism the name Hinayana, meaning the 'Lesser Vehicle'. The Northern school considered itself Mahayana, the 'Great Vehicle', because it built upon the earlier teachings, 'expanding' the doctrine to respond more to the needs of lay people, or so it claimed.

Theravada, doctrine stresses the three principal aspects of existence: *dukkha* (suffering, unsatisfactoriness, disease), *anicca* (impermanency, transience of all things) and *anatta* (non-substantiality or non-essentiality of reality: no permanent 'soul'). These concepts, when 'discovered' by Siddhartha Gautama in the 6th century BC, were in direct contrast to the Hindu belief in an eternal, blissful Self, or *Paramatman*, hence Buddhism was originally a 'heresy' against India's Brahmanic religion.

Gautama, an Indian prince-turned-ascetic, subjected himself to many years of severe austerities to arrive at this vision of the world and was given the title Buddha, 'the Enlightened' or 'the Awakened'. Gautama Buddha spoke of four noble truths which had the power to liberate any human being who could realise them. These four noble truths are:

- The truth of suffering – 'Existence is suffering.'
- The truth of the cause of suffering – 'Suffering is caused by desire.'
- The truth of the cessation of suffering – 'Eliminate the cause of suffering (desire) and suffering will cease to arise.'
- The truth of the path – 'The eight-fold path is the way to eliminate desire/extinguish suffering.'

The eight-fold path *(atthangika-magga)* consists of:

- right understanding
- right-mindedness (or 'right thought')
- right speech
- right bodily conduct
- right livelihood
- right effort
- right attentiveness
- right concentration

Many Cambodian monks are ordained for life.

The eight-fold path is also known as the Middle Way since it avoids both extreme austerity and extreme sensuality.

The ultimate goal of Theravada Buddhism is *nibbana* (Sanskrit: *nirvana*) which literally means the 'blowing-out' or 'extinction' of all causes of dukkha. Effectively it means an end to all corporeal existence – an end to that which is forever subject to suffering and which is conditioned from moment to moment by *karma*, or action. In reality, most Buddhists aim for rebirth in a 'better' existence rather than the supramundane goal of nibbana, which is highly misunderstood by Asians as well as westerners. Many Buddhists express the feeling that they are somehow unworthy of nibbana. By feeding monks, giving donations to temples and performing regular worship at the local wat (Buddhist temple) they hope to improve their

lot, acquiring enough merit *(punña* in the Pali language) to prevent or at least lessen the number of rebirths. The making of merit is an important social as well as religious activity. The concept of reincarnation is almost universally accepted by Cambodian Buddhists, and to some extent even by non-Buddhists.

The *Trilatna (Triratna)*, or Triple Gems, include the Buddha, the *dhamma* (the Teachings) and the Sangha (the Buddhist Brotherhood). The Buddha in his sculptural form is found on high shelves or altars in homes and shops as well as in temples. The dhamma is chanted morning and evening in every wat. The Sangha is represented by the street presence of orange-robed monks, especially in the early morning hours when they perform their alms rounds, in what has almost become a travel-guide cliche in motion.

Socially, every Buddhist male is expected to become a monk for a short period in his life, optimally between the time he finishes school and starts a career or marries. Men or boys under 20 years of age may enter the Sangha as novices and this is not unusual since a family earns great merit when one of its sons takes robe and bowl. Traditionally, the length of time spent in the wat is three months, during the Buddhist Lent *(phansaa* or *watsa)*, which begins in July and coincides with the rainy season. However, nowadays men may spend as little as a week or 15 days to accrue merit as monks.

Monks must follow 227 vows or precepts as part of the monastic discipline. Many monks ordain for a lifetime. Of these, a large percentage become scholars and teachers, while some specialise in healing and/or folk magic (although the latter is greatly discouraged by the current ruling party). There is no similar hermit-like order for nuns, but women are welcome to reside in temples as lay nuns, with shaved heads and white robes.

The women only have to follow eight precepts. Because discipline for these 'nuns' is much less arduous, they don't attain quite as high a social status as do monks. However, aside from the fact that they don't perform ceremonies on behalf of other lay persons, they engage in the same basic religious activities (meditation and study of dharma, ideal truth as set forth in the teaching of Buddha) as monks. The reality is that wats which draw sizeable contingents of eight-precept nuns are highly respected because women don't choose temples for reasons of clerical status – when more than a few reside at one temple it's because the teachings there are considered particularly strong.

Archaeologists have determined that before the 9th century, a period during which Sanskrit was used in ritual inscriptions, the Theravada school constituted the prevalent form of Buddhism in Cambodia. Inscriptions and images indicate that Mahayana Buddhism was in favour after the 9th century but was replaced in the 13th century by a form of Theravada Buddhism which arrived, along with the Pali language, from Sri Lanka via Thailand.

Between 1975 and 1979, the vast majority of Cambodia's Buddhist monks were murdered by the Khmer Rouge, who also damaged or destroyed virtually all of the country's more than 3000 wats. In the late 1980s, Buddhism was again made the state religion. At that time, Cambodia had about 6000 monks, who by law had to be at least 60 years old. The age requirements have been relaxed and young monks are once again a normal sight.

Islam

Cambodia's Muslims are descendants of Chams who migrated from what is now central Vietnam after the final defeat of the kingdom of Champa by the Vietnamese in 1471. Whereas their compatriots who remained in Vietnam were only partly Islamicised, the Cambodian Chams adopted a fairly orthodox version of Sunni Islam and maintained links with other Muslim communities in the region. Like their Buddhist neighbours, however, the Cham Muslims call the faithful to prayer by banging on a drum, rather than with the call of the *muezzin*, as in most Muslim lands.

Today, the Muslim community of Phnom Penh includes the descendants of people who emigrated from Pakistan and Afghanistan several generations ago, and a neighbourhood near Tuol Tom Pong Market is still known as the Arab Village. However, there are only about half a dozen Muslims fluent in Arabic, the language of the Koran, in all of Cambodia. In 1989, 20 Cambodian Muslims made the *hajj* (pilgrimage) to Mecca. *Halal* (killed according to Islamic law) meat is available in Phnom Penh in the O Russei, Tuol Tom Pong and Psar Char markets.

A small heretical community known as the Zahidin follows traditions similar to those of the Muslim Chams of Vietnam, praying once a week (on Friday) and observing Ramadan (a month of dawn-to-dusk fasting) only on the first, middle and last days of the month.

The Khmer Rouge seems to have made a concerted effort to annihilate Cambodia's Cham Muslim community.

Vietnamese Religions

During the 1920s, quite a few ordinary Cambodians became interested in Caodaism, a colourful syncretic religion founded in Vietnam.

LANGUAGE

The Khmer or Cambodian language is spoken by approximately nine million people in Cambodia, and is understood by many in bordering countries. Written Khmer is based on the ancient Brahmi script of southern India. Arguably one of the oldest languages in Southeast Asia, Khmer inscriptions have been dated back to the 7th century AD. Although separate and distinct from its Thai, Lao, and Burmese neighbours, Khmer shares with them the common roots of Sanskrit and Pali — a heritage of centuries of linguistic and cultural interaction and of their shared faith in Theravada Buddhism. More recently, many French words entered the Khmer language during the colonial period, especially medical and technical terms.

Unlike the languages of its bordering countries, Khmer is non-tonal, meaning that there are no special intonations of words which alter their meaning. This may be a relief for travellers in the region who have been frustrated in their attempts at tonal languages such as Thai, Vietnamese and Lao. However, the lack of tones is compensated by the complexity of the Khmer pronunciation. There are 33 consonants, often paired in seemingly bizarre combinations, and some 24 vowels and diphthongs. Further complicating the language is the haphazard transliteration system left over from the days of French rule, which does not reflect accurate pronunciation of Khmer words by English speakers.

On the positive side, Khmer grammar is very simple. There are no verb conjugations or gender inflections, no endings for single or plural, masculine or feminine. Adding a few words changes sentence tense to past, present, or future.

In any case, a bit of Khmer, even if butchered, will go a long way. The Khmers sincerely appreciate any effort to learn their language and are very supportive of visitors who give it even a halfhearted try. You will find that as your skill and vocabulary increases, so does your social standing; people go out of their way to complement you, moto-taxi fares and prices at markets drop, and you may even win a few friends.

The transliteration system used in this section has been designed for basic communications rather than linguistic perfection. Several Khmer vowels, however, have no English equivalent; thus such words can only be approximated by English spellings. Other words are written as they are pronounced and not necessarily according to the actual vowels used in the words. (Khmer placenames will follow their standard spellings.) As with any language, questions regarding exact pronunciations are best solved by asking a native speaker.

Though English is fast becoming Cambodia's dominant second language, the Khmer still cling to the Francophone pronunciation of the Roman alphabet and most foreign words. This is helpful to remember when spelling western words and names; thus 'ay—bee—cee' becomes 'ah—bey—sey', and so on. French speakers will definitely have an advantage when addressing the older generation, as most educated Khmers studied French at some point during their schooling. Many household items retain their French names as well, especially those which were introduced to Cambodia by the French, such as *robine*, 'faucet', and *ampuol*, 'light bulb'.

For those interested in further study of spoken and written Khmer, I recommend *Cambodian System of Writing and Beginning Reader*, *Modern Spoken Cambodian*, and any other books by Frank Huffman. Locally produced copies of most of these titles can be found at the book and stationery stalls around the eastern entrance to the Central Market in Phnom Penh.

Dialects

Although the Khmer language as spoken in Phnom Penh is generally intelligible nationwide, there are several distinct dialects in other areas of the country. Most notably, the Khmer of Takeo province tend to modify or slur hard consonant/vowel combinations, especially those which contain 'r'; thus *bram* ('five') becomes *pe-am*, *sraa* ('alcohol') becomes *se-aa*, and *baraang* ('French' or 'foreigner') becomes *be-ang*. In Siem Reap, sharp-eared travellers will notice a very Lao sounding lilt to the local speech. Here, certain vowels are modified, such as *poan* ('thousand') which becomes *peuan*, and *kh'sia* ('pipe'), which becomes *kh'seua*.

Vowels

aa	as the 'a' in 'father'
i	as the 'i' in 'kit'
uh	as the 'u' in 'but'
ii	as the 'ee' in 'feet'
ei	a combination of 'uh' and 'ii' above; 'uh-ii'
eu	similar to the French *peuple*; try pronouncing 'oo' while keeping the lips spread flat rather than rounded
euh	as 'euh' above, but pronounced short and hard
oh	as the 'o' in 'hose' but pronounced short and hard
ow	as the 'o' in 'glow'
u	as the 'u' in 'flute' but pronounced short and hard
uu	as the 'oo' in 'zoo'
ua	as the 'ou' in 'tour'
uah	as 'ua' above, but pronounced short and hard
aa-œ	a tough one with no English equivalent; like a combination of 'aa' and 'œ'. When placed between consonants it is often pronounced like 'ao'.
œ	as 'er' in 'her' but more open
eua	combination of 'eu' and 'a'
ia	as 'ee-ya', like 'beer' without the 'r'
e	as the 'a' in 'late'
ai	as the 'i' in 'side'
ae	as the 'a' in 'cat'
ay	as 'ai' above but slightly more nasal
ey	as the 'ay' in 'pray'
ao	as the 'ow' in 'cow'
av	another tough one with no English equivalent; like a very nasal 'ao'. The final 'v' is not pronounced.
euv	no English equivalent; like a very nasal 'eu'. The final 'v' is not pronounced.
ohm	as the 'ome' in 'home'
am	as the 'um' in 'glum'
oam	a combination of 'o' and 'am'
a, ah	shorter and harder than 'aa' above
eah	combination of 'e' and 'ah', pronounced short and hard
ih	as the 'ee' in 'teeth' pronounced short and hard
eh	as the 'a' in 'date' pronounced short

	and hard
awh	as the 'aw' in 'jaw' pronounced short and hard
oah	a combination of 'o' and 'ah', pronounced short and hard.
aw	as the 'aw' in 'jaw'

Vowels and diphthongs with an 'h' at the end should be pronounced hard and aspirated.

Consonants

Khmer uses some consonant combinations which may sound rather bizarre to the Westerner's ear and equally difficult for the Western tongue, such as 'j-r' in *j'rook*, 'pig', or 'ch-ng' in *ch'ngain*, 'delicious'. For ease of pronunciation such consonants are separated here with an apostrophe.

k	as the 'g' in 'go'
kh	as the 'k' in 'kind'
ng	as in the final sound of the word 'sing'; a difficult sound for Westerners to emulate. Practice by saying 'singing-nging-nging-nging' until you can say 'nging' clearly.
j	as the 'j' in 'jump'
ch	as in 'cheese'
ny	as in the final syllable of 'onion': 'nyun'.
t	a hard, unaspirated 't' sound with no direct equivalent in English. Similar to the 't' in 'stand'.
th	as the 't' in 'two', never as the 'th' in 'thanks'.
p	a hard, unaspirated 'p' sound, as the final 'p' in 'puppy'
ph	as the 'p' in 'pond', never as 'ph' in 'phone'
r	as in 'rum' but hard and rolling, with the tongue flapping against the palate. In rapid conversation it is often omitted entirely.
w	as the 'w' in 'would'. Contrary to the common transliteration system, there is no equivalent to the English 'v' sound in Khmer.

Greetings & Civilities

Hello.
> *johm riab sua/sua s'dei* ជំរាបសួរ / សួស្ដី

Goodbye.
> *lia suhn hao-y* លាសិនហើយ

See you later.
juab kh'nia th'ngay krao-y ជួបគ្នាថ្ងៃក្រោយ

Yes. **baat** បាទ
(used by men)
Yes. **jaa** ចាស
(used by women)
No. *te* ទេ
Please. *sohm* សូម
Thank you. *aw kohn* អរគុណ

You're welcome.
awt ei te/sohm anjœ-in
អត់អីទេ/ សូមអញ្ជើញ
Excuse me/I'm sorry.
sohm toh សុំទោស
Pardon? (What did you say?)
niak niyey thaa mait? អ្នកនិយាយថាម៉េច?

Small Talk

Hi. How are you?
niak sohk sabaay te? អ្នកសុខសប្បាយទេ?
I'm fine.
kh'nyohm sohk sabaay ខ្ញុំសុខសប្បាយ
Where are you going?
niak teuv naa? អ្នកទៅណា?
(NB This is a very common question
used when meeting people, even stran-
gers; an exact answer is not necessary.)
What is your name?
niak ch'muah ei? អ្នកឈ្មោះអី?
My name is ...
kh'nyohm ch'muah ... ខ្ញុំឈ្មោះ...

Where are you from?
niak mao pii prateh naa?
អ្នកមកពីប្រទេសណា?
I am from ...
kh'nyohm mao pii ... ខ្ញុំមកពី...
I'm staying at ...
kh'nyohm snahk neuv... ខ្ញុំស្នាក់នៅ...
Can I take a photo (of you)?
kh'nyohm aa-it thawt ruup niak baan te?
ខ្ញុំអាចថតរូបអ្នកបានទេ?

Forms of Address

The Khmer language reflects the social standing of the speaker and subject through various personal pronouns and 'politeness
words'. These range from the simple *baat* for
men and *jaa* for women, placed at the end of
a sentence, meaning 'yes' or 'I agree', to the
very formal and archaic *Reachasahp* or
'Royal language', a separate vocabulary reserved for addressing the King and very high
officials. Many of the pronouns are determined on the basis of the subject's age and
sex in relation to the speaker. Foreigners are
not expected to know all of these forms. The
easiest and most general personal pronoun is
niak, 'you', which may be used in most situations, with either sex. Men of your age and
older may be called *lowk*, or 'mister', women
of your age and older can be called *bawng
srei* ('older sister') or for more formal situations, *lowk srei* ('Madam'). *Bawng* is a good
informal, neutral pronoun for men or women
who are (or appear to be) older than you. For
third person, male or female, singular or plural, the respectful form is *koat* and the common form is *ke*.

Language Difficulties

Does any one here speak English?
tii nih mian niak jeh phiasaa awngle te?
ទីនេះមានអ្នកចេះភាសាអង់គ្លេសទេ?
Do you understand?
niak yuhl te/niak s'dap baan te?
អ្នកយល់ទេ /អ្នកស្ដាប់បានទេ?
I understand.
kh'nyohm yuhl / kh'nyohm s'dap baan
ខ្ញុំយល់ /ខ្ញុំស្ដាប់បាន
I don't understand.
*kh'nyohm muhn yuhl te / kh'nyohm s'dap
muhn baan te*
ខ្ញុំមិនយល់ទេ/ខ្ញុំស្ដាប់មិនបានទេ
How do you say ... in Khmer?
... kh'mai thaa mait?
...ខ្មែរថាម៉េច?
What does this mean?
nih mian nuh-y thaa mait?
នេះមានន័យថាម៉េច?
Please speak slowly!
sohm niyay yeut yeut
សូមនិយាយយឺតៗ
Write that word down for me.
sohm sawse piak nu ao-y kh'nyohm
សូមសរសេរពាក្យនោះឲ្យខ្ញុំ
Please translate for me.
sohm bawk brai ao-y kh'nyohm
សូមបកប្រែឲ្យខ្ញុំ

What is this called?
nih ke hav thaa mait?   នេះគេហៅថាម៉េច?

Getting Around

Where is the ...?
... neuv ai naa?   ... នៅឯណា?
bus station
  kuhnlaing laan ch'nual   កន្លែងឡានឈ្នួល
bus stop
  jamnawt laan ch'nual   ចំណតឡានឈ្នួល
train station
  s'thaanii roht plæng   ស្ថានីយរថភ្លើង
airport
  wial yohn hawh   វាលយន្តហោះ

What time does the ... leave?
... jein maong pohnmaan?
  ... ចេញម៉ោងប៉ុន្មាន?

bus	*laan ch'nual*	ឡានឈ្នួល
	laan ch'nual	ឡានឈ្នួល
train	*roht plæng*	រថភ្លើង
plane	*yohn hawh/*	យន្តហោះ/
	k'pal hawh	កប៉ាល់ហោះ

What time does the last bus leave?
*laan ch'nual johng krao-y jein teuv
maong pohnmaan?*
ឡានឈ្នួល ចុងក្រោយ ចេញទៅម៉ោងប៉ុន្មាន?

How can I get to ...?
phleuv naa teuv...   ផ្លូវណាទៅ...?
Is it far?
wia neuv ch'ngaay te? វានៅឆ្ងាយទេ?
Is it near?
wia neuv juht te?   វានៅជិតទេ?
Is it near here?
wia neuv juht nih te? វានៅជិតនេះទេ?

Go straight ahead.
teuv trawng   ទៅត្រង់
Turn left ...
bawt ch'weng   បត់ឆ្វេង
Turn right ...
bawt s'dam   បត់ស្ដាំ
at the corner
neuv kait j'rohng   នៅកាច់ជ្រុង
in front of
neuv khaang mohk   នៅខាងមុខ
next to
neuv joab   នៅជាប់

behind
neuv khaang krao-y   នៅខាងក្រោយ
opposite
neuv tohl mohk   នៅទល់មុខ

I want to get off (here)!
kh'nyohm jawng joh   ខ្ញុំចង់ចុះ
(tii nih)!   (ទីនេះ)!

How much is it to ...?
teuv ... th'lay pohnmaan? ទៅ... ថ្លៃប៉ុន្មាន?
That's too much!
th'lay pek!   ថ្លៃពេក!

Please take me to ...
sohm juun kh'nyohm teuv ...
  សូមជូនខ្ញុំទៅ ...
this address
aadreh/aasayathaan nih   អាស័យដ្ឋាននេះ
Here is fine, thank you.
chohp neuv tii nih kaw baan
ឈប់នៅទីនេះក៏បាន

north	*khaang jæng*	ខាងជើង
south	*khaang d'bowng*	ខាងត្បូង
east	*khaang kaot*	ខាងកើត
west	*khaang leit*	ខាងលិច

Around Town

Where is a ... ... *neuv ai naa?* ...នៅឯណា?

bank	*th'niakia*	ធនាគារ
cinema	*rowng kohn*	រោងកុន
consulate	*kohng sul*	កុងស៊ុល
embassy	*s'thaantuut*	ស្ថានទូត
hospital	*mohntii paet*	មន្ទីរពេទ្យ
market	*p'saa*	ផ្សារ
museum	*saramohntii*	សារមន្ទី
park	*suan*	សួន
post office	*praisuhnii*	ប្រៃសណីយ
temple	*wawt*	វត្ត

police station
poh polih/s'thaanii nohkohbaal
ប៉ុស្តិ៍ប៉ូលិស/ស្ថានីយនគរបាល
public telephone
turasahp saathiaranah
ទូរស័ព្ទសាធារណៈ
public toilet
bawngkohn saathiaranah
បង្គន់សាធារណៈ

How far is the ...?
... ch'ngaay pohnmaan?
... ឆ្ងាយប៉ុន្មាន?
I want to see the ...
kh'nyohm jawng teuv mœl...
ខ្ញុំចង់ទៅមើល...
I am looking for the ...
kh'nyohm rohk ...
ខ្ញុំរក...

What time does it open?
wia baok maong pohnmaan?
វាបើកម៉ោងប៉ុន្មាន?
What time does it close?
wia buht maong pohnmaan?
វាបិតម៉ោងប៉ុន្មាន?
Is it still open?
wia neuv baok reu te?
វានៅបើកឬទេ?
What ... is this?
... nih ch'muah ei?
...នេះឈ្មោះអី?
I want to change ...
kh'nyohm jawng dow ...
ខ្ញុំចង់ដូរ...
US dollars
dolaa amerik   ដុល្លាអាមេរិក

What is the exchange rate for US dollars?
muy dolaa dow baan pohnmaan?
មួយដុល្លាដូរបានប៉ុន្មាន?

Accommodation
Where is a ...?
... neuv ai naa?   ...នៅឯណា?
hotel
sahnthaakia/ohtail   សណ្ឋាគារ/អូតែល
cheap hotel
sahnthaakia/   សណ្ឋាគារ/
ohtail thaok   អូតែលថោក

I've already found a hotel.
kh'nyohm mian ohtail hao-y
ខ្ញុំមានអូតែលហើយ
I'm staying at ...
kh'nyohm snahk neuv ...
ខ្ញុំស្នាក់នៅ...
Could you write down the address, please?
sohm sawse aasayathaan ao-y kh'nyohm
សូមសរសេរអាសយដ្ឋានឱ្យខ្ញុំ

I'd like a room ...
kh'nyohm sohm bantohp ...   ខ្ញុំសុំបន្ទប់...
for one person
samruhp muy niak   សំរាប់មួយនាក់
for two people
samruhp pii niak   សំរាប់ពីរនាក់
with a bathroom
dail mian bantohp tuhk   ដែលមានបន្ទប់ទឹក
with a fan
dail mian dawnghahl   ដែលមានកង្ហារ
with a window
dail mian bawng-uit   ដែលមានបង្អួច

I am going to stay for ...
kh'nyohm nuhng snahk tii nih ...
ខ្ញុំនឹងស្នាក់ទីនេះ...
one day   *muy th'ngay*   មួយថ្ងៃ
one week   *muy aatuht*   មួយអាទិត្យ

Do you have a room?
niak mian bantohp tohmne te?
អ្នកមានបន្ទប់ទំនេទេ?
How much does it cost per day?
damlay muy th'ngay pohnmaan?
តំលៃមួយថ្ងៃប៉ុន្មាន?
Does the price include breakfast?
damlay bantohp khuht teang m'hohp pel pruhk reu?
តំលៃបន្ទប់គិតទាំងអាហារពេលព្រឹកឬ?
Can I see the room?
kh'nyohm aa-it mœl bantohp baan te?
ខ្ញុំអាចមើលបន្ទប់បានទេ?
I don't like this room.
kh'nyohm muhn johl juht bantohp nih te
ខ្ញុំមិនចូលចិត្តបន្ទប់នេះទេ
Do you have a better room?
niak mian bantohp l'aw jiang nih te?
អ្នកមានបន្ទប់ល្អជាងនេះទេ?
I'll take this room.
kh'nyohm yohk bantohp nih
ខ្ញុំយកបន្ទប់នេះ

Can I leave my things here until ... ?
kh'nyohm aa-it ph'nyaa-œ tohk eiwuhn r'bawh kh'nyohm neuv tii nih dawl... baan te?
ខ្ញុំអាចផ្ញើអីវ៉ាន់របស់ខ្ញុំនៅទីនេះដល់...បានទេ?

this afternoon   *l'ngiak nih*   ល្ងាចនេះ
this evening   *yohp nih*   យប់នេះ

Food

Where is a ...
... neuv ai naa? ...នៅឯណា?
cheap restaurant
  haang baay/ ហាងបាយថោក
  resturaan thaok
restaurant
  resturaan/ ភោជនីយដ្ឋាន
  phowjuhniiyathaan
food stall
  kuhnlaing luak m'howp កន្លែងលក់ម្ហូប
market
  p'saa ផ្សារ
I'm vegetarian.
  kh'nyohm tawm sait ខ្ញុំតមសាច់
I can't eat meat.
  kh'nyohm tawm sait. ខ្ញុំតម សាច់

Not too spicy please.
  sohm kohm twœ huhl pek
  សូមកុំធ្វើហ៊ីលពេក
No MSG please.
  sohm kohm dahk bii jeng
  សូមកុំដាក់ប៊ីចេង
This is delicious.
  nih ch'ngain nah
  នេះឆ្ងាញ់ណាស់

Shopping

How much is it?
  nih th'lay pohnmaan? នេះថ្លៃប៉ុន្មាន?
That's too much.
  th'lay pek ថ្លៃពេក
I'll give you ...
  kh'nyohm ao-y ... ខ្ញុំឱ្យ...
No more than ...
  muhn lœh pii ... មិនលើសពី..
What's your best price?
  niak dait pohnmaan? អ្នកដាច់ប៉ុន្មាន?

Health

Where is a ...
... neuv ai naa? ...នៅឯណា?
dentist *paet th'mein* ពេទ្យធ្មេញ
doctor *kruu paet* គ្រូពេទ្យ
hospital *mohntrii paet* មន្ទីរពេទ្យ
medicine *th'nam* ថ្នាំ
pharmacy
  kuhnlaing luak th'nam/ohsawt s'thaan
  កន្លែងលក់ថ្នាំ/ឱសថស្ថាន

I am ill.
  kh'nyohm cheu ខ្ញុំឈឺ
I'm suffering from ...
  kh'nyohm mian ... ខ្ញុំមាន...
My ... hurts
  ... r'bawh kh'nyohm cheu .របស់ខ្ញុំឈឺ
I feel nauseous.
  kh'nyohm jawng k'uat ខ្ញុំចង់ក្អួត
I feel weak.
  kh'nyohm awh kamlahng ខ្ញុំអស់កំលាំង
I keep vomiting.
  kh'nyohm k'uat j'raa-œn ខ្ញុំក្អួតច្រើន
I feel dizzy.
  kh'nyohm wuhl mohk ខ្ញុំវិលមុខ
I'm having trouble breathing.
  kh'nyohm pi baak dawk dawnghaom
  ខ្ញុំពិបាកដកដង្ហើម

I am allergic to ...
  kh'nyohm muhn treuv thiat ...
  ខ្ញុំមិនត្រូវធាតុ...
penicillin *penicillin* ប៉ីនីស៊ីលីន
antibiotics *awntiibiowtik* អង់ទីប៊ីយោទិក

I need medicine for ...
  kh'nyohm treuv kaa th'nam samruhp ...
  ខ្ញុំត្រូវការថ្នាំសំរាប់...

diarrhoea	*rowk joh riak*	រោគចុះរាក
dysentery	*rowk mual*	រោគមូល
fever	*krohn/*	គ្រុន/
	k'dav kh'luan	ក្ដៅខ្លួន
pain	*cheu*	ឈឺ
antiseptic	*th'nam*	ថ្នាំសំលាប់មេរោគ
	samlahp me	
	rowk	
aspirin	*parasetamol*	ប៉ារ៉ាសេតាម៉ុល
codeine	*codiin*	ខូឌីន
quinine	*kiiniin*	គីនីន
sleeping	*th'nam*	ថ្នាំងងុយដេក
pills	*ng'nguy dek*	

condoms
  sraom ahnaamai ស្រោមអនាម័យ
mosquito repellent
  th'nam kaa pia muh ថ្នាំការពារមូស
razor blade
  kambuht kao pohk កាំបិតកោរពុកមាត់
  moat

sanitary napkins
samlei ahnaamai សំឡីអនាម័យ
shampoo
sabuu kawk sawk សាប៊ូកក់សក់
shaving cream
kraim samruhp kao pohk moat
ប្រែមសំរាប់កោរពុកមាត់
sunblock cream
kraim kaa pia pohnleu th'ngay
ប្រែមការពារពន្លឺថ្ងៃ
toilet paper
krawdah ahnaamai ក្រដាស់អនាម័យ

Time & Dates
What time is it?
eileuv nih maong pohnmaan?
ឥឡូវនេះម៉ោងប៉ុន្មាន?

in the morning	*pel pruhk*	ពេលព្រឹក
in the afternoon	*pel r'sial*	ពេលរសៀល
in the evening	*pel l'ngiat*	ពេលល្ងាច
at night	*pel yohp*	ពេលយប់
today	*th'ngay nih*	ថ្ងៃនេះ
tomorrow	*th'ngay s'aik*	ថ្ងៃស្អែក
yesterday	*m'suhl mein*	ម្សិលមិញ

Monday	*th'ngay jahn*	ថ្ងៃចន្ទ
Tuesday	*th'ngay ahngkia*	ថ្ងៃអង្គារ
Wednesday	*th'ngay poht*	ថ្ងៃពុធ
Thursday	*th'ngay prohoah*	ថ្ងៃព្រហស្បតិ៍
Friday	*th'ngay sohk*	ថ្ងៃសុក្រ
Saturday	*th'ngay sav*	ថ្ងៃសៅរ៍
Sunday	*th'ngay aatuht*	ថ្ងៃអាទិត្យ

Numbers & Amounts
Khmers count in increments of five. Thus, after reaching the number five *(bram)*, the cycle begins again with the addition of one, ie 'five-one' *(bram muy)*, 'five-two' *(bram pii)*, and so on to 10, which begins a new cycle. This system is a bit awkward at first (for example, 18, which has three parts: 10, five, and three) but with practice it can be mastered.

You may be confused by a colloquial form of counting which reverses the word order for numbers between 10 and 20 and separates the two words with *duhn: pii duhn dawp* for

12, *bei duhn dawp* for 13, *bram buan duhn dawp* for 19, and so on. This form is often used in markets, so listen keenly.

1	*muy*	មួយ
2	*pii*	ពីរ
3	*bei*	បី
4	*buan*	បួន
5	*bram*	ប្រាំ
6	*bram muy*	ប្រាំមួយ
7	*bram pii/ bram puhl*	ប្រាំពីរ
8	*bram bei*	ប្រាំបី
9	*bram buan*	ប្រាំបួន
10	*dawp*	ដប់
11	*dawp muy*	ដប់មួយ
12	*dawp pii*	ដប់ពីរ
16	*dawp bram muy*	ដប់ប្រាំមួយ
20	*m'phei*	ម្ភៃ
21	*m'phei muy*	ម្ភៃមួយ
30	*saamsuhp*	សាមសិប
40	*saisuhp*	សែសិប
100	*muy roy*	មួយរយ
1000	*muy poan*	មួយពាន់
a million	*muy lian*	មួយលាន
1st	*tii muy*	ទីមួយ
2nd	*tii pii*	ទីពីរ
3rd	*tii bei*	ទីបី
4th	*tii buan*	ទីបួន
10th	*tii dawp*	ទីដប់

Emergencies
Help!
juay kh'nyohm phawng! ជួយខ្ញុំផង!
It's an emergency!
nih jia reuang bawntoan នេះជារឿងបន្ទាន់
Call a doctor!
juay hav kruu paet mao!
ជួយហៅគ្រូពេទ្យមក!
Call the police!
juay hav polih mao!
ជួយហៅប៉ូលីសមក!

| toilets | *bawngkohn* | បង្គន់ |

Where are the toilets?
bawngkohn neuv ai naa? បង្គន់នៅឯណា?
Could you help me please?
niak aa-it juay kh'nyohm baan te?
អ្នកអាចជួយខ្ញុំបានទេ?

Could I please use the telephone?
kh'nyohm braa-œ turasahp baan te?
ខ្ញុំប្រើទូរស័ព្ទបានទេ?

I wish to contact my embassy/consulate.
kh'nyohm jawng hav s'thaantuut /
kohngsuhl r'bawh prawteh kh'nyohm

ខ្ញុំចង់ហៅស្ថានទូត/កុងស៊ុលរបស់ប្រទេសខ្ញុំ

I've been robbed.
kh'nyohm treuv jao   ខ្ញុំត្រូវចោរប្លន់។
plawn

Stop!
chohp!   ឈប់!
Watch out!
prawyaht!   ប្រយ័ត្ន!

Is this path safe to walk on?
phleuv nih mian sohwatthaphiap dai
reu te?
ផ្លូវនេះមានសុវត្ថភាពដែរឬទេ?

Are there any landmines in this area?
neuv m'dohm nih mian miin reu te?
នៅម៉ុំនេះមានមីនឬទេ?

Facts for the Visitor

PLANNING
When to Go

Cambodia can be visited any time of year. You might want to coordinate your trip, however, with one of the annual festivals – check the Public Holidays & Special Events section of this chapter.

The ideal months to be in Cambodia are December and January. At this time of year humidity levels are relatively low and there is little likelihood of rain. From early February, temperatures start to rise until the hottest month, April, in which temperatures can reach 38°C. Some time in April or early May the south-west monsoon brings rain and cooler weather. The wet season, which lasts from April to October, need not be a bad time to visit Cambodia. Angkor, for example, is surrounded by lush foliage and the moats are full of water at this time of year. If you are planning to visit the hill tribe regions of the north-east, however, the wet season should be avoided.

Maps

Tourist maps of Cambodia and Phnom Penh are available in Phnom Penh and Siem Reap, though they are fairly poor. The Periplus *Cambodia Travel Map* at 1:1,100,000 scale is probably the best around and is available in Phnom Penh and Bangkok bookshops. The Nelles Verlag *Vietnam, Laos & Cambodia* map at 1:1,500,000 scale is another good map of the country.

What to Bring

The usual rule applies: bring as little as possible. Phnom Penh is surprisingly well stocked with travel provisions, so if you have forgotten or lost anything it should be possible to replace it there. Nevertheless, it is always best to be prepared. The following is a comprehensive rundown of what you might consider taking.

Backpacks A good backpack is one outlay you will never regret. Look into buying a frameless or internal-frame pack – these are generally easier to deal with in crowded travel conditions, and also more comfortable to walk with. Also consider buying a pack that converts into a carry bag by way of a hood that zips over the shoulder and waist straps – it is less likely to be damaged on airport carousels and is more presentable if you ever need to discard the backpacker image.

A daypack is essential for carrying things around after you've dumped your backpack at the hotel or wherever. A beltpack is OK for maps, extra film and other miscellanea, but don't use it for valuables such as your travellers' cheques and passport (see the Dangers & Annoyances section in this chapter for precautions against theft).

Clothes Cambodia is blessed with year-round warm to pressure-cooker hot weather. You will need little in the way of clothes. Essentials, of course, are underwear, swimming gear (if you're heading down to Sihanoukville), a pair of jeans and a pair of shorts, a few T-shirts and shirts, a pair of runners or shoes, some sandals or thongs (flip-flops), and a lightweight jacket or raincoat (if you're in Cambodia for the rainy season).

Sleeping Bag Should you, shouldn't you? As is the case almost everywhere else in South-East Asia, you will not need a sleeping bag. For a start, it will be too hot most of the time to get any use out of it unless you stay in an air-con room. The fastidious might like to come prepared with a 'sheet sleeping bag' (two sheets sewn together), of the kind used in European youth hostels, but the bedding provided in Cambodia is generally very clean.

Necessities Almost any essentials you forget can be picked up in Phnom Penh, though prices are generally higher than at home (depending of course on where that is).

Absolutely essential is a good pair of sunglasses, and sunscreen (UV) lotion. The latter can be bought at the Lucky Supermarket in Phnom Penh.

An alarm clock is essential for getting up on time to catch your flight, bus or whatever – make sure yours is lightweight and bring extra batteries or a battery charger (size AA rechargeable batteries can be bought in most towns in Cambodia).

The following is a checklist of things you might consider packing. You can delete whatever you like from this list:

- photocopy of passport, documents (vaccination certificate, diplomas, marriage licence photocopy, student ID card), visa photos (about 20)
- money belt or vest, padlock, daypack
- long pants, short pants, long-sleeved shirt, T-shirt, nylon jacket, underwear, socks, thongs or sandals
- raincover for backpack, umbrella or rain poncho
- sunglasses, contact lens solution
- deodorant, shampoo, soap, razor, razor blades, shaving cream, sewing kit, spoon, sunhat, tampons, toothbrush, toothpaste, comb, nail clippers, tweezers
- compass, Swiss army knife, leakproof water bottle, alarm clock, camera & accessories, extra camera battery, shortwave radio, Walkman, address book, pens, notepad, torch (flashlight) with batteries & bulbs
- mosquito repellent, sunscreen, vitamins, laxative, condoms, contraceptives, medical kit (the Health section in this chapter has a contents list), special medications you use

SUGGESTED ITINERARIES

Due to security risks and the arduous nature of travel in Cambodia, travel options around the country are still limited. Before planning any 'adventurous' trips upcountry, it is essential that you check on the security situation with your embassy and/or with NGOs (Non-Government Organisations) in Phnom Penh. Cambodia is still in a state of civil war. Risks that backfire could have repercussions not just for you individually but also for the whole travel industry in Cambodia.

At present the only real travel itinerary in

Cambodia is a flight to Phnom Penh and then a trip by plane or boat to Siem Reap and Angkor Wat. Most embassies recommend that their nationals fly to Siem Reap, but very few budget travellers take heed of this advice. Most visitors to Cambodia seem to spend four or five days in and around Phnom Penh before heading up to Angkor Wat for around three days to a week of exploring the ruins.

A possible side trip for those who have more time and want to see more of the country is a visit to Sihanoukville. This seaside 'resort' is still in its infancy, and by South-East Asian standards the beaches are nothing to write home about. On the other hand, there are not many beach retreats left in Asia that have so few visitors – it's a great place to escape the crowds.

The other area of Cambodia attracting a trickle of hardcore travellers is the Ratanakiri region in the north-east of the country. At the time of writing this area was difficult to get to due to a shortage of flights. A small number of travellers have made their way up there via the Mekong River to Stung Treng, from where it is a rough 10 hour trip by road to Ban Lung, the provincial capital of Ratanakiri. Definitely check on the security situation before making this trip. Although Ratanakiri is free of Khmer Rouge activity, the upper reaches of the Mekong from Kratie to Stung Treng are not.

TOURIST OFFICES

Cambodia only has a handful of tourist offices, and these have little to offer the independent traveller. See the Phnom Penh chapter and the Siem Reap entry of the Angkor chapter for information on tourist offices there. Cambodia has no tourist offices abroad and it is unlikely that Cambodian embassies will be of much assistance in planning a trip, besides providing visas.

VISAS & DOCUMENTS
Passport

Not only is a passport essential but you also need to make sure that it's valid for at least six months beyond the *end* of your trip –

most countries will not allow you a visa if you have less than six months validity left on your passport.

It's also important to make sure that there is plenty of space left in your passport. Do not set off on a six month trek across Asia with only two blank pages left – a Cambodian visa alone takes up one page. It is sometimes possible to have extra pages added to your passport, but most people will be required to get a new passport. This is possible for most foreign nationals in Cambodia but it can be time consuming.

Losing a passport is not the end of the world, but it is a serious inconvenience. To expedite the issuance of a new passport, make sure that you have the information on your data pages written down somewhere, or better still make a photocopy of these pages and keep it separate from your passport.

Visas

Most nationalities receive a one month visa on arrival at Pochentong airport. The cost is US$20 and you require one passport photo. It is a good idea to bring a supply of extra passport photographs with you, though these are readily obtainable in Phnom Penh.

Travellers arriving overland from Ho Chi Minh City (Saigon) will have to obtain a visa before they reach the Moc Bai border crossing, but these are easy to get in Vietnam nowadays.

Visa Extensions Visa extensions can usually be granted in Phnom Penh (see under Information in the Phnom Penh chapter for details). Theoretically, extensions are simply a matter of having the cash to hand, but in practice they can sometimes be difficult to obtain. One passport photograph is required for visa extensions. One week costs US$20; one month US$30; three months US$60; six months US$100; and one year US$150.

Photocopies

As already mentioned in the Passport entry above, it is sensible to make a copy of the data pages in your passport and keep it sep-

arate from your passport. It is also a good idea to do the same thing with your airline tickets, credit cards and any other important documentation you may be travelling with. To be extra careful, leave copies of these with someone at home – this way you can get the information you need even if everything you have gets stolen.

It is recommended that you store your photocopies with an emergency cash stash – say, US$50 to US$100.

Travel Permits

The Cambodian government no longer requires that foreign travellers obtain travel permits for destinations outside Phnom Penh. This does not mean, however, that it is safe to go everywhere in the country. Check with your embassy or with Phnom Penh NGOs before making any potentially dangerous trips.

Onward Tickets

Customs officials at Pochentong airport are not in the habit of checking air tickets and onward tickets are not required. It is possible to fly into Cambodia and exit overland to Vietnam.

Travel Insurance

A travel insurance policy that covers theft, property loss and medical expenses is more essential for Cambodia than for most other parts of South-East Asia. Theft is less a problem in Cambodia than you might imagine, but in the event of serious medical problems or an accident you will probably need to be airlifted to Bangkok, an expense that stretches beyond the average traveller's budget.

There are a wide variety of travel insurance policies available, and it is wise to check with a reliable travel agent about which will best suit you in Cambodia. The policies handled by STA Travel (which has branches in Bangkok) are usually good value.

Wherever you buy your travel insurance, always check the small print:

- Some policies specifically exclude 'dangerous activities' such as scuba diving and motorcycling. If you are going to be riding a motorbike in Cambodia, check that your policy covers you.
- Check whether your medical coverage requires you to pay first and claim later; if this is the case you will need to keep all documents relating to your medical treatment.
- In the case of Cambodia, it is essential that you check to see that your medical coverage includes the cost of emergency evacuation.

Driving Licence

For obvious reasons, car hire is not available in Cambodia and it is very unlikely you will find any use for a driving licence. Motorbikes are available for hire in Phnom Penh, but nobody is checking licences.

Student & Youth Cards

Student and youth cards won't get you anywhere in Cambodia, though they may be useful in Thailand. In general, the availability of cheap counterfeit student cards in places like Bangkok has done much to rob the student card of whatever value it once had.

International Health Certificate

There are no direct flights from areas where infection with yellow fever is a possibility so an International Health Certificate is not necessary for Cambodia. See Immunisation in the Health section of this chapter for details of recommended vaccinations.

EMBASSIES
Cambodian Embassies Abroad

Cambodian diplomatic representation abroad is still thin on the ground, though the situation is gradually improving.

Australia
    No 5 Canterbury Crt, Deakin, Canberra, ACT 2600 (☎ 273 1259, fax 273 1053)
China
    No 9 Dongzhimenwai Dajie, 100600, Beijing (☎ 532 2101, fax 532 3507)
France
    4 Rue Adolphe Yvon, 75016 Paris (☎ 45.03.47.20, fax 45.03.47.40)

Germany
    Grüner Weg 8, 53343 Wachtberg Pech, Bonn (☎ /fax 328572)
India
    B47 Soami Nagar, New Delhi, 110017 (☎ /fax 642 3782)
Indonesia
    4th Floor, Panin Bank Plaza, Jalan 52 Palmerah Utara, Jakarta 11480 (☎ 548 3716, fax 548 3684)
Japan
    8-6-9 Akasaka, Minato-ku, 107 Tokyo (☎ 3478-0861, fax 3478-0865)
Laos
    Thanon Saphan Thong Neua, Vientiane (☎ /fax 314951)
Russia
    Strarokonyushenny Per 16, Moscow (☎ /fax 956 6573)
Thailand
    185 Rajadamri Rd, Bangkok 10330 (☎ 254-6630, fax 253-9859)
USA
    4500 16th St, NW, Washington, DC 20011 (☎ 726-7742, fax 726-8381)
Vietnam
    71 Tran Hung Dao St, Hanoi (☎ 253 789, fax 265 225)
    Consulate: 41 Phung Khac Khoan St, Ho Chi Minh City (☎ 292 751, fax 292 744)

Besides the above, Cambodia also has embassies in Bulgaria, Cuba, the Czech Republic, Hungary and North Korea.

Foreign Embassies in Cambodia

These are all based in Phnom Penh. There is quite a number of them nowadays, though some travellers will find their nearest embassy is in Bangkok. Most embassies in Phnom Penh will happily provide information to their nationals about the current security situation in Cambodia and can replace your passport in the event that it is lost or stolen. Embassies will not, however, provide funds for onward travel, though some will contact your relatives at home to enable them to send money. See the Phnom Penh chapter for a list of foreign embassies in Cambodia.

CUSTOMS

If Cambodia has customs allowances, it is keeping close-lipped about them. A 'reasonable amount' of duty free items are allowed

Phnom Penh

Top: A tri-lingual sign above a Phnom Penh street.
Middle Left: Bicycles form the basis of Cambodia's transport system.
Middle Right: Tuol Sleng serves as an unpleasant reminder of Khmer Rouge atrocities.
Bottom: A street scene in the New Market area.

CHRIS TAYLOR

CHRIS TAYLOR

Around Cambodia
Top: A stupa at Tonlé Bati, near Phnom Penh.
Bottom: Sunset over the coastal town of Sihanoukville.

GLENN BEANLAND

TONY WHEELER

TONY WHEELER

Angkor
Top: Intricate carvings adorning one of the towers at Angkor Wat.
Bottom Left: A battle scene from a bas relief at the Bayon, Angkor Thom.
Bottom Right: Dancing apsaras on the outer walls of the Bayon, Angkor Thom.

TONY WHEELER

TONY WHEELER

TONY WHEELER

TONY WHEELER

Angkor
Top Left: The South Gate of the fortified city of Angkor Thom.
Top Right: Lolei, a part of the Roluos Group, dates from the 9th century.
Bottom Left: The corridors of the 12th-century Preah Khan, built by Jayavarman VII.
Bottom Right: The causeway leading to the South Gate at Angkor Thom.

into the country. Travellers arriving by air might bear in mind that alcohol and cigarettes sell at duty free (and lower) prices on the streets of Phnom Penh – a carton of Marlboro costs just US$7!

Like any other country, Cambodia does not allow travellers to import weapons, explosives or narcotics.

MONEY
Costs
For the most part, Cambodia is an inexpensive country to travel in. Budget travellers who have arrived from Vietnam will find that accommodation rates are cheaper in Cambodia but food costs are slightly higher.

Rock bottom travellers can probably manage Phnom Penh on around US$10 a day, though there's not a great deal to be said for travelling this way – there is much that you will have to miss out on. Accommodation can be as cheap as US$2-3 in Phnom Penh and Siem Reap (elsewhere, you will be looking at a minimum of US$5). It is generally possible to eat fairly well for US$2-3, less if you go native and live off inexpensive soups and noodles (though you drastically increase the risk of spending your Cambodia trip in search of a toilet this way).

Transportation is a major expense if you are carefully watching your finances. The slow boat services between Phnom Penh and Siem Reap have a certain risk factor but will always attract passengers due to the fact they are cheap. Travelling by train costs next to nothing, but at the time of writing was (rightly) off limits to foreign travellers. The only bus services worth considering (and even these were not recommended by foreign embassies in Cambodia) are the daily services to Sihanoukville and to Ho Chi Minh City (Saigon).

Visitors to Angkor will have to factor in the cost of entrance fees, which now seem to have finally settled down to US$20 for one day, US$40 for three days and US$60 for one week. An additional expense out at Angkor is the government ruling against travellers visiting the ruins without a guide. A guide with a motorbike will cost a minimum of US$6 per day. It's almost impossible to visit Angkor for less than US$20 per day.

Mid-range travellers are probably the best served in Cambodia. In Phnom Penh and Siem Reap there is an excellent range of accommodation from US$15 to US$25, and if you are happy spending US$5 or slightly more on meals Phnom Penh in particular can be quite a gourmet experience. Having a little extra money also allows you the luxury of flying one way or return to Siem Reap, and perhaps renting a taxi to visit sights around Phnom Penh.

Carrying Money
A lightweight money belt that can be worn comfortably and discreetly inside your clothes is the best bet for the bulk of your travel savings – a pair of nylon stockings with one leg folded inside the other can hold a lot of travellers' cheques and other documents. It can be tied inconspicuously around your waist inside your clothes without any discomfort. Some travellers use a pouch around the neck that rests inside their shirts, though this is usually fairly conspicuous.

Cash
Cambodia is one country where US dollars are extremely useful. Indeed, if you have enough cash, you will never have to make a trip to the bank. Hardened travellers make the point that your trip ends up being slightly more expensive if you rely on US dollars rather than riel, but in reality there's very little in it. If you pay for something worth 2000r with US$1 you will always get 500r change, and generally enough riel will accumulate in your wallet to pay for small items in riel anyway.

The only other cash currency that can be useful is Thai baht, though it is much less widely used than the US dollar. Any other currency will have to be changed at the bank into US dollars or riel.

Travellers' Cheques
Travellers' cheques can only be changed at a limited number of banks in Phnom Penh and Siem Reap. If you are travelling upcountry,

you should change enough money before you go. It is best to have US dollar cheques in Cambodia, though it is also possible to change most major European currencies and Japanese yen. Generally you will be looking at a minimum of 2% commission on changing travellers' cheques.

Credit Cards

Except for top-end hotels and major purchases such as air tickets, credit cards are not particularly worthwhile. Cash advances are generally only available on Visa and carry prohibitive processing fees. The exception to the latter rule is the Cambodian Commercial Bank, which has branches in Phnom Penh and Siem Reap, and allows advances of up to US$2000 on JCB, MasterCard and Visa with no commission charged.

Telegraphic Transfers

It would be a good idea to ask at your embassy about the best way to have money sent to Cambodia if you need it in a hurry. The most reliable bank for telegraphic transfers is the Cambodian Commercial Bank at 26 Monivong Blvd, Phnom Penh. The money will probably be routed through the Siam Commercial Bank at 1060 Petchaburi Rd, Bangkok, Thailand, and this information may be useful for the bank that is sending the money. Ideally, you should organise telegraphic transfers in Bangkok rather than Phnom Penh – it will be quicker this way.

Currency

Cambodia's currency is the riel, abbreviated here by a lower-case 'r' written after the sum. From around 200r to the US dollar in mid-1989 the riel has plummeted in value and now seems to have settled at around 2600r to the US dollar.

Cambodia's second currency is the US dollar, which is accepted everywhere and by everyone, though your change may arrive in riel. If two currencies seems a little excessive, perhaps the Cambodians are making up for lost time: during the Pol Pot era, the country had *no* currency. The Khmer Rouge

abolished money and blew up the National Bank building in Phnom Penh.

The sinking fortunes of the riel meant that until recently it was hardly worth the paper it was printed on. The government has responded by creating new higher-value denominations, though denominations of 5000r and upwards are still a fairly rare sight. The riel comes in notes with the following values: 100, 200, 500, 1000, 2000, 5000, 10,000, 20,000, 50,000 and 100,000. Coins in denominations of 100, 200 and 500 have been issued but these are also rarely seen.

Currency Exchange		
A$1	=	2070r
DM1	=	1720r
FFr1	=	510r
J¥	=	2400r
NZ$1	=	1770r
Thai B	=	103r
UK£1	=	4040r
US$1	=	2600r
Viet d	=	240r

Changing Money

In the interests of making life as simple as possible, organise a supply of US dollars before you arrive in Cambodia. But if you have cash in another major currency, you will be able to change it without any hassle in Phnom Penh or Siem Reap. The same goes for travellers' cheques. The Cambodian Commercial Bank is the best bank in Phnom Penh and Siem Reap for changing money. A commission of 2% is charged.

Black Market

There is no longer a black market in Cambodia. Exchange rates on the street are the same as those offered by the banks.

Tipping & Bargaining

Tipping is not expected in Cambodia but, as is the case anywhere, if you meet with exceptional service or out-of-the-way kindness, a tip is always greatly appreciated. Salaries remain extremely low in Cambodia.

Bargaining is the rule in markets, when hiring vehicles and sometimes even when taking a room. The Khmers are not the ruthless hagglers that Thais and Vietnamese can be, however, and care should be taken not to come on too strong. A persuasive smile and a little friendly quibbling is usually enough to get a good price.

POST & COMMUNICATIONS

Post is now routed by air through Bangkok, which makes Cambodia a much more reliable place to send mail and parcels from. Telephone connections with the outside world have also improved immensely, though they are not cheap.

Poste Restante

The Phnom Penh GPO has a poste restante box at the far left-hand end of the post counter. Basically anybody can pick up your mail, so it is not a good idea to have anything valuable sent there.

Postal Rates

Postal rates are listed in the Phnom Penh GPO. A 10g airmail letter to anywhere in the world costs 1500r, while a 100g letter costs 4800r anywhere in Asia, 5400r to Australia, 5600r to Europe and 7100r to the USA.

Parcel rates are 18,000r for 500g to anywhere in Asia, 20,600r to Australia, 21,800r to Europe and 29,400r to the USA. There is a 2000r additional fee to send items by registered mail – it is well worth it.

Letters and parcels sent farther afield than Asia can take up to two or three weeks to reach their destination.

Telephone

Domestic Most hotels in Phnom Penh will allow you to make local calls free of charge. Numbers starting with 015, 017 or 018 are cellular phone numbers. Local phone calls can also be made on the Telstra public pay phones that are common in Phnom Penh and Siem Reap. It can sometimes be difficult to get through to numbers outside Phnom Penh, and there is no directory information service.

International It is now easy to place an international call due to the Telstra public phone system. You will need to get a phone card, which in Phnom Penh can be bought at the Telstra office at 58 Norodom Blvd and at various other outlets (hotels, restaurants, the GPO). Phone cards come in denominations of US$2, US$5, US$20, US$50 and US$100.

International calls are expensive in Cambodia. To keep expenses to a minimum, ring on a Saturday or Sunday, when a discount of 20% prevails. Calls to Australia cost US$3.80 per minute, and to Europe and the USA are US$4.80 per minute.

Before inserting your card into a Telstra public phone, always check that there is a readout on the LCD unit. If there isn't, it probably means there is a power cut – inserting your card during a power cut wipes the value off the card.

Home Country Direct Making reverse-charge (collect) calls in Cambodia is a hassle, but a home country direct service has been set up for the USA and Australia; other countries will soon follow. For more information ring Telstra (☎ 426022) in Phnom Penh.

Home country direct calls allow you to reverse charges or have the call charged to a Telstra or AT&T telecard. For the USA ring 1-800-881-001 and for Australia ring 1-800-881-061. No telephone card is required for these numbers.

Fax If possible, save your faxes for somewhere else. They can cost as much as US$6 a page in Cambodia. Some of the more popular mid-range hotels in Phnom Penh have reliable business centres that can send and receive faxes. The best are the Golden Gate Hotel, the Goldiana Hotel and the Cathay Hotel. Phnom Penh's top-end hotels all have expensive business centres. The FCC (Foreign Correspondents' Club) in Phnom Penh is another good place to send and receive faxes.

Email At the time of writing, the information superhighway bypassed Cambodia, and short-term visitors were basically forced to access their internet accounts via international calls. This is likely to change in the near future. Ask around at the FCC for the latest, or at your hotel if you are staying in top-end digs (though it is unlikely that Phnom Penh hoteliers will be savvy to the internet).

BOOKS
Lonely Planet
Besides the book you hold in your hands, Lonely Planet also publishes guides to neighbouring countries that you may visit on your travels. *South-East Asia on a shoestring* is our overall guide to travel on the South-East Asian trail. Also available are country guides to *Vietnam, Laos, Myanmar (Burma)* and *Thailand*, as well as phrasebooks for the languages of those countries, and travel atlases for *Thailand, Vietnam* and *Laos*.

Guidebooks
It's worth looking out for a copy of the *Great Little Guide – Cambodia & Angkor* when you are in Cambodia (it is also available in Bangkok). Put together and frequently updated by Roland Neveu, this pocket-sized book is packed with no-nonsense nuts and bolts information in dodgy (but never indecipherable) English. Another useful book, especially for anyone planning to spend a length of time in Phnom Penh, is the *Guide to Phnom Penh*, compiled by the Women's International Group. All proceeds from the book are donated to Cambodian charities, and it is packed with useful tips on living in Phnom Penh.

A Guide to Phnom Penh – The Gateway to Cambodia by Robert Philpotts (Blackwater Books) is slightly dated now (it was last updated in 1993), but is still a good background read on the Cambodian capital and is charmingly illustrated with line drawings by the author.

Travellers with an earnest archaeological bent heading out to Angkor are advised to pick up a copy of *Angkor – An Introduction*

to the Temples by Dawn Rooney (Odyssey). This book is packed with illustrations and fascinating reading on Angkor. Also recommended is the pocket-size *Angkor – Heart of an Asian Empire* by Bruno Dagens (New Horizons). The emphasis in this book is more on the discovery and restoration of the ruins of Angkor, but it is lavishly illustrated and dripping with interesting asides.

Travel
There are not a lot of travel books about Cambodia around. The classic is Norman Lewis' *A Dragon Apparent*, an account of a 1950 foray into an Indochina which was soon to disappear. In the course of his travels, Lewis makes a circuit from Phnom Penh around the Tonlé Sap with a pause in Angkor. The book has been reissued by Picador as part of *The Norman Lewis Omnibus*.

Another elusive book is the quaintly titled *Mistapim in Cambodia*, an entertaining account of a year spent travelling and living in Cambodia in the late 1950s by Christopher Pym. Bert's Books & Guesthouse in Phnom Penh had some rare copies of this book at the time of writing.

On a more scholarly note, *To Angkor* (Société d'Éditions Géographiques, Maritimes et Coloniales (SEGMC), Paris, 1939) is the English version of the French work *Vers Angkor* (Librairie Hachette, Paris, 1925). *Indochina* (SEGMC, Paris, 1939), an English-language condensation of the two-volume set *Indochine du Nord* and *Indochine du Sud*, has the same spread on Cambodia as *To Angkor*. The most comprehensive section on Cambodia is to be found in the augmented and excellent 2nd edition of *Indochine du Sud* (SEGMC, Paris, 1939).

Francophone fans of antiquarian books may want to track down *Voyage au Cambodge* by Louis Delaporte (Librairie C Delgrave, Paris, 1880).

Angkor
See the Guidebooks entry earlier for *Angkor – An Introduction to the Temples* by Dawn Rooney and *Angkor – Heart of an Asian Empire* by Bruno Dagens, two first-rate introductions

to Angkor that make good supplemental guides.

Angkor: An Introduction by George Coedes (Oxford University Press) gives excellent background information on Angkorian Khmer civilisation. You might also look for Malcolm MacDonald's *Angkor & the Khmers* (Oxford University Press); *Arts & Civilization of Angkor* by Bernard Groslier & Jacques Arthaud (Fredrick A Prager, New York, 1958); and, in French, *Histoire d'Angkor* by Madeleine Giteau (Presses Universitaires de France, Paris, 1974).

The Art of Southeast Asia by Philip Rawson (Thames & Hudson, 1967) has recently been reprinted by Asia Books in Thailand and has excellent chapters on Angkor. *Angkor* by Michael Freeman & Roger Warner (Houghton Mifflin, 1990) is a big, glossy, coffee-table book on Angkor.

A recent coffee-table release is *Passage Through Angkor* by Mark Standen (Indochina News Corp, 1995). Standen, a newcomer to photography, has come up with some of the most striking images ever produced of Angkor. If you want a photographic memento of Angkor, this is the best there is.

National Geographic has run some memorable features on Cambodia and Angkor. Some of the relevant issues are available at Bert's Books & Guesthouse in Phnom Penh. In particular, look out for 'The Temples of Angkor' (May 1982, pp 548-89) and 'Kampuchea Wakens from a Nightmare' (May 1982, pp 590-623). The temples feature contains a fine fold-out map of the Angkor region as it must have been at the height of its power.

History

The best widely available history of Cambodia is David Chandler's *History of Cambodia*. It is available in Cambodia and Bangkok, published by Silkworm Books. Chandler has also documented recent Cambodian history in two more excellent titles: *The Tragedy of Cambodian History – Politics, War & Revolution since 1945* (Yale University Press, 1991) and *Brother Number One – A Political Biography of Pol Pot* (Westview Press, 1991).

Look out for Milton Osbourne's *Sihanouk –Prince of Light, Prince of Darkness* (Silkworm Books, 1994). This superbly written book provides a no-holds-barred look at the man who has played such a crucial role in the shifting fortunes of Cambodia's modern history. Besides providing a fascinating glimpse into the life of Sihanouk, the book also works well as a history of modern Cambodia.

The expansion of the Vietnam War into Cambodian territory and events through the mid-1970s are superbly documented by William Shawcross in his award-winning book *Sideshow: Kissinger, Nixon & the Destruction of Cambodia* (The Hogarth Press, London, and Simon & Schuster, New York, 1979). Also highly recommended is *How Pol Pot Came to Power* by Ben Kiernan (Verso, 1985).

Cambodia: Year Zero by François Ponchaud (1978; originally published in French as *Cambodge: Année Zéro* in 1977) is an account of life in Cambodia under the Khmer Rouge. Other works on this period include *The Stones Cry Out: A Cambodian Childhood, 1975-1980* (Hill & Wang, New York, 1986) by Molyda Szymusiak, originally published in French as *Les Pierres Crieront: Une Enfance Cambodgienne, 1975-1980* (La Découverte, Paris, 1984); *The Cambodian Agony* by David Ablin (1987); and *The Murderous Revolution* by Martin Stuart-Fox (1985).

The atrocities of the Khmer Rouge are documented by *Kampuchea, Decade of Genocide: Report of the Finnish Enquiry Commission* (Zed Books, London, 1984) edited by Kimmo Kiljunen. *Brother Enemy*, an excellent work by Nayan Chanda (Collier, 1986), examines events in Indochina since 1975.

William Shawcross' work *The Quality of Mercy: Cambodia, Holocaust & Modern Conscience* (André Deutsch, UK, and Simon & Schuster, USA, 1984) looks at the contradictions inherent in the massive international famine-relief operation mounted in 1979 and 1980. This still highly relevant title is available in Thailand in a paperback edition published by DD Books.

NEWSPAPERS & MAGAZINES

Despite occasional tirades by the government about foreign press interference in the country's 'internal affairs', Cambodia has a lively local English-language press. Bookshops in Phnom Penh have a wide range of English and French-language newspapers and magazines.

Local Publications

The *Cambodia Daily* nearly lives up to its name, appearing at newsstands and restaurants daily on weekdays – it takes a break on the weekends. It is an excellent overview of international agency stories with some local input, and also has Khmer and Japanese supplements. It costs just 1000r. The Friday edition has a useful 'This Week's Calendar' section.

The *Cambodge Soir* is a French paper that comes out twice weekly. It is available in bookshops and most of the restaurants frequented by French patrons around Phnom Penh.

The *Cambodia Times* and *Cambodia Business News* are published weekly and provide a government perspective (not as biased as you might think) on local and international news.

The *Phnom Penh Post* provides a very good overview of events in Cambodia. As well as informative feature stories, it has a lift-out map of Phnom Penh with restaurants and business services. It costs 2000r and deserves your support.

International Publications

The Bangkok Post and the *Nation* are Thai English-language dailies that are widely available in Phnom Penh, usually by mid-afternoon of the day of publication. The Foreign Correspondents' Club (FCC) has copies you can read free of charge if you pop in for a coffee, a snack or a meal.

The bookshop at the Sofitel Cambodiana Hotel is the best stocked in Phnom Penh when it comes to newspapers. The French newspaper section is comprehensive. Several-days-old copies of *The Australian* are usually also on sale. Other English-language newspapers on sale include the *Asia Times*, *International Herald Tribune* and *The European*.

On the magazine front, Phnom Penh bookshops have current copies of *The Economist*, *Far Eastern Economic Review*, *Asiaweek*, *Time*, *Newsweek* and others. The bookshop at the Sofitel Cambodiana Hotel also has a good range of French magazines.

RADIO & TV
Radio

Unless you have a shortwave radio, there is not a great deal of interest on Cambodian airwaves. The Cambodian radio station in Phnom Penh has an English-language news broadcast at 9 pm every evening. French speakers should tune in to Radio France International, which is relayed from Paris.

If you have a shortwave radio, it is possible to pick up the BBC World Service, Radio Australia and so on.

TV

Most of the mid-range hotels in Phnom Penh have satellite TV reception nowadays, which means that you should have access to the BBC World Service, CNN, Star TV, Channel V (the regional answer to MTV) and possibly even the Australian ABC. Without satellite reception, you are restricted to Channel 2 (which is French).

PHOTOGRAPHY & VIDEO
Film & Equipment

Print film and processing are cheap in Cambodia. A roll of ASA 100 Kodak Gold (36 exposures), for example, costs US$2.50, or US$3.50 for 400 ASA. Konika film is cheaper again. The cheapest places for fast printing are the Konika photolabs, which can be found all over Cambodia. The Konika shops generally charge US$4 for 36 standard prints. Kodak photolabs are more expensive at US$6.

The only slide film available at the time of writing was Ektachrome Elite (100 ASA), and it costs US$5 for a roll of 36 exposures. If you are a serious photographer bring a supply of Velvia, or whatever it is you use – slide film is readily available in Bangkok. Do not have slide film processed in Cambodia.

At the very least, wait until you get to Bangkok.

General camera supply needs can be satisfied in Phnom Penh. Camera batteries should be easy to replace providing you don't require anything too obscure.

Photography

The best light conditions in Cambodia begin around 20 minutes after sunrise and last for just one to 1½ hours. The same applies for the late afternoon light, which begins to assume a radiant warm quality around 1½ hours before sunset. From 10 am to around 3.30 pm you can expect the light to be hard and contrasty – there's not much you can do with it. Bear in mind that you have much more leeway with exposures in print film than you do in slide film. Snaps taken in poor light conditions often turn out OK in the printing process; with slides you either get it right or you don't.

If you've forked out a lot of money on photographic gear and have a lot of film with you, it is worthwhile doing some reading about getting the best out of it. Also look critically at published photographs and think about how the photographers achieved the results. There are, after all, a lot of tricks you can use to give your travel shots a professional edge.

Video

Properly used, a video camera can give a fascinating record of your holiday. As well as videoing the obvious things – sunsets, spectacular views – remember to record some of the ordinary everyday details of life in the country. Often the most interesting things occur when you're actually intent on filming something else. Remember too that, unlike still photography, video 'flows' – so, for example, you can shoot scenes of countryside rolling past the train window, to give an overall impression that isn't possible with ordinary photos.

Video cameras these days have amazingly sensitive microphones, and you might be surprised how much sound will be picked up. This can also be a problem if there is a lot of ambient noise – filming by the side of a busy road might seem OK when you do it, but viewing it back home might simply give you a deafening cacophony of traffic noise. One good rule to follow for beginners is to try to film in long takes, and don't move the camera around too much. Otherwise, your video could well make your viewers seasick! If your camera has a stabiliser, you can use it to obtain good footage while travelling on various means of transport, even on bumpy roads. And remember, you're on holiday – don't let the video take over your life, and turn your trip into a Cecil B de Mille production.

Make sure you keep the batteries charged, and have the necessary charger, plugs and transformer for the country you are visiting. In most countries, it is possible to obtain video cartridges easily in large towns and cities, but make sure you buy the correct format. It is usually worth buying at least a few cartridges duty free to start off your trip.

Finally, remember to follow the same rules regarding people's sensitivities as for a still photography – having a video camera shoved in their face is probably even more annoying and offensive for locals than a still camera. Always ask permission first.

Restrictions

The Cambodian armed forces don't seem too concerned about foreigners photographing bridges and so on, but most of these were built by foreigners anyway. It would still be sensible to exercise some restraint. Charging up to an armed convoy and snapping away might result in unpleasant consequences.

Photographing People

The usual rules apply. Be polite about photographing people; don't push cameras into their faces, and have some respect for monks and people at prayer. It shouldn't be necessary to say this, but unfortunately there are a lot of amateur photographers out there who think that they're on assignment for *National Geographic*. In general, the Khmers are remarkably courteous people and if you ask nicely they'll agree to have their photograph taken.

Airport Security

The X-ray machines at Pochentong airport are safe to put your film through. If you are carrying 1000 ASA or higher film, you should store it separately and ask to have it inspected by hand. Some professional photographers refuse to put any film through any X-ray machine. This is an unnecessary precaution, but then it is their livelihood.

TIME

Cambodia, like Vietnam, Thailand and Laos, is seven hours ahead of GMT/UTC. When it is noon in Cambodia it is 10 pm the previous evening in San Francisco, 1 am in New York, 5 am in London and 3 pm in Sydney.

ELECTRICITY

Electricity in Phnom Penh and most of the rest of Cambodia is 220V, 50 Hz (cycles). Power is in short supply in Cambodia, however, and power cuts are frequent. Most mid-range and top-end hotels and restaurants have their own generators, but if you are staying downmarket you can expect to be without electricity for long periods every day.

Plugs & Sockets

Electric power sockets are generally of the round two-pin variety. Three-pin plug adaptors can be bought at the markets in Phnom Penh.

WEIGHTS & MEASURES

Cambodia uses the metric system. For those unaccustomed to this system, there is a metric/imperial conversion chart at the end of the book.

LAUNDRY

Laundry is never a problem in Cambodia. All hotels provide a laundry service and, unless you are holed up in some top-end joint where they charge you to switch on the lights, it is either free or very cheap.

TOILETS

Although the occasional squat toilet turns up here and there, the general rule (particularly in hotels) is the sit-down variety. If you get out into the sticks, you will find that hygiene conditions deteriorate somewhat, but Cambodia is still a cleaner country than say China or India. Public toilets are nonexistent.

WOMEN TRAVELLERS

Insofar as Cambodia can be described as safe, women will generally find the country to be a hassle-free place to travel in. Foreign women are unlikely to be targeted by local men, but at the same time it pays to be careful. As is the case anywhere in the world, walking or riding a bike alone late at night is risky; and if you're planning a trip off the beaten trail it would be best to find a travel companion.

Despite the prevalence of prostitution and women's roles as 'beer girls', dancing companions and the like in the entertainment industry, foreign women will probably find Khmer men to be courteous and polite. It's best to keep things this way by being restrained in your dress. Khmer women dress fairly conservatively, and it's best to follow suit, particularly when visiting wats. In general, long-sleeved shirts and long trousers or skirts are preferred.

GAY & LESBIAN TRAVELLERS

While Cambodian culture is tolerant of homosexuality, the scene is certainly nothing like that of neighbouring Thailand. Public displays of affection, whether heterosexual or homosexual, are frowned on.

DISABLED TRAVELLERS

Depending on your disability, Cambodia is not going to be an easy country to get around in. Local labour at least is inexpensive, which means that you can hire a guide for around US$10 a day or less. Travellers with major disabilities would be advised to look into a tour.

SENIOR TRAVELLERS

Senior travellers are not eligible for anything in the way of discounts in Cambodia – all foreigners are rich as far as Cambodians are concerned (and they are right, comparatively). Depending on how nimble you are on your feet, it is not recommended that you take adventurous options such as the boats that travel between Phnom Penh and Siem Reap.

TRAVEL WITH CHILDREN

Travellers considering visiting Cambodia with children should pick up a copy of Lonely Planet's *Travel with Children*. If you are just planning a visit to Angkor and Phnom Penh, there should be no problems. More adventurous travel in Cambodia with children is not recommended.

USEFUL ORGANISATIONS

Cambodia hosts a huge number of Non-Government Organisations (NGOs). The best way to find out who exactly is represented in Cambodia is to call in to the Cooperation Committee for Cambodia (CCC) (☎ 426009), at 35, 178 St, Phnom Penh. This organisation has a handy list of all NGOs, both Cambodian and international.

The following list comprises the more prominent international NGOs operating out of Phnom Penh. There are many more.

Action Internationale Contre la Faim (AICF) – 14, 57 St (☎ 426934)
American Friends Service Committee (AFSC) – 30, 352 St (☎ 426400)
American Refugee Committee (ARC) – 53, 360 St (☎ 426115)
Australian Catholic Relief (ACR) – 17, 213 St (☎ 426200)
Australian People for Health Education & Development Abroad (APHEDA) – 10, 302 St (☎ 426034)
Cambodian-British Centre for Teacher Education 26, 122 St (☎ 723705)
Cambodia Canada Development Program (CCDP) – 198, 370 St (☎ 015-194582)
Cambodia Development Resource Institute (CDRI) – 56, 318 St (☎ 426103)
Care International – 4B, 302 St (☎ 426233)
Catholic Office for Emergency Relief & Refugees (COERR) – 30, 232 St (☎ 364306)
Community Aid Abroad (CAA) – 17, 294 St (☎ 360563)
CONCERN – 27, 71 St (☎ 426049)
Coopération Internationale pour le Développement et la Solidarité (CIDSE) – 15, 306 St (☎ 426369)
Enfants du Cambodge – 61, 21 St (☎ 360040)
Groupe de Recherche et d'Échanges Technologiques (GRET) – 1 Mao Tse Toung Blvd (☎ 015-911435)
International Committee of the Red Cross (ICRC) – 18 Samdech Sothearos Blvd (☎ 360071)
Japan International Volunteer Centre (JIVC) – 35, 169 St (☎ 366385)
Lutheran World Service (LWS) – 37, 592 St (☎ 426350)

Médecins sans Frontières, Holland/Belgium (MSF-HB) – 8, 211 St (☎ 246521)
Médecins sans Frontières, France (MSF France) – 26, 334 St (☎ 426252)
Mennonite Central Committee (MCC) – 29, 228 St (☎ 426592)
Mines Advisory Group (MAG) – 201 Sisowath Quay (☎ 360495)
Oxfam UK – 64, 57 St (426261)
Partnership for Development in Kampuchea (PADEK) – 38, 57 St (☎ 426224)
Quaker Service Australia (QSA) – 13, 302 St (☎ 362732)
Redd Barna (Norwegian Save the Children) – 9, 322 St (☎ 362143)
Save the Children Fund, UK (SCF-UK) – 77, 392 St (☎ 362157)
United Nations Children's Fund (UNICEF) – 11, 75 St (☎ 426005)
United Nations Development Programme (UNDP) – 53, 334 St (☎ 426217)
United Nations High Commission for Refugees (UNHCR) – 66-68 Monivong Blvd (☎ 362150)
United Nations Human Rights Centre (UNHRC) – 45, 85 St (☎ 015-913446)
Volunteer Service Overseas (VSO) – 18, 282 St (☎ 426734)
World Health Organization (WHO) – 120, 228 St (☎ 426205)
World Food Programme (WFP) – 250, 63 St (☎ 426205)
World Vision International (WVI) – 24, 360 St (☎ 426052)

DANGERS & ANNOYANCES
Security

Sadly the civil war drags on in Cambodia, and this should be at the top of your thoughts when you plan any trips in the country. Do not fall victim to the gung-ho mentality that taking risks makes for good travel anecdotes. It's not worth it. Since 1994, seven foreign visitors have been murdered in Cambodia.

This guidebook takes a cautious approach to travel in Cambodia. This is because real dangers still linger. The government has forbidden railway employees to sell tickets to foreigners for good reason, and many of Cambodia's roads are chock-a-block with checkpoints by day and Khmer Rouge controlled by night. Always make a point of checking on the latest security situation before making a trip that you know not many travellers undertake. Moreover, do not rely only on information provided by locals –

Out of Sight, Out of Mined

In a supplement to the *Phnom Penh Post* (10-23 February, 1995) sponsored by NGOs and the US government, an article paints a hypothetical picture of Britain terrorised by 60 million landmines planted in over 14,000 battlefields. Because many of these landmines are planted in agriculturally and industrially productive parts of the country, the job of providing for national needs becomes harder to fulfil. The hospitals fill with injured and dying. As tourists shun the country, industry relocates overseas and foreign investment dries up. The government declares a national emergency. The scale of the disaster is such that the military lacks the resources to find all the landmines – most will be discovered by people stepping on them. In just three years, some 245,000 Britons become amputees. Many turn to begging and crime to support themselves.

This essentially is the situation in Cambodia. The country is littered with some four to eight million unexploded mines. Over 35,000 Cambodians have lost limbs due to mines. This is the highest per-capita rate of amputees in the world – one in 246 people. After malaria and tuberculosis, mines are Cambodia's number-one killer.

The cost to an extensively mined country is enormous. In a developing country like Cambodia, the UN reckons that the lifetime rehabilitation of a landmine victim costs US$3000. Spread over 35,000 victims the cost is US$105 million. Then there are indirect costs, such as the deaths of grazing livestock. Mines hamper rural development too. Much of Cambodia's agricultural land is mined, making it impossible to farm and causing shortages of food.

There are number of groups working in Cambodia to alleviate the problem of mines. The Cambodian Mine Action Centre (CMAC) was foreign trained but recently became an all-Cambodian government agency. The Hazardous Areas Life (Support) Organisation (HALO) was one of the pioneers of mine clearance in Cambodia and now has eight teams working in Pursat, Banteay Meanchey and Siem Reap. The Mines Advisory Group (MAG) is a British outfit that has been training Cambodians in de-mining. It has launched programmes which train mine victims and all-women teams in mine clearance. The Campagna Française d'Assistance Specialisée (COFRAS) is working in Siem Reap Province to clear sites of historical importance.

Most sensible travellers will not be wandering around mined areas while they are in Cambodia. Nevertheless, there are some points worth bearing in mind while you are in the country.

- Always check with locals that paths are unmined.
- Never leave a safe path.
- Never *ever* touch anything that looks remotely like a mine.
- If you find yourself accidentally in mined area, only retrace your steps if you can clearly see your footprints; if not, you should stay where you are and call for help – as advisory groups put it, better to spend a day standing in a minefield than a lifetime as an amputee.
- If someone is injured in a minefield, even if they are crying out for help, do not rush in; find the help of someone who knows how to safely enter a mined area.
- Play it safe and stick to the main tourist attractions of Cambodia. No-one is handing out medals to gung-ho travellers. ∎

they often undertake dangerous trips as a matter of necessity and have no way of assessing the risks for a foreigner.

Undetonated Mines, Mortars & Bombs

Never, ever touch any rockets, artillery shells, mortars, mines, bombs or other war material you may come across. In Vietnam most of this sort of stuff is 15 or more years old, but in Cambodia it may have landed there or been laid as recently as the previous night. In fact, a favourite tactic of the Khmer Rouge has been to lay mines along roads and in rice fields in an effort to maim and kill civilians, thus – so their twisted logic concludes – furthering the rebel cause by demoralising the government. The only concrete results of this policy are the many limbless people you see all over Cambodia. The most heavily mined part of the country is the Battambang area, but mines are a problem all over Cambodia. In short: *do not* stray from well marked paths under any circumstances, even around the monuments of Angkor.

Snakes

Visitors to Angkor and other overgrown archaeological sites should beware of snakes, including the small but deadly light-green Hanuman snake.

Theft & Street Crime

Given the number of guns about in Cambodia, there is less armed theft than you might suppose. Still, motorcycle theft is a problem in Phnom Penh. There is no need to be overly paranoid, just cautious. Riding alone late at night is probably not a good idea.

Pickpocketing and theft by stealth is more a problem in Vietnam and Thailand than in Cambodia. Again, though, it pays to be careful. Don't make it any easier for thieves by putting your passport and wads of cash in your back pocket. As a precaution, keep a 'secret' stash of cash separately from the bulk of your funds.

Traffic Accidents

Traffic conditions in Cambodia are chaotic, though no worse than in many other under-developed countries. If you are riding a bike in Phnom Penh you should stay alert and take nothing for granted. The horn is used to alert drivers of your presence – listen out behind and get out of the way if it's a car or a truck.

None of the moto (motorbike taxi) drivers in Cambodia use or provide safety helmets. Fortunately most of them drive at sensible speeds. If you encounter a reckless driver, tell them to slow down or pay them off and find another.

Having a major traffic accident in Phnom Penh would be bad enough, but if you have one in rural Cambodia you are in big trouble. Somehow you will have to get back to Phnom Penh for medical treatment.

LEGAL MATTERS

Contrary to popular belief – and at least one guidebook – marijuana is not legal in Cambodia. Traditionally used in Khmer cooking, there would no doubt be much local opposition to a major crackdown on its availability. Still, if you are a smoker, be discreet. It's probably only a matter of time before the Cambodian police turn the busting of foreigners into a lucrative sideline.

The above applies equally to other narcotic substances, which are also illegal according to the Cambodian constitution.

Moral grounds alone should be enough to deter foreigners from seeking under-age sexual partners in Cambodia, but unfortunately in some cases this is not enough. Paedophiles are treated as criminals in Cambodia and several have served or are serving jail sentences as a result. Countries such as Australia have also introduced legislation which will see nationals prosecuted on their home ground for having under-age sex abroad.

BUSINESS HOURS

Government offices, which are open Monday to Saturday, theoretically begin the working day at 7 or 7.30 am, breaking for a siesta from 11 or 11.30 am to 2 or 2.30 pm and ending the day at 5.30 pm. However, it is a safe bet that few people will be around early in the morning or after 4 or 4.30 pm.

Banking hours tend to vary according to the bank, but you can reckon on core hours of 8.30 am to 3.30 pm. The Foreign Trade Bank is open from 7.30 to 11.30 am on Saturdays.

PUBLIC HOLIDAYS & SPECIAL EVENTS

The festivals of Cambodia take place according to the lunar calendar so the dates vary from year to year:

Chaul Chnam – Held in mid-April, this is a three day celebration of Khmer New Year; Khmers make offerings at wats, clean out their homes and exchange gifts of new clothes.

Chat Preah Nengkal – Held in mid to late May, this is the Royal Ploughing ceremony, a ritual agricultural festival led by the royal family.

International Workers' Day – 1 May

P'chum Ben – Held in late September, this is a kind of All Souls' Day, when respects are paid to the dead through offerings made at wats.

HM the King's Birthday – 30 October to 1 November

Bon Om Tuk – Held in early November, this celebrates the reversal of the current of the Tonlé Sap River (with the onset of the dry season, water backed up in the Tonlé Sap Lake begins to empty into the Mekong; in the wet season the reverse is the case).

Independence Day – 9 November

The Chinese inhabitants of Cambodia celebrate their New Year in late January or early to mid-February – for the Vietnamese, this is Tet.

ACTIVITIES

Tourism in Cambodia is still in its infancy and as yet there is little in the way of activities besides sightseeing. Hiking is possible to a limited extent in Ratanakiri, and snorkelling and diving are available in Sihanoukville.

LANGUAGE COURSES

The only courses available in Cambodia at present are in Khmer, and these are aimed at expat residents of Phnom Penh rather than at travellers. If you are going to be based in Phnom Penh for some time, however, it would be well worth learning basic Khmer. Ring the Cambodian Development Resource Institute (☎ 368053) for information about classes – courses run for two months at a time.

WORK

Jobs are available in Phnom Penh and elsewhere around Cambodia. The obvious categories are English/French teaching work and volunteer work with one of the many non-government organisations (NGOs) operating in the country. For information about work opportunities with the NGOs call into the CCC (see the Useful Organisations section in this chapter), which has a noticeboard for positions vacant and may also be able to give advice on where to look. If you are thinking of applying for work with NGOs, you should bring copies of your educational certificates and work references with you.

Other places to look for work include the Classifieds sections of the *Phnom Penh Post* and the *Cambodia Daily*. The FCC in Phnom Penh has a noticeboard with job postings, as does Bert's Books & Guesthouse.

Do not expect to make a lot of money working in Cambodia. But if you want to learn more about the country and help the locals get the place up and running again, it may well be a very worthwhile experience.

ACCOMMODATION

The accommodation situation in Cambodia has changed immensely over the last five years. There is now a wide range of options to suit all budgets in Phnom Penh, and in Siem Reap new hotels are springing up everywhere. Elsewhere around Cambodia, options are fairly limited, however.

Budget hostels only exist in Phnom Penh, Siem Reap and Sihanoukville. Costs hover around US$3 for a bed, and slightly more in Sihanoukville, where there is little competition. In other parts of Cambodia, the standard rate for the cheapest hotels is US$5 – in many places this will be the standard rate for all hotels in town.

In Phnom Penh and Siem Reap, which see a steady flow of traffic, hotels improve significantly once you start spending more than US$10. For US$15 or less it is usually possible to find an air-con room with satellite TV and attached bathroom. If you spend between US$20 and US$30 you can get something quite luxurious.

Top-end accommodation is only available in Phnom Penh and Siem Reap, and most of it is poor value. This will change when the Singapore Raffles Group completes its renovations of the Grand D'Angkor in Siem Reap and Le Royal in Phnom Penh.

FOOD

Cambodian food is closely related to the cuisine of neighbouring Thailand and Laos and, to a lesser extent, Vietnam, but there are some distinct local dishes. The overall consensus is that Khmer cooking is like Thai without the spices.

Phnom Penh is far and away the best place to try Khmer cuisine, though Siem Reap also has some good restaurants. In Phnom Penh you also have the choice of excellent Thai, Vietnamese, Chinese, French and Mediterranean cooking.

Rice is the principal staple and the Battambang region is the country's rice bowl. Most Cambodian dishes are cooked in a wok, known locally as a *chhnang khteak*.

Local Food

A Cambodian meal almost always includes a soup, or *samla*, dish but this is eaten at the same time as the other courses, not as a separate starter. *Samla machou banle* is a popular fish soup with a sour flavour rather like the hot & sour dishes of neighbouring Thailand. Other soups include *samla chapek* (ginger-flavoured pork soup) or *samla machou bangkang* (a prawn soup closely related to the popular Thai *tom yam).*

Much of the fish eaten in Cambodia is freshwater, from the great Tonlé Sap Lake or Mekong River. *Trey aing,* or grilled fish, is a Cambodian speciality (*aing* means 'grilled' in Khmer and can be applied to many dishes). Traditionally, the fish is eaten in pieces which are wrapped in lettuce or spinach leaves and dipped into a fish sauce known as *tuk trey,* a close relative of Vietnam's *nam pla* or *nuoc mam* but with the addition of ground peanuts. *Trey noueng phkea* is fish stuffed with small dried prawns, *trey chorm hoy* is steamed whole fish, and *trey chean noeung spei* is fried fish served with vegetables.

Cambodian 'salad' dishes are also popular and delicious although quite different from the western idea of a cold salad. *Phlea sach ko* is a beef and vegetable salad, flavoured with coriander, mint leaves and lemon grass. These three herbs find their way into the flavouring of many Cambodian dishes.

Khao phoune is one of the most common Cambodian dishes and is found everywhere from street stalls to homes. Closely related to Malaysia's *laksa* dishes, the fine rice noodles are prepared in a sauce enriched with coconut milk.

At weddings and other festivities, sweet specialities like *ansam chruk,* sticky rice balls stuffed with banana, are served. *Nom bat* and *nom kom* are sticky rice cakes, or there is *phleay,* a pastry and palm sugar concoction which is fried and rolled in grated coconut. The large fruit known as jackfruit is used to make a pudding known as *sangkcha khnor.*

Fast Food

As of early 1996 there was no fast food in Cambodia. Rumour had it, however, that McDonald's was poised to set up a branch in Phnom Penh. Others will undoubtedly follow.

Vegetarian

If you are not a strict vegetarian and can deal with fish sauces and the like, you should have few problems when it comes to ordering meals. In Phnom Penh many of the international restaurants feature vegetarian meals, though naturally these are not budget options. In Khmer and Chinese restaurants, stir-fried vegetable dishes are readily available, as are vegetarian fried rice dishes. If you eat fish, you can sample Khmer cooking at its best.

Self-Catering

The French influence is most clearly seen in the delicious bread, baked every day and sold in the markets. It is very cheap (around 200r). The international supermarkets of Phnom Penh have excellent supplies of goodies such as salami, pastrami and cheeses. Supplementing these with some vegetables from the markets, you can put together your own meals at a very reasonable cost.

DRINKS
Nonalcoholic Drinks

All the well known soft drinks are available in Cambodia. There are also a lot of lesser known drinks for sale, most of them produced in other Asian countries. It is best to buy canned drinks rather than the bottled drinks sold from the roadside if you want to avoid stomach upsets. Locally produced mineral water is available at 500r per bottle.

In Phnom Penh, ice *(tuk kak)* is produced with treated water, but the transportation of it in huge blocks often involves dragging it along the ground. It is probably best to avoid it. Drinking tap water is to be avoided, especially in the provinces.

Coffee is sold in most restaurants. It is either served black or *café au lait* – with generous dollops of condensed milk, which makes it very sweet. Chinese-style tea is popular and in many Khmer and Chinese restaurants a pot of it will automatically appear as soon as you sit down.

Alcoholic Drinks

The local beer is Angkor, which is produced by an Australian joint venture based in

Sihanoukville. Most Khmer restaurants have a bevy of 'beer girls', each of whom represents a beer brand. They are always friendly, and will leave you alone if you prefer not to drink beer. Brands represented include Angkor, Heineken, Tiger, San Miguel, Carlsberg, VB, Foster's and Grolsch. Beer sells for around US$1.30 a can in restaurants.

In Phnom Penh, foreign wines and spirits are sold at very reasonable prices. The local spirits are best avoided, though some expats say that Sra Special, a local whiskey-like concoction, is not bad. At around 1000r a bottle it's a cheap route to oblivion.

ENTERTAINMENT
Cinemas
See the Phnom Penh chapter for information about venues that sometimes screen foreign films. Cinemas are best avoided. Even if you can understand the proceedings, Cambodia's cinemas tend to be scruffy, hot, and sometimes dangerously overcrowded.

Discos
Phnom Penh is the place for disco nightlife. There are several clubs that see a good mix of locals and expats. Nightlife in Phnom Penh tends not to get going until fairly late – an 11 pm boogie seems to be the popular thing to do, after a leisurely meal and some drinks at a bar.

Nightclubs
Outside Phnom Penh, nightlife is dominated by the 'dancing restaurant'. These clubs are aimed at men, though it's unlikely that a foreign woman accompanied by a foreign man would have any trouble in these places. Music alternates between a live band and a DJ usually, and the women charge the men to dance with them. The women are generally not employed by the bar. Some of these places, particularly in Sihanoukville, are very opulent.

Traditional Dance
Public performances of Khmer traditional dance are few and far between. In Phnom Penh, the Cambodiana Hotel stages performances once a week, and performances are also held in Siem Reap. Check in the local English newspapers for news of any upcoming events.

Pubs/Bars
Again, Phnom Penh is the place for pubs and bars. Elsewhere around Cambodia, drinking takes place in market areas, in restaurants and in 'dancing restaurants'.

SPECTATOR SPORT
Sports events are held from time to time at the Olympic Stadium in Phnom Penh. Kick boxing is popular in Cambodia and can be interesting to watch. Check the local English-language newspapers for news of events at the stadium.

THINGS TO BUY
The checked cotton scarves everyone wears on their heads, around their necks or, if bathing, around their midriffs, are known as *kramas*. Fancier coloured versions are made of silk or a silk-cotton blend. Some of the finest cotton kramas come from the Kompong Cham area.

For information on where in Phnom Penh to find antiques, silver items, jewellery, gems, colourful cloth for sarongs and *hols* (variegated silk shirts), wood carvings, papier-mâché masks, stone copies of ancient Khmer art, brass figurines and oil paintings, see Things to Buy in the Phnom Penh chapter.

Also see the Phnom Penh chapter for information on buying craft items produced by Cambodian mine victims, handicapped people and women's groups. The proceeds go to good causes, and the products themselves are very fine.

Getting There & Away

AIR
Airports & Airlines

Cambodia has just one international airport: Phnom Penh's Pochentong airport. There is talk of establishing direct flights from Malaysia to Sihanoukville, a service that, if it starts up, will provide a direct connection with the Malaysian-financed Naga Island casino. Flights from Bangkok to Siem Reap have not materialised and probably won't in the near future.

Flights to Cambodia itself are limited, and most of them originate either in Bangkok or Hong Kong. Bangkok has the most flights to Phnom Penh, and it is usually possible to get on a flight with either Thai or Royal Air Cambodge at short notice. From Hong Kong, there are regular flights with Dragonair and with Royal Air Cambodge. Other regional centres with flights to Cambodia are Singapore (Silk Air/Royal Air Cambodge) and Kuala Lumpur (Malaysia Air/Royal Air Cambodge). There are also flights to and from Vietnam and Laos.

There are no direct flights to or from Australia, Europe or the USA.

Buying Tickets

If you plan to buy your ticket in Bangkok or Hong Kong, it's a good idea to shop around. In Bangkok, the Banglamphu area, in particular Khao San Rd, is a good place to buy tickets for Cambodia. In Hong Kong, most of the budget travel agencies are in Tsimshatsui, Kowloon. In Hong Kong these days there are rarely problems with agents 'forgetting' to issue tickets, but this can occasionally occur in Bangkok. It's often better to pay a little bit more and go with a reputable agency.

Travellers with Special Needs

If you have any special needs, you should let the airline know as soon as possible and make a point of reminding them when you reconfirm and when you check in. Airlines can cater for victims of accidents, for passengers travelling with babies, for vegetarians, for almost anyone providing they are given notice.

Children under the age of two travel for 10% of the standard fare, or free with some airlines. 'Skycots', nappies (diapers) and baby food should be provided with some advance notice. Children aged between two and 12 generally travel at between half and two-thirds the full fare; they are allowed a baggage allowance.

The USA

Competition between Asian airlines flying to South-East Asia has resulted in discounted tickets. Good places to start looking are the travel sections of daily newspapers such as the *New York Times*, the *Chicago Tribune*, the *LA Times*, or whatever your local newspaper is. Agents such as Council Travel and Student Travel Network are well established and have offices in most major American cities. CIEE and STA are other travel agent chains that are well represented.

From the US west coast, fares to Bangkok and Hong Kong (the two best access points for Cambodia) cost around US$700/1000 one-way/return. Flights from the east coast are more expensive.

Canada

Check with the travel sections of newspapers like the *Vancouver Sun* and the *Toronto Globe & Mail* for details of agents and ticket prices they offer. Travel CUTS is probably the most well established agency chain, and they have offices throughout Canada.

Australia

The best agencies to check ticket prices with in Australia are STA Travel and Flight Centre. It may be a good idea to compare the prices they give you with prices posted in the travel sections of daily newspapers such as

Air Travel Glossary

Apex Tickets Apex stands for Advance Purchase Excursion fare. These tickets are usually between 30 and 40% cheaper than the full economy fare, but there are restrictions. You must purchase the ticket at least 21 days in advance (sometimes more) and must be away for a minimum period (normally 14 days) and return within a maximum period (90 or 180 days). Stopovers are not allowed, and if you have to change your dates of travel or destination, there will be extra charges to pay. These tickets are not fully refundable – if you have to cancel your trip, the refund is often considerably less than what you paid for the ticket. Take out travel insurance to cover yourself in case you have to cancel your trip unexpectedly – for example, due to illness.

Baggage Allowance This will be written on your ticket; you are usually allowed one 20-kg item to go in the hold, plus one item of hand luggage. Some airlines which fly transpacific and transatlantic routes allow for two pieces of luggage (there are limits on their dimensions and weight).

Bucket Shops At certain times of the year and/or on certain routes, many airlines fly with empty seats. This isn't profitable and it's more cost-effective for them to fly full, even if that means having to sell a certain number of drastically discounted tickets. They do this by off-loading them onto bucket shops (UK) or consolidators (USA), travel agents who specialise in discounted fares. The agents, in turn, sell them to the public at reduced prices. These tickets are often the cheapest you'll find, but you can't purchase them directly from the airlines. Availability varies widely, so you'll not only have to be flexible in your travel plans, you'll also have to be quick off the mark as soon as an advertisement appears in the press.

Bucket-shop agents advertise in newspapers and magazines and there's a lot of competition – especially in places like Amsterdam and London which are crawling with them – so it's a good idea to telephone first to ascertain availability before rushing from shop to shop. Naturally, they'll advertise the cheapest available tickets, but by the time you get there, these may be sold out and you may be looking at something slightly more expensive.

Bumped Just because you have a confirmed seat doesn't mean you're going to get on the plane – see Overbooking.

Cancellation Penalties If you have to cancel or change an Apex or other discount ticket, there may be heavy penalties involved; insurance can sometimes be taken out against these penalties. Some airlines impose penalties on regular tickets as well, particularly against 'no show' passengers.

Confirmation Having a ticket written out with the flight and date on it doesn't mean you have a seat until the agent has confirmed with the airline that your status is 'OK'. Prior to this confirmation, your status is 'on request'.

Courier Fares Businesses often need to send their urgent documents or freight securely and quickly. They do it through courier companies. These companies hire people to accompany the package through customs and, in return, offer a discount ticket which is sometimes a phenomenal bargain. In effect, what the courier companies do is ship their freight as your luggage on the regular commercial flights. This is a legitimate operation – all freight is completely legal. There are two shortcomings, however: the short turnaround time of the ticket, usually not longer than a month; and the limitation on your luggage allowance. You may be required to surrender all your baggage allowance for the use of the courier company, and be only allowed to take carry-on luggage.

Discounted Tickets There are two types of discounted fares – officially discounted (such as Apex – see Promotional Fares) and unofficially discounted (see Bucket Shops). The latter can save you more than money – you may be able to pay Apex prices without the associated Apex advance booking and other requirements. The lowest prices often impose drawbacks, such as flying with unpopular airlines, inconvenient schedules, or unpleasant routes and connections.

Economy Class Tickets Economy-class tickets are usually not the cheapest way to go, though they do give you maximum flexibility and they are valid for 12 months. If you don't use them, most are fully refundable, as are unused sectors of a multiple ticket.

Lost Tickets If you lose your airline ticket, an airline will usually treat it like a travellers' cheque and, after inquiries, issue you with a replacement. Legally, however, an airline is entitled to treat it like cash, so if you lose a ticket, it could be forever. Take good care of your tickets.

MCO An MCO (Miscellaneous Charges Order) is a voucher for a value of a given amount, which resembles an airline ticket and can be used to pay for a specific flight with any IATA (International Air

Transport Association) airline. MCOs, which are more flexible than a regular ticket, may satisfy the irritating onward ticket requirement, but some countries are now reluctant to accept them. MCOs are fully refundable if unused.

No Shows No shows are passengers who fail to show up for their flight for whatever reason. Full-fare no shows are sometimes entitled to travel on a later flight. The rest of us are penalised (see Cancellation Penalties).

Open-Jaw Tickets These are return tickets which allow you to fly to one place but return from another, and travel between the two 'jaws' by any means of transport at your own expense. If available, this can save you backtracking to your arrival point.

Overbooking Airlines hate to fly with empty seats, and since every flight has some passengers who fail to show up (see No Shows), they often book more passengers than they have seats available. Usually the excess passengers balance those who fail to show up, but occasionally somebody gets bumped. If this happens, guess who it is most likely to be – the passengers who check in late.

Promotional Fares These are officially discounted fares, such as Apex fares, which are available from travel agents or direct from the airline.

Reconfirmation You must contact the airline at least 72 hours prior to departure to 'reconfirm' that you intend to be on the flight. If you don't do this, the airline can delete your name from the passenger list and you could lose your seat.

Restrictions Discounted tickets often have various restrictions on them, such as necessity of advance purchase, limitations on the minimum and maximum period you must be away, restrictions on breaking the journey or changing the booking or route etc.

Round-the-World Tickets These tickets have become very popular in the last few years; basically, there are two types – airline tickets and agent tickets. An airline RTW ticket is issued by two or more airlines that have joined together to market a ticket which takes you around the world on their combined routes. It permits you to fly pretty well anywhere you choose using their combined routes as long as you don't backtrack, ie keep moving in approximately the same direction east or west. Other restrictions are that you (usually) must book the first sector in advance and cancellation penalties then apply. There may be restrictions on how many stopovers you are permitted. The RTW tickets are usually valid for 90 days up to a year.

The other type of RTW ticket, the agent ticket, is a combination of cheap fares strung together by an enterprising travel agent. These may be cheaper than airline RTW tickets, but the choice of routes will be limited.

Standby This is a discounted ticket where you only fly if there is a seat free at the last moment. Standby fares are usually only available directly at the airport, but sometimes may also be handled by an airline's city office. To give yourself the best possible chance of getting on the flight you want, get there early and have your name placed on the waiting list. It's first come, first served.

Student Discounts Some airlines offer student-card holders 15% to 25% discounts on their tickets. The same often applies to anyone under the age of 26. These discounts are generally only available on ordinary economy-class fares. You wouldn't get one, for instance, on an Apex or a RTW ticket, since these are already discounted.

Tickets Out An entry requirement for many countries is that you have an onward or return ticket, in other words, a ticket out of the country. If you're not sure what you intend to do next, the best solution is to buy the cheapest onward ticket to a neighbouring country or a ticket from a reliable airline which can later be refunded if you do not use it.

Transferred Tickets Airline tickets cannot be transferred from one person to another. Travellers sometimes try to sell the return half of their ticket, but officials can ask you to prove that you are the person named on the ticket. This may not be checked on domestic flights, but on international flights, tickets are usually compared with passports.

Travel Periods Some officially discounted fares, Apex fares in particular, vary with the time of year. There is often a low (off-peak) season and a high (peak) season. Sometimes there's an intermediate or shoulder season as well. At peak times, when everyone wants to fly, both officially and unofficially discounted fares will be higher, or there may simply be no discounted tickets available. Usually the fare depends on your outward flight – if you depart in the high season and return in the low season, you pay the high-season fare. ■

The Australian, *The Age* in Melbourne and the *Sydney Morning Herald*, among others.

There are usually low and high season rates for flights from Australia to South-East Asia. The high season applies during the school holiday December-January period – flights can often be heavily booked at this time as well as more expensive.

Return fares from Sydney and Melbourne to Bangkok cost from A$700 to A$900. Hong Kong is more expensive, with ticket prices from A$900.

New Zealand

Air New Zealand and Cathay Pacific fly directly from Auckland to Hong Kong. Apex fares are the best option. The cheapest one way/return tickets on the Hong Kong/Auckland run are around US$740/1060.

UK

The Sunday editions of most of the major dailies have travel sections with advertising for ticket prices to South-East Asia. The London listings magazine *Time Out* is also a good place to start your search.

Two of the best agencies for budget flights to South-East Asia are Trailfinders and STA. Many of the rock-bottom prices are with airlines that fly via Eastern Europe or the Middle East. Round-trip prices of around £350 are available with airlines such as Biman, Bangladeshi, Balkan, Qatar Airways. One-way flights for around £210 can be had with Aeroflot. Return flights to Hong Kong will cost around £500.

Asia

All travellers going to Cambodia will have to either transit in or fly from one of the regional air centres. Bangkok is the most likely option, but not the only one.

Thailand Flights to Phnom Penh from Bangkok are available with Thai and Royal Air Cambodge. There is not much in the way of discounting available on these flights, but it may be worth shopping around a little. Royal Air Cambodge is the cheaper of the two at around US$120/220 one way/return. Thai Airways flights cost around US$140/280.

The best area to shop around for tickets is Banglamphu. Khao San Rd has a large number of travel agents catering almost exclusively to foreign budget travellers.

Hong Kong Dragonair and Royal Air Cambodge fly between Hong Kong and Phnom Penh. Royal Air Cambodge is the cheaper of the two, with flights at US$190/300 one-way/return. Dragonair costs US$210/310. There is no discounting on flights to and from Hong Kong, so it makes little difference who you buy your ticket with.

Singapore Silk Air and Royal Air Cambodge have flights to/from Singapore to Phnom Penh. Royal Air Cambodge tickets cost around US$210/300 one-way/return, while Silk Air flights are around US$210/360.

Malaysia Flights between Kuala Lumpur and Phnom Penh are offered by Malaysia Air Line and Royal Air Cambodge. One-way flights with both airlines are around US$200. Return flights are around US$310 with Royal Air Cambodge and US$360 with Malaysia Air.

Vietnam Vietnam Airlines does the short hop from Ho Chi Minh City (Saigon) to Phnom Penh for US$70/130 one-way/return; Royal Air Cambodge costs US$65/110. Royal Air Cambodge is probably the better airline.

Laos Daily flights between Vientiane and Phnom Penh cost US$150/300 one-way/return.

LAND
Vietnam

The only fully functioning land crossing in or out of Cambodia is at Moc Bai in Vietnam. The trip by bus or by taxi between Phnom Penh and Ho Chi Minh City (Saigon) should only take five to six hours, but delays are frequent. See the Getting There & Away section of the Phnom Penh chapter for details.

Thailand

A trickle of adventurous travellers have made their way between Trat in Thailand and Koh Kong in Cambodia. This border crossing is not officially open to foreign travellers and the journey is dangerous. It is not recommended.

The border crossing between Aranyaprathet in eastern Thailand and Poipet (Poay Pet) in western Cambodia is extremely dangerous due to Khmer Rouge activity in this part of Cambodia. If you hear that this border has become safe to cross, it would be wise to confirm it with your embassy.

DEPARTURE TAXES

Domestic departure taxes in Cambodia were US$4 at the time of writing, but were said to be rising to US$5. International departure tax from Pochentong airport is US$15.

ORGANISED TOURS

In the early days of Cambodia travel, organised tours were a near necessity. The situation has changed over the last four or five years and it is much easier nowadays to organise your own trip. Budget and midrange travellers in particular are best off going it alone. If you are on a tight schedule, you may like to book a return flight to Siem Reap before you leave to ensure that you get the time you want at Angkor. Once you get to Angkor, guides and drivers are plentiful.

All the same, Cambodia is not the easiest of countries to travel in and some travellers will no doubt feel more secure visiting with a tour. Some major operators are listed below.

From Australia

Orbitours (☎ (02) 9221 7322; fax (02) 9221 7425), GPO Box 3309, Sydney 2000, is a major tour operator for English-speaking visitors from other countries as well as Australia. They operate tours ex-Bangkok which can also combine Cambodia with the other countries in Indochina.

From the UK

Regent Holidays (UK) (☎ (1179) 9211711; fax (0272) 9254866), 13 Small St, Bristol BS1 1DE, is a major operator from the UK.

From Thailand

In Bangkok, Diethelm Travel is the major operator for tours to Indochina. Its office in Bangkok can be found at the Kian Gwan Building II, 140/1 Wireless Rd, Bangkok 10500 (☎ 2559150/60/70; fax 256-0248/9). Diethelm also has offices in Phnom Penh (see the Phnom Penh chapter for details) and in Ho Chi Minh City (Saigon).

WARNING

The information in this chapter is particularly vulnerable to change: prices for international travel are volatile, routes are introduced and cancelled, schedules change, special deals come and go, and rules and visa requirements are amended. Airlines and governments seem to take a perverse pleasure in making price structures and regulations as complicated as possible. You should check directly with the airline or a travel agent to make sure you understand how a fare (and ticket you may buy) works. In addition, the travel industry is highly competitive and there are many lurks and perks.

The upshot of this is that you should get opinions, quotes and advice from as many airlines and travel agents as possible before you part with your hard-earned cash. The details given in this chapter should be regarded as pointers and are not a substitute for your own careful, up-to-date research.

Getting Around

Transportation in Cambodia is still fairly primitive. The train system is off limits to foreigners; there is little in the way of bus routes; and the boats that ply the Mekong and the Tonlé Sap Lake still carry an element of risk. Share taxi services are best for visiting the sights around Phnom Penh. Until security problems are resolved, it is recommended that long-distance travel in Cambodia be undertaken by air.

AIR
Domestic Air Services
Royal Air Cambodge, established as a joint venture with Malaysia Helicopter Services in 1994, has flights to limited destinations around Cambodia. Angkor is well serviced and it is usually possible to get on a flight at short notice. Some travellers even manage to get a flight out to Angkor immediately upon arrival at Phnom Penh's Pochentong airport. But demand for flights to other destinations around the country often exceeds supply; it is not always easy to get seats.

The Royal Air Cambodge fleet comprises two Boeing 737-400s, which are used for international flights, and two ATR 72s, which are used for domestic flights. Plans to expand the fleet will hopefully result in more domestic flights.

There are seven flights a day from Phnom Penh to Siem Reap (Angkor); the cost is US$55/110 one-way/return. For Battambang, there are five flights a week; the cost is US$45/90 one-way/return. Flights going to Ratanakiri are scheduled five times a week; the cost is US$55/100 one-way/return. Other destinations are Sihanoukville (four times a week) for US$40/70; Koh Kong (four times a week) for US$50/100; Stung Treng (three times a week) for US$45/90; and Mondulkiri (twice a week) for US$50/100.

The baggage weight limit for domestic flights is only 10 kg per passenger but unless you are way over the limit it is unlikely you will have to pay excess baggage.

The airport tax for domestic flights, US$4 at the time of writing, is reportedly poised to rise to US$5.

Helicopter
If you're absolutely loaded or are on an expense account, you might consider chartering a Soviet-built helicopter for sightseeing or aerial photography. A round-trip excursion from Phnom Penh to Angkor for up to a dozen people costs around US$6000. Helicopters can be hired by the hour for around US$2000.

BUS
Bus travel is no longer forbidden for foreigners, but most travellers sensibly give the buses a miss. The only services used regularly by foreigners are those from Phnom Penh to Ho Chi Minh City (Saigon) and to Sihanoukville. Most foreign embassies advise against using the latter, but this may change as Sihanoukville becomes a more popular destination.

TRAIN
For good reason, Cambodia's rail system is off limits to foreigners. It is frequently the target of Khmer Rouge attacks.

If it wasn't being blown up all the time, Cambodia's rail system would consist of around 645 km of single-track metre-gauge lines. The 382 km north-western line, built before WWII, links Phnom Penh with Pursat (165 km from the capital), Battambang (274 km from the capital) and, in peacetime, Poipet (Poay Pet) on the Thai border. The 263 km south-western line, completed in 1969, connects the capital with Takeo (75 km from Phnom Penh), Kampot (160 km from the capital), Kep (get off at Damnak Chang Aeu) and the port of Sihanoukville.

The civil war of recent years has led to some unique developments in the Cambodian rail system. Each train is equipped with a tin-roofed armoured carriage sporting a huge machine gun and numerous gun ports

Lives on the Line

According to the government director of railways, the Khmer Rouge has a railway policy of its own. It goes: 'cut the railway into pieces.' This should be warning enough for most travellers to keep off the trains in Cambodia but, just in case it isn't, the government also has a policy of not selling tickets to foreigners. This has been in force since an attack on a passenger train on 26 July, 1994, in which 13 Khmer civilians were killed and three foreigners – an Australian, a Briton and a Frenchman – were taken hostage, marched off into the jungle and later shot.

Even locals, who are used to the security problems that bedevil Cambodia, complain that the railways are pure chaos. All but the very poor avoid the trains. From January to July of 1995, for example, 327 stretches of railway and 12 bridges were blown up on the Phnom Penh-Battambang-Sisophon line. The (theoretically) daily service on this line ran just three times during that period.

Of course, you might point to the fact that there are some 800 to 1000 government troops defending Cambodia's 600 km of railways. But poorly paid government troops are part of the problem. At checkpoints on the Phnom Penh-Battambang route troops armed with AK 47s and grenade launchers arbitrarily exact 'tolls' from hapless passengers. Government troops were implicated in the kidnapping and murder of the three foreigners mentioned already, probably in conjunction with the Khmer Rouge.

In the long term, Cambodia hopes to resuscitate its railway network. A long-mooted plan involves extending a line from Sisophon into Thailand and from Sihanoukville to Vietnam, raising the exciting prospect of a new Asian overland route. Until this happens, however, and the trains are declared safe, keep away from them. ∎

---

in its half-height sides. In addition, the first two cars of the train operate as mine sweepers. Travel on these carriages is free and, despite the risks, very popular.

CAR & MOTORCYCLE

Motorcycles are handy for short-distance driving, but they are not recommended for use over long distances. Car hire is only available with a driver. This is for the best, given the risks entailed in driving yourself around Cambodia.

Road Network

Cambodia's highways are conveniently numbered from one to seven. National Route 1 links Phnom Penh with Ho Chi Minh City (Saigon) via Svay Rieng and the Moc Bai border crossing, which is five km east of the Cambodian town of Bavet. National Route 2 heads south from the capital, passing through Takmau and Takeo on its way to Vietnam's An Giang Province and the city of Chau Doc. National Route 3 links the capital with the southern coastal city of Kampot. National Route 4 connects Phnom Penh and the country's only port, Sihanoukville,

which is on the Gulf of Thailand, south-west of the capital.

National Route 5 heads north from Phnom Penh, circling around to the south of the Tonlé Sap and passing through Kompong Chhnang, Pursat, Battambang and Sisophon on its way north-westward to the Thai frontier. National Route 6 splits off from National Route 5 at the Prek Kdam Ferry over the Tonlé Sap River, heading northward and then north-westward on a route that goes to the north of the Tonlé Sap and passes through Kompong Thom, Siem Reap and Sisophon on its way to Thailand. National Route 7 splits from National Route 6 at Skun, heading eastward to Kompong Cham and eventually to Memot (Memut), Kratie, Stung Treng and the Lao border; the latter sections are currently impassable.

Road Rules

If there are road rules in Cambodia it is doubtful that anyone is following them. The best advice, if you ride a motorbike in Cambodia, is to take nothing for granted and assume that your fellow motorists are visually-challenged psychopaths. Slow down to a standstill before crossings and develop a habit of constant vigilance.

Rental

Motorbikes are available for rent in Phnom Penh. Costs are US$5 per day and upwards depending on the motorbike. The cheapest models are 100 cc Hondas. Bear in mind that medical facilities are less than adequate in Cambodia and that the driving is erratic. A motorbike can be useful for visiting out-of-town attractions in the Phnom Penh area. Cross-country biking is dangerous.

BICYCLE

Cambodia is unfortunately not a country for cyclists. At present and for the foreseeable future the security risks are too great.

HITCHING

There is a severe shortage of transport in Cambodia, so most trucks – the only vehicles other than large buses able to negotiate the country's dilapidated roads – are likely to be extremely crowded. Expect to pay for your ride. Don't even think of hitching until after the war is definitely over!

BOAT

Cambodia's 1900 km of navigable waterways are an important element in the country's transportation system. Phnom Penh, some 320 km from the mouth of the Mekong, can be reached by ocean-going vessels with a draft of less than 3.3 metres. North of the capital, the Mekong is navigable as far north as Kratie; from September to January, boats can make it as far as Stung Treng.

The most popular boat services with foreigners are those that run between Phnom Penh and Siem Reap. The new express services do the trip in as little as four hours. They are, however, dangerously overcrowded and occasionally the target of attacks by fishing people.

For information on ferry services to/from Phnom Penh, see the Getting There & Away section of the Phnom Penh chapter.

LOCAL TRANSPORT
Bus

The only real local bus services running in Cambodia are those in Phnom Penh. For the most part, buses are not yet a practical way of getting around.

Taxi

The taxi situation has been steadily improving in Cambodia over the past few years.

The ubiquitous cyclo, a cheap mode of transport in Cambodia.

Whereas taxi hire was once only available through government ministries, there are now many private operators working in Cambodia. Even in Phnom Penh, you'll be hard pressed finding a taxi for short hops.

Moto

The moto is generally a 100 cc Honda. The drivers almost universally wear a blue cap. Motos are a quick, if somewhat dangerous, way of making short hops around towns and cities. Prices range from 500r to US$1, depending on the distance you travel.

Moto drivers assume you know the cost of a trip and prices are rarely agreed before starting.

Cyclo

As in Vietnam and Laos, the samlor or cyclo is a quick, cheap way to get around urban areas. In Phnom Penh, cyclo drivers can either be flagged down on main roads or found hanging out around marketplaces and major hotels. In Phnom Penh and elsewhere around Cambodia the cyclo is fast losing ground to the moto.

Remorque-Kang & Remorque-Moto

The *remorque-kang* is a trailer pulled by a bicycle; a trailer hitched to a motorbike is called a *remorque-moto*. Both are used to transport people and goods, especially in rural areas. They are not seen so much nowadays in urban Cambodia.

Phnom Penh

Phnom Penh sits at the confluence of the Mekong River, the Bassac River and the Tonlé Sap River. Once considered the loveliest of the French-built cities of Indochina, its charm has managed to survive the violence of its recent history and the present invasion of Hondas and investors.

Most of Phnom Penh's attractions are low key, which means that many travellers spend only a short time there. This is a pity. Phnom Penh is a city that is rediscovering itself and, once you have done the obligatory sightseeing circuit, it is a fascinating city to take in at leisure. The French left a legacy of now crumbling colonial architecture, some of which has been tastefully renovated; sidewalk restaurants have sprung up all over town; crowds gather on the recently developed riverfront area at dusk and on Sunday afternoons; and, as the wats come back to life, monks in saffron robes can be seen wandering around town with alms bowls.

History

Legend has it that Phnom Penh was founded when an old woman named Penh found four Buddha images that had come to rest on the banks of the Mekong. She housed them on a nearby hill, and the town that emerged around the hill came to be known as Phnom Penh – the Hill of Penh.

The story, however, gives no clue as to why Angkor was abandoned in the 1440s and Phnom Penh chosen as the site of the new Cambodian capital. The move has been much lamented as evidence of cultural decline, but it nevertheless made a good deal of practical sense. Angkor was poorly situated for trade and subject to attacks from the Siamese (Thai) kingdom of Ayudhya (Ayuthaya). Phnom commanded a more central position in the Khmer territories and was perfectly located for riverine trade with Laos and China via the Mekong Delta. The Tonlé Sap River provided access to the rich fishing grounds of the Tonlé Sap Lake.

By the mid-16th century trade had turned Phnom Penh into a regional power. Indonesian and Chinese traders were drawn to the city in large numbers. A century later, however, Vietnamese incursions into Khmer territory had robbed the city of access to sea lanes, and Chinese merchants driven south by the Manchu Qing dynasty began to monopolise trade. The landlocked and increasingly isolated kingdom became a buffer between ascendent Thais and Vietnamese. In 1772 the Thais burnt Phnom Penh to the ground. Although the city was rebuilt, in the years that followed until the French took over in 1863, Phnom Penh was buffeted by the rival hegemonic interests of the Thai and Vietnamese courts. Its population is thought never to have risen above 25,000.

The population of Phnom Penh was approximately 500,000 in 1970. After the spread of the Vietnam War to Cambodian territory, the city's population swelled with refugees, reaching about two million in early 1975. The Khmer Rouge took over the city on 17 April 1975 and immediately forced the entire population into the countryside as part of its radical social programme.

During the next four years, many tens of thousands of former Phnom Penhois – including the vast majority of the capital's educated people – were killed. Repopulation of the city began when the Vietnamese arrived in 1979. Today the population of the city has grown again to around 812,000.

Orientation

A minor hurdle to orientation in Phnom Penh is the frequency with which street names get changed. The current denominations, which date back to 1993, seem to have settled in, but there is still a chance that some of them will change again. Mao Tse Toung Blvd (where appropriately you will find the Chinese Embassy), for example, will probably re-emerge as something else when the current roadworks are completed.

The major boulevards of Phnom Penh run north-south, parallel to the banks of the Tonlé Sap and Brassac rivers. Monivong Blvd cuts north-south through the centre of town, passing just west of the New Market. Its northern sector is the main shopping drag, and is also home to some of the longest-running hotels in town. Norodom Blvd also runs north-south, from Wat Phnom, and is largely administrative; the northern end contains a number of banks, while farther south is mainly government ministries. Samdech Sothearos Blvd runs north-south along the riverfront past the Royal Palace, Silver Pagoda and National Assembly building. The major east-west boulevards are Pochentong Blvd in the north of town, Preah Sihanouk Blvd, which passes the Victory Monument and ends just south of the Sofitel Cambodiana Hotel, and Mao Tse Toung Blvd (also known as Issarak Blvd). Mao Tse Toung Blvd, a ring road of sorts, also runs north-south.

Intersecting the main boulevards is a network of hundreds of numbered smaller streets. As a rule of thumb, streets running east-west have even numbers that get higher the farther south they are in town, while north-south running streets have odd numbers that get higher the farther west you go.

Most buildings around town have signs with both their street number and the number of the street. Finding a building purely by its address, however, is not always easy as numbers are rarely sequential. It's not unusual to find house No 23 next door to house No 13, followed by No 11. Sometimes separate buildings on the same street share the same number. Try and get a cross-reference for an address: ie close to the intersection of 107 St and 182 St. The letters 'EO' after a street address stand for *étage zéro*, which means 'ground floor' in French.

Maps Local maps of Phnom Penh, touted around the restaurants by children, are generally poor. The *Phnom Penh Post* includes a map with regularly updated listings, though entries are sponsored by advertisers and are far from comprehensive. The *Cam-bodia – Travel Map* published by Periplus is available at the Cambodiana Hotel bookshop and includes a large fold-out map of Phnom Penh at a scale of 1:17,000. It is a colourful production, but while the streets are accurately listed many of the items included are either out of date or incorrectly placed on the map.

Information

Tourist Offices Due to lack of funds, you can basically forget about useful tourism information in Phnom Penh. The tourist office at Pochentong international airport has information on certain hotels around town and can provide bookings, but other than this you are effectively on your own.

The head office of Phnom Penh Tourism is across from Wat Ounalom at the oblique intersection of Mohavithei Sothearos Blvd and Sisowath Quay. The office is officially open from 7 to 11 am and from 2 to 5 pm. It's a sleepy place with nothing in the way of useful information; for the most part it restricts its activities to running the Lotus D'or sightseeing boat service.

The Ministry of Tourism (☎ 426876) is in a white, two-storey building on the western corner of Monivong Blvd and 232 St. Inside chaos prevails; it should be possible to organise a guide with some persistence.

Foreign Embassies An ever-growing number of countries are establishing embassies in Phnom Penh. More will undoubtedly come.

Australia
    11, 254 St (☎ 426000/1; fax 426003)
Bulgaria
    227 Norodom Blvd (☎ 723181/2; fax 726491)
Canada
    c/o Australian Embassy (see above)
China
    156 Mao Tse Toung Blvd
    (☎ 426271; fax 426972)
Cuba
    98, 214 St (☎ 724181)
France
    1 Monivong Blvd (☎ 30021)
Germany
    76-78, 214 St (☎ 426381; fax 427746)

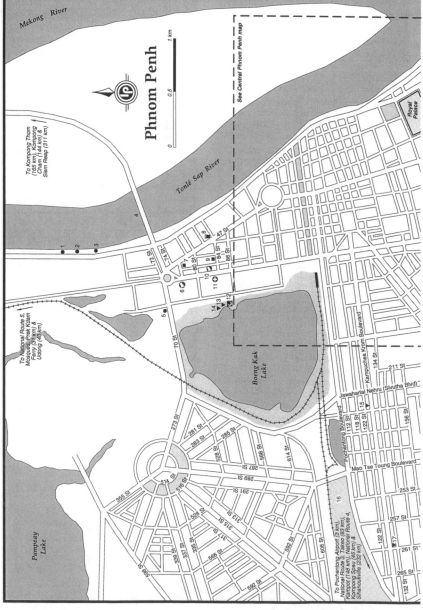

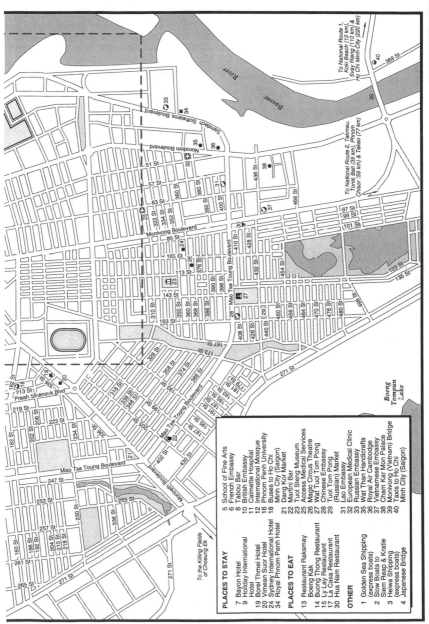

PLACES TO STAY

7 Bayon Hotel
9 Holiday International Hotel
19 Borei Thmei Hotel
20 Vimean Suor Hotel
24 Sydney International Hotel
34 Royal Phnom Penh Hotel

PLACES TO EAT

13 Restaurant Raksmay Boeng Kak
14 Buong Thong Restaurant
15 Ly Lay Restaurant
17 La Casa Restaurant
30 Hua Nam Restaurant

OTHER

1 Golden Sea Shipping (express boats)
2 Slow Boats to Siem Reap & Kratie
3 Heiwa Shipping (express boats)
4 Japanese Bridge
5 School of Fine Arts
6 French Embassy
8 Tabou Bar
10 British Embassy
11 Calmette Hospital
12 International Mosque
16 Phnom Penh University
18 Buses to Ho Chi Minh City (Saigon)
21 Dang Kor Market
22 Martini Bar
23 Tuol Sleng Museum
25 Access Medical Services
26 Magic Circus Theatre
27 Wat Tuol Tom Pong
28 Chinese Embassy
29 Tuol Tom Pong (Russian) Market
31 Lao Embassy
33 European Medical Clinic
33 Russian Embassy
35 Wat Than Handicrafts
36 Royal Air Cambodge
37 Vietnamese Embassy
38 Cham Kar Mon Palace
39 Monivong (Vietnam) Bridge
40 Taxis to Ho Chi Minh City (Saigon)

Hungary
463 Monivong Blvd (☎ 722781; fax 426216)
India
777 Monivong Blvd (☎ 722981)
Indonesia
179, 51 St (☎ 426148; fax 426571)
Japan
75 Norodom Blvd (☎ 427161; fax 426162)
Laos
15-17 Mao Tse Toung Blvd (☎ 426441; fax 427454)
Malaysia
161, 51 St (☎ 426176; fax 426004)
Philippines
33, 294 St (☎ 428048; fax 428592)
Poland
767 Monivong Blvd (☎ 426250)
Russia
213 Samdech Sotheros Blvd
(☎ 723081; fax 426776)
Thailand
4 Monivong Blvd (☎ 426124)
USA
27, 240 St (☎ 426436; fax 426437)
UK
27-29, 75 St (☎ 427124; fax 428295)
Vietnam
436 Monivong Blvd (☎ 018-810694)

Visa Extensions Visa extensions are granted
by the Direction des Étrangers on 200 St,
near the corner of Norodom Blvd. Officially,
visa extensions are a straightforward matter.
One photograph is required, the application
form costs 2000r, and visa extensions of one
month cost US$30, three months US$60, six
months US$100 and one year (!) US$150. In
practice, however, some applicants have
found it difficult to get extensions. Try and
look presentable, smile, and come prepared
with a fistful of dollars.

Money The best bank for changing money
and obtaining credit card advances is the
Cambodian Commercial Bank, on the corner
of Pochentong Blvd and Monivong Blvd. It
takes most travellers' cheques and can also
organise credit card advances for MasterCard,
JCB and Visa. A limit of US$2000 is
imposed on cash advances, but there is no
charge. Most other banks around town only
deal with Visa and charge 2% commission.

Travellers' cheques can also be changed at
the Foreign Trade Bank, at 24 Norodom
Blvd, and next door at the Bangkok Bank.

The Banque Indosuez, at 77 Norodom Blvd,
is another place that changes travellers'
cheques. Both the Diamond and Sofitel
Cambodiana hotels have exchange counters,
but they are only available for guests.

Other banks include:

Asia Bank
86 Norodom Blvd
Cambodia Asia Bank
252 Monivong Blvd
May Bank
2 Norodom Blvd
Standard Chartered Bank
95a Preah Sihanouk Blvd
Thai Farmers Bank
2, 114 St

Post The GPO is just east of Wat Phnom on
13 St. It is open from 6.30 am to 9 pm daily.
The GPO offers postal services as well as
domestic and international telegraph and
telephone links.

Telephone The best way to dial locally or
internationally is with the Telstra card
phones that are scattered around town. Cards
are available at the Telstra Office (☎ 426022),
58 Norodom Blvd and at the Foreign
Correspondents' Club (FCC) and other
outlets. You are rarely far from a card phone
in Phnom Penh, but some key locations are:
in front of the National Museum; in front of
the FCC; and in front of Lucky Supermarket
(Preah Sihanouk Blvd).

Fax Many of the mid-range hotels and all of
the top-end hotels around town have fax
services. Sending faxes from Phnom Penh is
expensive, and it generally costs money to
receive them too. The FCC has a business
centre where faxes can be sent and received.

Travel Agencies The area near the Pacific
Hotel on Monivong Blvd has a few budget
travel agencies, including Pich Tourist Co
(☎ 246585), which also has a reasonable
bookshop.

One of the most reliable outfits in town is
Diethelm Travel (☎ 426648), at 8 Samdech
Sotheros Blvd, behind the FCC. Diethelm

also has offices in Siem Reap, Bangkok and Ho Chi Minh City (Saigon), making it a good agency for regional flights and tours. Another popular agency is East West Tours (☎ 427118), at 84 Samdech Sothearos Blvd, just south of the Regent Park Hotel. Like Diethelm, this office has a counterpart in Bangkok and is a reliable operator. Transpeed Travel (☎ 427366), at 19, 106 St in the same building as Thai Airways, is another good option for flight bookings.

Bookshops The availability of English and French publications in Phnom Penh has improved immensely over the last few years. The New Market is still a good place to seek out discount (largely photocopied) books on Cambodia, but if you are starved of more entertaining reading there is a number of bookshops around town with reasonably wide-ranging supplies of reading fodder.

Bert's Books, at 79 Sisowath Quay, is the best place in town for browsing. The shelves here are simply groaning with stock shipped in from the US. If you are looking for anything in particular ask Bert – he's set up arguably the best second-hand bookshop in Asia and is knowledgeable about his stock to boot.

For new books and magazines, the bookshop on the ground floor of the Sofitel Cambodiana Hotel is one of the best stocked in town. It has a very good selection of French newspapers, magazines and books, as well as a modest selection of English coffee-table publications, novels and weeklies such as *Far Eastern Economic Review*, *The Economist*, *Time*, *Newsweek* and *Asiaweek*.

Bookazine, at 228 Monivong Blvd, has a reasonable selection of Penguins, magazines and a good range of books on Cambodia. The International Stationery & Book Centre is mainly devoted to dictionaries, but it also stocks some locally produced maps.

Libraries The National Library, on 90 St near Wat Phnom, is in a delightful old building but only has a small selection of reading material for foreign visitors. Most of the books were destroyed during the Pol Pot era. Opening hours are from 8 to 11 am and 2 to 5 pm.

French speakers should call into the French Cultural Centre on 184 St (near the corner of Monivong Blvd). It has a good range of reading material.

Clubs & Associations A good opportunity to meet local expats is via the Hash House Harriers, usually referred to simply as 'the Hash'. A weekly run/walk takes place every Sunday. Participants meet in front of the railway station at 2.45 pm, and entry is US$5; the entry fee includes refreshments at the end.

The Foreign Correspondents' Club, at 363 Sisowath Quay, unlike many FCCs around the world, is open to all comers and is a great place to meet people, enjoy a few drinks and a meal. Membership is US$150 per year for local residents, US$75 for overseas members. Membership provides access to the members' room (which has online news services), business facilities, 20% discount on food and drinks and reciprocal rights to other FCCs.

Look out for announcements of performances by the Phnom Penh Players in the *Cambodia Daily* and the *Phnom Penh Post* while you are in town. The players are local residents who perform a play every several months.

Laundry Most hotels around town offer reasonably priced laundry services – in some cases free. For dry cleaning, try Penley Dry Cleaning at the corner of 13 St and 136 St.

Medical Services SOS International Medical Centre (☎ 015-962914), 83 Mao Tse Toung Blvd, is one of the best medical services around town; as you might expect, costs for a consultation are on par with those overseas. Office hours are from 9 am to 5 pm Monday to Friday, 9 am to noon Saturday.

Access Medical Services (☎ 015-913358), at the corner of 63 St and 310 St, is another reliable clinic. Office hours are from 8 am to noon and 2 to 5 pm Monday to Friday, and 8 am to noon Saturday.

The Calmette Hospital (☎ 725373), at Monivong Blvd, is French administered and the best of the local hospitals.

For dental problems, go to the European

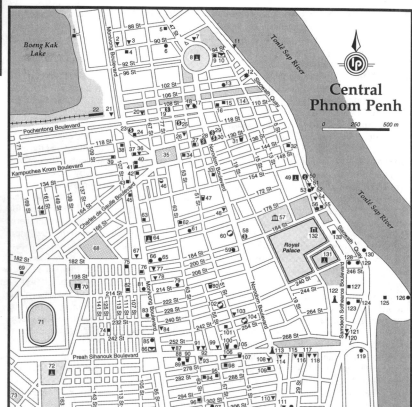

Central
Phnom Penh

Medical Clinic (☎ 018-812055), at 195 Norodom Blvd. Office hours are 8 am to noon and 2.30 pm to 6 pm Monday to Friday, 8 am to 1 pm Saturday.

Emergency In the event of a medical emergency you will probably have to be flown to Bangkok. The SOS International Medical Centre (☎ 015-912765) has a 24 hour emergency service and can also organise evacuation. The European Dental Clinic (☎ 018-812055) also has an after hours service.

To contact the police in an emergency, ring 722467 or 018-811542.

Dangers & Annoyances Phnom Penh is not as dangerous as many people imagine, but it is still important to take care. Armed theft is on the increase. It is not sensible to ride a motorbike alone late at night.

Those out clubbing in the evenings can expect to be stopped at checkpoints from time to time. Ostensibly police checkpoints are there to check for firearms, but occasionally foreigners will be nabbed for a cigarette or a dollar. You are under no obligation to fork out.

The restaurant areas of Phnom Penh (particularly places with outdoor seating) are

PLACES TO STAY

1 Cloud Nine Guesthouse
4 Le Royal Hotel
5 Sharaton Cambodia Hotel
9 Wat Phnom Hotel
12 Bert's Books & Guesthouse
15 Last Home Guesthouse
10 Oathay Hotel
24 Dusit Hotel
27 Hawaii Hotel
32 Hotel Indochine
33 Landmark Boulevard Hotel
34 La Paillote Hotel & Restaurant
37 Allson Hotel
38 Monoram Hotel
39 Morakat Hotel
40 Asie Hotel
41 Singapore Hotel
42 Diamond Hotel
43 Paradis Hotel
44 Juliana Hotel
45 Pailin Hotel
55 Hotel New Paris
62 Lotus Guesthouse
63 Mittapheap Hotel
69 Sangkor Hotel
74 Narin's Guesthouse
75 Capital Guesthouse
76 Hong Kong Hotel/Lucky! Lucky! (Motorbike Rental)
82 No 20 Guesthouse
89 Tokyo Hotel
94 Amara Hotel
95 Goldiana Hotel
96 Champs Elysées Hotel
98 Golden Gate Hotel
101 Lucky Inn
109 Rama Inn
116 Hotel Shinwa
124 Bophar Toep Hotel
125 Sofitel Cambodiana Hotel
127 Regent Park Hotel
133 Renakse Hotel

PLACES TO EAT

2 Chez Lipp Restaurant
3 Seven Seven Super- market/Café

7 Il Padrino Restaurant
11 Tonlé Sap Restaurant
18 Le Cuistot
20 Happy Neth Pizza
21 Indian Restaurant
26 Cathouse Tavern
36 Mamak's Corner/Kababeesh Restaurants
48 Chao Praya Restaurant
51 Wagon Wheel Restaurant
52 Pon Lok Restaurant
54 FCC (Foreign Correspondent's Club of Cambodia)
67 King's Bar
77 Tropicana Café Bar
78 La Pacha
84 Royal India Restaurant
87 Singapore Chicken Rice/Cordon Bleue Restaurants
91 King of King's Restaurant
92 California II Restaurant
93 Phnom Kiev Restaurant
99 Nagasaki
103 Baggio's Pizza
106 Cactus
108 L'Atmosphére
110 Ban Thai Restaurant
111 Troika
114 The Mex
115 Greenhouse II Restaurant
117 Bamboo House Restaurant
118 Red
120 Saigon House/ EID Restaurants
121 Chiang Mai Restaurant

OTHER

6 National Library
8 Wat Phnom
10 GPO
13 Thai Airways/Dragonair
14 Old Market (Psar Char)
17 NCDP Handicrafts
19 Canadia Bank
22 Railway Station
23 Cambodian Commercial Bank
25 Thai Farmers' Bank

28 Maybank
29 Foreign Trade Bank of Cambodia
30 Bangkok Bank
31 Sharky's (Disco)
35 New Market
46 Local (City) Bus Station
47 Heart of Darkness Bar
49 Wat Ounalom
50 Phnom Penh Tourism
53 Diethelm Travel
56 UNESCO
57 National Museum
58 Banque Indosuez
59 Immigration (Direction des Étrangers) Bureau
60 Japanese Embassy
61 Cooperation Committee for Cambodia (CCC)
64 Wat Koh
65 French Cultural Centre (Centre Culturel Français)
66 Ministry of Culture
68 O Russei Market
70 Wat Sampao Meas
71 Olympic Stadium
72 Wat Moha Montrei
73 Olympic Market
79 Bangkok Airways
80 Le Saint Tropez (Disco)
81 International Stationery & Book Centre
83 Ministry of Tourism
85 Suntan Food Market
86 Post & Telecom- munications Office
88 Lucky Supermarket
90 Ettamogah Pub
97 Khemara Handicrafts
100 Fire Club (Disco)
102 US Embassy
104 Australian Embassy
105 Vietnam Airlines
107 Irish Rover Pub
112 Prayuvong Buddha Factories
113 Victory Monument
119 Cambo Fun Park
122 Cambodia-Vietnam Monument
123 East-West Tours
126 Naga Floating Casino
128 National Assembly Building
129 Foreign Ministry
130 Chatomuk Theatre
131 Silver Pagoda
132 Royal Palace

infested with beggars. Generally, however, there is little in the way of push and shove. If you give to beggars, do as the locals do and keep the denominations small – this way hopefully foreigners will not become special targets of beggars.

Royal Palace

Phnom Penh's Royal Palace, which stands on the site of the former citadel, Banteay Kev (built in 1813), fronts Samdech Sothearos Blvd between 184 St and 240 St. Since Sihanouk's return to Cambodia, visitors are only allowed to visit the palace's Silver Pagoda and its surrounding compound. Entry is not, at present, permitted to the rest of the palace complex. The Silver Pagoda is open to the public daily from 8 to 11 am and from 2 to 5 pm. The entry fee is US$2. There is an additional US$2 charge to bring a still camera into the complex; movie or video cameras cost US$5. Photography is not permitted inside the pagoda.

Chan Chaya Pavilion Performances of classical Cambodian dance were once staged in Chan Chaya Pavilion, through which guests enter the grounds of the Royal Palace. These days, the Sofitel Cambodiana Hotel is one of the few venues that hosts the country's traditional classical dance performances.

Throne Hall The Throne Hall, topped by a 59m-high tower inspired by the Bayon Temple at Angkor, was inaugurated in 1919 by King Sisowath; the present cement building replaced a vast wooden structure built on this site in 1869. The Throne Hall was used for coronations and ceremonies such as the presentation of credentials by diplomats. Most of the items once displayed here were destroyed by the Khmer Rouge.

Silver Pagoda The Silver Pagoda, so named because the floor is covered with over 5000 silver tiles weighing one kg each, is also known as Wat Preah Keo (Pagoda of the Emerald Buddha). It was constructed of wood in 1892 during the rule of King Norodom, who was apparently inspired by Bangkok's Wat Phra Keo, and rebuilt in 1962. The Silver Pagoda and its contents were preserved by the Khmer Rouge in order to demonstrate to the outside world their concern for the conservation of Cambodia's cultural riches. Although some 60% of the pagoda's contents were destroyed under Pol Pot, what's left is spectacular. This is one of the few places in all of Cambodia where objects embodying some of the brilliance and richness of Khmer civilisation can still be viewed.

The staircase leading to the Silver Pagoda is made of Italian marble. Inside, the Emerald Buddha, said to be made of Baccarat crystal, sits on a gilt pedestal high atop the dais. In front of the dais stands a life-size gold Buddha decorated with 9584 diamonds, the largest of which weighs 25 carats. Created in the palace workshops during 1906 and 1907, the gold Buddha weighs some 90 kg. Directly in front of it, in a Formica case, is a miniature silver-and-gold stupa containing a relic of Buddha brought from Sri Lanka. To either side is an 80 kg bronze Buddha (to the left) and a silver Buddha (to the right). On the far right, figurines of solid gold tell the story of the Buddha.

Behind the dais is a standing marble Buddha from Myanmar (Burma) and a litter, used by the king on coronation day, designed to be carried by 12 men; parts are made of 23 kg of gold. To either side are silver models of King Norodom's stupa and Wat Preah Keo's library. At the back of the hall is a case containing two gold Buddhas, each decorated with diamonds weighing up to 16 carats; the lower figure weighs 4.5 kg, the upper 1.5 kg.

Along the walls of the pagoda are examples of extraordinary Khmer artisanship, including bejewelled masks used in classical dance and dozens of solid and hollow gold Buddhas. The many precious gifts given to Cambodia's monarchs by foreign heads of state appear rather spiritless when displayed next to such diverse and exuberant Khmer art.

The epic of the *Ramayana* is depicted on a colossal mural, created around 1900, painted on the wall enclosing the pagoda compound; the story begins just south of the eastern gate. It is being restored with the assistance of Poland.

Other structures in the complex (listed clockwise from the north gate) include: the Mondap (library), which used to house richly illuminated sacred texts written on palm leaves; the stupa of King Norodom (reigned 1860 to 1904); an equestrian statue of King Norodom; the stupa of King Ang Duong (reigned 1845 to 1859); a pavilion housing a huge footprint of the Buddha; Phnom Mondap, an artificial hill at the top of which is a structure containing a bronze footprint of the Buddha from Sri Lanka; the stupa of one of Prince Sihanouk's daughters; a pavilion for celebrations held by the royal family; the stupa of Prince Sihanouk's father, King Norodom Suramarit (reigned 1955 to 1960); and a bell tower, whose bell is rung to order the gates to be opened or closed. ■

CHRIS TAYLOR

CHRIS TAYLOR

CHRIS TAYLOR

Phnom Penh
Top: The imposing Chan Chaya Pavilion at the Royal Palace.
Middle: Detail from a mural of the Ramayana epic in the Silver Palace.
Bottom: Phnom Penh's French architecture survives in various states of repair.

CHRIS TAYLOR

TONY WHEELER

Phnom Penh
Top: Students receiving training in classical dance at the School of Fine Arts.
Bottom: Fishing boats on the Mekong River, a familiar sight in Phnom Penh.

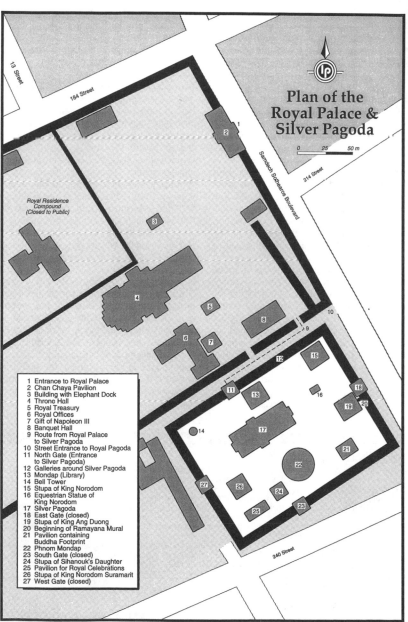

Plan of the Royal Palace & Silver Pagoda

13 Street
184 Street
Samdech Sothearos Boulevard
214 Street
240 Street

Royal Residence Compound (Closed to Public)

0   25   50 m

1 Entrance to Royal Palace
2 Chan Chaya Pavilion
3 Building with Elephant Dock
4 Throne Hall
5 Royal Treasury
6 Royal Offices
7 Gift of Napoleon III
8 Banquet Hall
9 Route from Royal Palace
   to Silver Pagoda
10 Street Entrance to Royal Pagoda
11 North Gate (Entrance
   to Silver Pagoda)
12 Galleries around Silver Pagoda
13 Mondap (Library)
14 Bell Tower
15 Stupa of King Norodom
16 Equestrian Statue of
   King Norodom
17 Silver Pagoda
18 East Gate (closed)
19 Stupa of King Ang Duong
20 Beginning of Ramayana Mural
21 Pavilion containing
   Buddha Footprint
22 Phnom Mondap
23 South Gate (closed)
24 Stupa of Sihanouk's Daughter
25 Pavilion for Royal Celebrations
26 Stupa of King Norodom Suramarit
27 West Gate (closed)

Museums
National Museum The National Museum of Cambodia is housed in a graceful terracotta structure of traditional design (built 1917-20) just north of the Royal Palace. It is open Tuesday to Sunday from 8 to 11 am and from 2 to 5 pm; entry is $2. Photography is prohibited inside. The School of Fine Arts (École des Beaux-Arts) has its headquarters in a structure behind the main building.

Guides who speak French and English are available, and there is also a booklet – *Khmer Art in Stone* – available at the front desk for US$3, which gives a rundown with locations of the most important objects on display. The museum comprises four courtyards which face onto a garden courtyard. The most significant displays of sculpture are in the courtyards to the left and straight ahead of the entrance.

Some highlights include the eight-armed statue of Vishnu from the 6th or 7th century, the statue of Shiva (circa 877-866) and the sublime statue of Jayavarman VII seated (circa 1181-1218), his head bowed slightly in a meditative pose. Elsewhere around the museum are displays of pottery and bronzes dating from the pre-Angkor periods of Funan and Chenla (4th to 9th centuries), the Indravarman period (9th and 10th centuries), the classical Angkor period (10th to 14th centuries), as well as more recent works.

See the Sculpture section of the Facts About the Country chapter for more information about some of the exhibits displayed in the National Museum.

Tuol Sleng Museum In 1975, Tuol Svay Prey High School was taken over by Pol Pot's security forces and turned into a prison known as Security Prison 21 (S-21). It soon became the largest such centre of detention and torture in the country. Over 17,000 people held at S-21 were taken to the extermination camp at Choeung Ek to be executed; detainees who died during torture were buried in mass graves in the prison grounds. S-21 has been turned into the Tuol Sleng Museum, which serves as a testament to the crimes of the Khmer Rouge. The museum's entrance is on the western side of 113 St just north of 350 St, and it is open daily from 7 to 11.30 am and from 2 to 5.30 pm; entry is US$2.

Like the Nazis, the Khmer Rouge were meticulous in keeping records of their barbarism. Each prisoner who passed through S-21 was photographed, sometimes before and after being tortured. The museum displays include room after room in which such photographs of men, women and children cover the walls from floor to ceiling; virtually all the people pictured were later killed. You can tell in what year a picture was taken

---

Bats in the Belfry
The elegant curves of the National Museum make for a picturesque sight framed against the pink and mauve of a sunset. It's also about this time of day that great flocks of bats stream out from the museum's roof. Readers with a particular interest in bats, should note that most of the denizens of the museum roof belong to a recently identified species: the Cambodian freetail.

Some bat experts (there's an expert for everything nowadays) claim that the National Museum has the largest bat population of any artificial structure in the world. The problem is that bat droppings are corrosive. As they fell through the ceiling, the exhibits were gradually being destroyed. Meanwhile, museum patrons had to do their sightseeing in a miasma of bat guana.

Fortunately the Australians have come to the rescue. In an agreement that saw the 'Treasures of the National Museum of Cambodia' exhibited in the Australian National Gallery, the Australian International Development Assistance Bureau (AIDAB) has undertaken to help maintain the contents of the museum and do something about the bats. It was considered ecologically unsound to remove them altogether (the final solution?), so a second artificial ceiling has been constructed to stop the droppings falling through. Let's just hope it holds up under the weight. ■

by the style of number board that appears on the prisoner's chest. Several foreigners from Australia, France and the USA were held here before being murdered. Their documents are on display.

As the Khmer Rouge 'revolution' reached ever greater heights of insanity, it began devouring its own children. Generations of torturers and executioners who worked here killed their predecessors and were in turn killed by those who took their places. During the first part of 1977, S-21 claimed an average of 100 victims a day.

When Phnom Penh was liberated by the Vietnamese army in early 1979, they found only seven prisoners alive at S-21. Fourteen others had been tortured to death as Vietnamese forces were closing in on the city. Photographs of their gruesome deaths are on display in the rooms where their decomposing corpses were found. Their graves are nearby in the courtyard.

Altogether, a visit to Tuol Sleng is a profoundly depressing experience. There is something about the sheer ordinariness of the place that makes it even more horrific: the surburban setting, the plain school buildings, the grassy playing area where several children kick around a ball, rusted beds, instruments of torture and wall after wall of harrowing black-and-white portraits conjure up images of humanity at its worst. Tuol Sleng is not for the squeamish.

Killing Fields of Choeung Ek Between 1975 and 1978, about 17,000 men, women, children and infants (including nine westerners), detained and tortured at S-21 prison (now Tuol Sleng Museum), were transported to the extermination camp of Choeung Ek. They were bludgeoned to death to avoid wasting precious bullets.

The remains of 8985 people, many of whom were bound and blindfolded, were exhumed in 1980 from mass graves in this one-time longan orchard; 43 of the 129 communal graves here have been left untouched. Fragments of human bone and bits of cloth are scattered around the disinterred pits. Over 8000 skulls, arranged by sex and age, are visible behind the clear glass panels of the Memorial Stupa, which was erected in 1988.

The Killing Fields of Choeung Ek are 15 km from central Phnom Penh. To get there, take Monireth Blvd south-westward out of the city from the Dang Kor Market bus depot. The site is 8.5 km from the bridge near 271 St. A memorial ceremony is held annually at Choeung Ek on 9 May.

Wats & Mosques
Wat Phnom Set on top of a tree-covered knoll 27m high, Wat Phnom is the only hill in town. According to legend, the first pagoda on this site was erected in 1373 to house four statues of Buddha deposited here by the waters of the Mekong and discovered by a woman named Penh – see the introduction to this chapter. The main entrance to Wat Phnom is via the grand eastern staircase, which is guarded by lions and *naga* (snake) balustrades.

Today, many people come here to pray for good luck and success in school exams or business affairs. When a petitioner's wish is granted, he or she returns to make the offering (such as a garland of jasmine flowers or bananas, of which the spirits are said to be especially fond) promised when the request was made.

The *vihara* (temple sanctuary) was rebuilt in 1434, 1806, 1894 and, most recently, in 1926. West of the vihara is an enormous stupa containing the ashes of King Ponhea Yat (reigned 1405 to 1467). In a small pavilion on the south side of the passage between the vihara and the stupa is a statue of a smiling and rather plump Madame Penh.

A bit to the north of the vihara and below it is an eclectic shrine dedicated to the genie Preah Chau, who is especially revered by the Vietnamese. On either side of the entrance to the chamber in which a statue of Preah Chau sits are guardian spirits bearing iron bats. On the tile table in front of the two guardian spirits are drawings of Confucius, and two Chinese-style figures of the sages Thang Cheng (on the right) and Thang Thay (on the left). To the left of the central altar is an eight-armed statue of Vishnu.

Down the hill from the shrine is a royal stupa sprouting full-size trees from its roof. For now, the roots are holding the bricks together in their net-like grip, but when the trees die the tower will slowly crumble. If you can't make it out to Angkor, this stupa gives a pretty good idea of what the jungle can do (and is doing) to Cambodia's monuments.

Curiously, Wat Phnom is the only attraction in Phnom Penh that is in danger of turning into a circus. Beggars, street urchins, women selling drinks and children selling birds in cages (you pay to set the bird free – locals claim the birds are trained to return to their cage afterwards) pester everyone who turns up to slog the 27m to the summit. Fortunately it's all high-spirited stuff, and it's difficult to be annoyed by the vendors, who, after all, are only trying to eke out a living.

Wat Ounalom Wat Ounalom, the headquarters of the Cambodian Buddhist patriarchate, is across the road from Phnom Penh Tourism. It was founded in 1443 and comprises 44 structures. As you might expect, it received a battering during the Pol Pot era, but today the wat is coming back to life. The head of the country's Buddhist hierarchy lives here along with an increasing number of monks.

On the 2nd floor of the main building, to the left of the dais, is a statue of Samdech Huot Tat, Fourth Patriarch of Cambodian Buddhism, who was killed by Pol Pot. The statue, made in 1971 when the patriarch was 80, was thrown in the Mekong but retrieved after 1979.

Nearby, a bookcase holds a few remnants of the once-extensive library of the Buddhist Institute, which was based here until 1975 and is being re-established. To the right of the dais is a statue of a former patriarch of the Thummayuth sect, to which the royal family belongs.

On the 3rd floor of the building is a marble Buddha of Burmese origin broken into pieces by the Khmer Rouge and later reassembled. On the right front corner of the dais on the 3rd floor are the cement remains of a Buddha from which the Khmer Rouge stripped the silver covering. In front of the dais to either side are two glass cases containing flags – each 20m long – used during Buddhist celebrations. The walls are decorated with scenes from the life of the Buddha, which were painted when the building was constructed in 1952.

Behind the main building is a stupa containing an eyebrow hair of the Buddha. There is an inscription in Pali over the entrance.

Wat Lang Ka Wat Lang Ka, on Preah Sihanouk Blvd by the Victory Monument, is another wat that is enjoying a new lease of life. It is a colourful place with plenty of new paint and young monks in saffron robes strolling around. It was the second of Phnom Penh's wats repaired by the post-1979 government (the first was Wat Ounalom). Around the main building are reconstructed stupas. Both the ground level and 2nd-floor chambers of the vihara have been newly painted with scenes from the life of Buddha.

Wat Koh Wat Koh, on Monivong Blvd between 174 St and 178 St, is one of Phnom Penh's oldest pagodas. It was established centuries ago (around the time when Wat Phnom was founded) but only became popular with the masses after the lake surrounding its very small vihara was filled in during the 1950s.

Wat Moha Montrei Wat Moha Montrei, which is one block east of the Olympic Market, is on the southern side of Preah Sihanouk Blvd between 163 St and 173 St (across from the Olympic Stadium). It was named in honour of one of King Monivong's ministers, Chakrue Ponn, who initiated the founding of the pagoda *(moha montrei* means 'the great minister'). The cement vihara, topped with a 35m-high tower, was completed in 1970. Between 1975 and 1979, the building was used to store rice and corn.

Note the assorted Cambodian touches incorporated in the wall murals of the vihara, which tell the story of Buddha. The angels accompanying Buddha to heaven are dressed as classical Khmer dancers, and the assembled officials wear white military uniforms of the Sihanouk period. Along the wall to the left of the dais is a painted and carved wooden lion from which religious lessons are preached four times a month. The gold-coloured wooden throne nearby is used for the same purpose. All the statues of Buddha here were made after 1979

International Mosque This completely rebuilt mosque is beside the Boeng Kak Lake. It was built with US$350,000 in donations from Saudi Arabia. Prayers are held five times daily.

Nur ul-Ihsan Mosque Nur ul-Ihsan Mosque in Khet Chraing Chamres, founded in 1813, is seven km north of central Phnom Penh on National Route 5. According to local people, it was used by the Khmer Rouge as a pigsty and reconsecrated in 1979. It now serves a small community of Cham and ethnic Malay Muslims. Next to the mosque is a *madrasa* (religious school). Visitors must remove their shoes before entering the mosque.

Not many of the moto drivers know Nur ul-Ihsan Mosque, so you may need to ask around a bit to get out there. Buses leave from O Russei Market towards Khet Prek Phnou, passing the mosque en route.

An-Nur an-Na'im Mosque The original An-Nur an-Na'im Mosque was built in 1901 and razed by the Khmer Rouge. A new, more modest brick structure – topped with a white dome holding a star and crescent aloft – has been constructed by the local Muslim community. The mosque is in Chraing Chamres II about one km north of Nur ul-Ihsan Mosque.

Markets
New Market The dark-yellow Art Deco New Market is also referred to as the Central market, a reference to its location and size. Psar Thmay, as it is called in Khmer, means New Market, however, and most English-speaking locals will know it better by this name.

The central domed hall resembles a Babylonian ziggurat, and has four wings filled with shops selling gold and silver jewellery, antique coins, fake name-brand watches and other such items. Around the main building are stalls offering *kramas*, (checked scarves) stationery, household items, cloth for sarongs, flowers, etc. There are food stalls on the structure's western side, which faces Monviong Blvd.

The New Market is undoubtedly the best of Phnom Penh's markets for browsing. It is the cleanest and has the widest range of products for sale. Opening hours are from early morning until early evening.

Tuol Tom Pong Market This market is at the corner of 440 St and 163 St, south of Mao Tse Toung Blvd. It's the best place in town for souvenir shopping, having a large range of real and fake antiquities. Items for sale include miniature Buddhas, silk, silver jewellery, gems, CDs, videos, ganja (both ready-rolled and roll-your-own), and a host of other goodies. It's well worth popping in for a browse.

O Russei Market 'Luxury' foodstuffs, costume jewellery and imported toiletries are sold in hundreds of stalls at O Russei Market, which is on 182 St between 111 St and 141 St. The complex also includes scores of food stalls.

Olympic Market A great deal of wholesaling is done at the Olympic Market, which is near the Olympic Stadium and Wat Moha Montrei. Items for sale include bicycle parts, clothes, electronics and assorted edibles. There are dozens of food stalls in the middle of the market.

Dang Kor Market Dang Kor Market is just north of the intersection of Mao Tse Toung Blvd and Pokambor Blvd, where the modern Municipal Theatre building stands. Not much of interest is sold here, though there are food stalls in the centre of the market area.

Old Market The Old Market (Psar Char) on 110 St lives up to its name. It's a scruffy place that deals in household goods, clothes and jewellery. Small restaurants, food vendors and jewellery stalls are scattered throughout the area.

Other Sights

The following sites of interest are listed from north to south.

Japanese Bridge The real name of the 700m Japanese Bridge, which spans the Tonlé Sap River, is the Chruoy Changvar Bridge. It was blown up in 1975. Long a symbol of the devastation visited upon Cambodia, it was repaired in 1993 with US$23.2 million of Japanese funding.

Those who have seen the film *The Killing Fields* will be interested to note that it was here on the afternoon of 17 April 1975 – the day Phnom Penh fell – that *New York Times* correspondent Sydney Schanberg and four companions were held prisoner by Khmer Rouge fighters and threatened with death.

School of Fine Arts West of the Japanese Bridge on 70 St is the School of Fine Arts. This is an active school devoted to training students in the arts of music and dance, and is not a tourist attraction. It is possible, however, to call in early in the morning and watch children rehearsing classical Khmer dance on a dais to the rear of the school. Request permission from the teachers to watch the lessons or to take photographs.

French Embassy The French Embassy, on the northern end of Monivong Blvd, was for many years used as an orphanage whose apparently larcenous residents were blamed by local people for every theft in the neighbourhood. Today the embassy is back in place, and a high wall surrounds the massive complex – the French have returned to Cambodia in a big way, promoting French language and culture in their former colony.

When Phnom Penh fell in 1975, about 800 foreigners and 600 Cambodians took refuge in the French Embassy. Within 48 hours, the Khmer Rouge informed the French vice-consul that the new government did not recognise diplomatic privileges and that if all the Cambodians in the compound were not handed over, the lives of the foreigners inside would also be forfeited. Cambodian women married to foreigners could stay, he was told; Cambodian men married to foreign women could not. The foreigners stood and wept as their servants, colleagues, friends, lovers and husbands were escorted out of the embassy gates. At the end of the month, the foreigners were taken out of the country by truck. Almost none of the Cambodians were ever seen again.

National Library The National Library (Bibliothèque Nationale), which is open from 7 to 11.30 am and 2 to 5.30 pm daily except Mondays, is on 90 St next to the Hotel Le Royal. The Khmer Rouge turned the graceful building, constructed in 1924, into a stable and threw many of the books out into the streets, where they were picked up by people who donated them back to the library after 1979.

Today, the National Library has about 100,000 volumes, including many crumbling books in French. Part of the English-language collection consists of books taken from the US Embassy when it was sacked after the communist takeover in 1975. Cornell University is assisting the National Library to preserve its collection of palm-leaf manuscripts.

English St There is a cluster of private language schools teaching English (and some French) one block west of the National Museum on 184 St between Norodom Blvd and the back of the Royal Palace compound. Between 5 and 7 pm, the whole area is filled with students who see learning English as the key to making it in post-war Cambodia. This is a good place to meet local young people.

Olympic Stadium Known collectively as the National Sports Complex, the stadium is near the intersection of Preah Sihanouk Blvd and Monireth Blvd. It includes a sports arena (which doubles as the site of government-sponsored political rallies) and facilities for swimming, boxing, gymnastics, volleyball and other sports.

Cambo Fun Park Just south of the Cambodiana Hotel, the Cambo Fun Park is the only amusement park in Phnom Penh since the old Boeng Kak Amusement Park was demolished. It opens at around 3 pm and entrance is 1000r. By 7 pm it is usually packed with school children queuing impatiently to risk their lives on what appear to be some very rickety rides – the management boasts that the whole thing was built in just 20 days.

Victory Monument The Victory Monument, at the intersection of Norodom Blvd and Preah Sihanouk Blvd, was built in 1958 as an Independence Monument. It is now a memorial to Cambodia's war dead. Wreaths are laid here on national holidays. Nearby, beside Samdech Sothearos Blvd, is the Cambodia-Vietnam (or Liberation) Monument, built to a Vietnamese design in 1979.

Prayuvong Buddha Factories In order to replace the countless Buddhas and ritual objects smashed by the Khmer Rouge, a whole little neighbourhood of private workshops producing cement Buddhas, nagas, gingerbread ornamentation and small stupas has grown up on the grounds of Wat Prayuvong. While the graceless cement figures, painted in gaudy colours, are hardly works of art, they are part of an effort by the Cambodian people to restore Buddhism to a place of honour in their reconstituted society.

The Prayuvong Buddha factories are on the eastern side of Norodom Blvd about 300m south of the Victory Monument (between 308 St and 310 St).

Former US Embassy The former US Embassy is on the north-eastern corner of the intersection of Norodom Blvd and Mao Tse Toung Blvd. Much of the US air war in Cambodia (1969 to 1973) was run from here.

The building now houses the Department of Fisheries of the Ministry of Agriculture.

On the morning of 12 April 1975, 360 heavily armed US Marines brought in by helicopter secured a landing zone several hundred metres from the embassy. Within hours, 276 people – Americans, Cambodians and others – were evacuated by helicopter relay to US ships in the Gulf of Thailand. Among the last to leave was US Ambassador John Gunther Dean, carrying the embassy's US flag under his arm.

Cham Kar Mon Palace Cham Kar Mon Palace, on the west side of Norodom Blvd between 436 St and 462 St, was once the residence of Prince Sihanouk. The palace, whose name means 'silkworm fields', is now used by visiting heads of state.

Mekong Island Very few individual travellers bother with this tourist development. The island lies north of Phnom Penh and is reached via an organised boat trip that leaves from the Sofitel Cambodiana Hotel. There are elephant rides, classical dancing, handicraft production and so on. Boats leave at 9.30 am and return at 3 pm. All up, including lunch, the trip costs US$32. Bookings can be made at the Cambodiana Hotel or at Mekong Island Tours (☎ 427225), 13, 240 St.

It's possible to visit the island itself without taking the tour boat, but bribes will be required if you want to get in to see the tourist operations. If you want to visit the island this way (it involves an inexpensive ferry ride), ask one of the English speaking moto drivers about how to do it.

Places to Stay

The Phnom Penh hotel scene has made great strides over past three or four years. Where once there were just a few ineptly run government 'institutions', there is now a wide selection of guesthouses, mid-range *pensions* and hotels and even a few top-end choices.

The best hotel deals in Phnom Penh nowadays fall into the mid-range category. For the most part, it is still slim pickings for budget travellers, though there are signs that the situation is gradually improving. Similarly, top-end travellers will often find that Phnom Penh's top hotels fall short of international standards; there is often far better value for money at the mid-range hotels.

For the time being, traffic conditions, while slightly chaotic, are not as bad as they are in many Asian cities. Provided you are happy to jump on a moto or take a cyclo, it makes little difference where in town you are based. Some of the best mid-range deals, for example, are down in the south of town near the Victory Monument, but even from here it is only a 10 minute moto drive to the centre of town.

Places to Stay – bottom end

The most popular guesthouses are scattered around town, which makes checking them out for comfort difficult. The longest-running, though by no means the best, is the *Capital Guesthouse* (☎ 364104), on 182 St not far from O Russei Market. The owners have expanded operations into two adjacent buildings under the names *Happy Guesthouse* and *Capital II* – the latter is almost exclusively the domain of Japanese travellers. Basic singles/doubles (no bathroom, often no window) are US$3/4, while rooms with bathrooms cost US$5/6.

The Capital and its neighbours come in for a lot of criticism. Locals and some travellers allege that the hotel is a hotbed of vice. And if this were not enough to keep most people away, it's in a grotty, noisy part of town. All the same, it is often close to full.

There are some more wholesome alternatives to the Capital not far away. *Narin's Guesthouse* is probably the pick of the pack. It's a clean, family-run place that provides excellent meals. The guesthouse is at 50, 125 St, and has an overflow annex a few doors down. Clean rooms with windows and shared bathroom cost US$3 for a single, US$5 for a double. The annex also has a double with bathroom for US$6, but it's very rarely free.

Around the corner from the Capital on 111 St is the family-run *Seng Sokhom House*. It's a friendly place with a pleasant veranda area to sit out on. Rooms cost US$5 with bathroom and US$3 without. Next door is the *No 20 Guesthouse*, which charges a flat US$5 for its no-frills rooms – it might be an option if everything else in the area is full.

Elsewhere around town, the two most popular spots are *Bert's Books & Guesthouse* (☎ 015-916411) and *Cloud Nine Guesthouse* (formerly known as No 9 Guesthouse). Cloud Nine has a great location on the Boeng Kak Lake, and there's a wooden pavilion area with hammocks on the lake itself. The food here is very good, with some excellent curries courtesy of the Tamil-Malaysian management. It's advisable that you check any valuables in with management here if you stay – the rooms are not particularly secure. Dorm accommodation costs US$2. The nearby *No 10 Guesthouse* takes the overflow from Cloud Nine when it's full.

Bert of Bert's Books & Guesthouse runs a tighter ship than Cloud Nine, which tends to attract a lot of hang-loose heavy smokers. As Bert will explain, his guesthouse is a converted bordello (emphasis on 'converted' – Bert takes a dim view of prostitution); downstairs has been converted into a wonderfully cluttered second-hand bookshop; upstairs there are 15 rooms and a couple of veranda areas that provide views of the Tonlé Sap River. There is a continuous supply of coffee, soft drinks and beer, and if you book ahead meals are provided in the evening on a rickety bamboo awning. The ever-fussing Bert and his Khmer wife Mrs Bert were about to have their first child as this book was being researched, so by the time you have this book in your hands there will be a baby Bert. Pop in and say hello even if you don't stay. Rooms cost US$6 with bathroom and US$3.50 without.

Finally, a new arrival on the guesthouse scene is the *Last Home* (☎ 724917), a German-run place at 47 108 St. The name will apparently be meaningful to fans of science fiction and fantasy, and a bar under construction at the back of the 1st floor will continue the theme when it's completed. For the time being Last Home has a bit of a crash-pad atmosphere, but this will no doubt improve if the place takes off. A mattress on the floor of a high-ceilinged room costs US$2, singles cost US$4.50 and spacious doubles are US$5; bathroom facilities are communal.

Places to Stay – middle

If you are happy spending US$10 to US$20 for a room in Phnom Penh there are some excellent deals to be had around town. The average price for a double with air-con, attached bathroom, TV (sometimes with satellite) and laundry service is US$15, though occasionally prices dip to US$10 or lower for a single.

As with the guesthouses, there is no single mid range hotel area. The stretch of Monivong Blvd between Pochentong Blv and Preah Sihanouk Blvd is the old hotel district, but many of the hotels in this area have been renovated and refurbished into the top-end category; those that haven't are generally poor value. Some of the best deals in town are south of Preah Sihanouk Blvd, but there are also some good deals elsewhere.

At the bottom end of the middle bracket, a popular option is the *Lotus Guesthouse* (☎ 362409), on the corner of 63 St and 172 St. Rooms are functional, with attached bathroom (no hot water), and cost US$10 for singles/doubles. There is a restaurant downstairs.

On the waterfront, at the corner of 144 St, is the *Hotel Indochine* (☎ 427292), a very friendly place with spacious air-con rooms with attached bathroom for US$10/12 for singles/doubles. Given it's prime location, this place will probably get the renovation treatment at some stage, but for the moment it is very good value.

Down in the south of town is the *Amara Hotel* (☎ 362824), on the corner of 63 St and 280 St. The Amara looks slightly the worse for wear, but it has a business centre, and singles/doubles with air-con and bathroom are just US$10/13. There are also functional triples available for US$15.

The *Cathay Hotel* (☎ 427178) has been around for a while, and is a popular place

with resident journalists and photographers, who swear by the hotel's answering service and business facilities. The rooms are a good deal too. Air-con rooms on the 1st and 2nd floors cost US$20, while those prepared to puff their way up several flights of stairs get the same rooms for US$15 on the 3rd and 4th floors (this is a common situation in Phnom Penh). One of the highpoints of this hotel (besides its central location) are the encircling verandas on every floor. The Cathay is just north of the corner of 19 St and 110 St.

Not far from the Cathay, at 2, 67 St, is the *Fortune Hotel* (☎ 428216). It does a steady business with regular visitors to Phnom Penh and seems to have cleaned up its once slightly seedy image. Singles/doubles cost US$15. The *Wat Phnom Hotel* (☎ 725320) is also US$15 for a room and is not far away on the Wat Phnom circle road. The Wat Phnom is a little tired these days – the rooms are musty and look the worse for wear.

A favourite with long-termers is the *Golden Gate Hotel* (☎ 427618). Unfortunately it is not unusual for this extremely friendly Chinese-run hotel to be full – it's a good idea to ring ahead and book. The Golden Gate has a downstairs restaurant, verandas, and areas to sit down with magazines provided; the rooms are spotless, have air-con and are fitted with satellite TV and minibars. There is also a free laundry service. Costs are US$15/17 for a single/double. It is close to the corner of 57 St and 278 St.

If the Golden Gate is full, the *Tokyo Hotel* (☎ 722247) is not far away, at 13, 278 St. It is good value with rooms at US$15. Another nearby option is the *Champs Elysees Hotel* (☎ 724153) at 185, 63 St. This place deserves to be more popular than it is. The staff are helpful and the doubles at US$17 are among the best in town at this price. Two room apartments are available at US$27, and there are also some triples for US$22 and a couple of singles without bathrooms for US$13.

Also close to the Golden Gate, but a definite notch up in price and comfort is the *Goldiana Hotel* (☎ 723085). The only thing it is possible to fault this excellently run place on is the gaudiness of the pink décor in the rooms. Standard doubles cost US$25, spacious deluxe rooms US$35 and suites US$50. The standard doubles here would cost US$50 or upwards at any of the self-proclaimed three or four-star hotels around town. The restaurant downstairs is Chinese, but the food is very average.

The *Tai Seng Hotel* (☎ 427220), at 56 Monivong Blvd, has a good location just west of Wat Phnom and is heavily promoted by the tourist office at Pochentong airport. Rooms here cost US$25, or US$20 on the higher floors – some of these have good views of the Boeng Kak Lake. The hotel also has a reasonably good restaurant.

There are very few good mid-range deals to be had on the Monivong Blvd commercial stretch nowadays. The *Asie Hotel* (☎ 427825), at the corner of Monivong Blvd and Kampuchea Krom Blvd, has some singles at US$25, but they are grim, windowless coffins; other rooms range from US$30. One of the better deals in this area is the *Morakat Hotel* (☎ 725540), at the corner of 107 St and Kampuchea Krom Blvd. Rooms on the lower floors are US$20, while rooms higher up are US$15. This place gives commissions to taxi drivers who deliver guests, so if you come in by taxi from Pochentong you will probably be advised to stay here.

On Charles de Gaulle Blvd opposite the Olympic Market there are a few more budget mid-range places. The best of these is the *Borei Thmei Hotel* (☎ 428711), where spacious, clean, air-con doubles are US$15/20. The nearby *Sangkor Hotel* (☎ 427144) and the *Vimean Suor Hotel* (☎ 364070) offer the same rates, but are not quite as welcoming or comfortable.

If you are looking for some colonial ambience and you don't mind dodgy electrical fittings and dealing with staff who spend most of their working hours nodding off, the *Renakse Hotel* (☎ 722457), opposite the Silver Pagoda, is a gloriously torpid place to be based. Somewhere in this rambling warren of deserted rooms are singles for US$22 and doubles for US$27 – rumour has it this place will be renovated soon, so get in quick.

For more upmarket accommodation, one of the best choices around is the *Hawaii Hotel* (☎ 426652), on the corner of 51 and 136 St near the New Market. The Hawaii has Chinese and Thai restaurants, and the rooms are US$30 for singles, US$40 for doubles and US$50/60 for suites plus 10%. Discounts of 10% are available for a stay of a week or more.

The *Rama Inn* (☎ 362161) is just west of the corner of Norodom Blvd and 280 St. It's a charming place with a leafy garden, coffee shop and bar. Rooms here are US$35/45 and it attracts a lot of long-termers. Another popular place with long-term residents is the *Sydney International Hotel* (☎ 427907), inconveniently located just west of the intersection of Monivong Blvd and 360 St. This place is recogniseable by the oversize Foster's can outside and a miniature Sydney Opera House outside the foyer. As you might expect, it's popular with the Aussie contingent. Rooms range from US$30-50, though discounts are sometimes available.

Some other mid-range hotels (Phnom Penh is swarming with them) include:

Anco Hotel – 320 Monivong Blvd (☎ 428052), standard mid-range place with doubles at US$20

Bophar Toep Hotel – opposite Sofitel Cambodiana Hotel (☎ 724251), noisy place with attached karaoke/dancing club; seedy rooms at US$15

Bayon Hotel – 2, 75 St (☎ 427281), new French-run hotel with bar and restaurant plus video room with over 1500 titles; singles/doubles US$30/40; deluxe rooms from US$50

Dusit Hotel – 2, 118 St (☎ 427483), sprawling place not far from New Market; singles US$15, doubles US$20; some very good US$25 doubles and apartments at US$35-45

East Paris Hotel – couple of doors down from FCC on Sisowath Quay (☎ 360618); great location, good views of river; closed for renovations at time of writing; formerly US$15 for spacious double

Hong Kong Hotel – 419 Monivong Blvd (☎ 427108), standard fare with attached Cantonese restaurant; popular with the Chinese business set; rooms at US$20/25

Paradis Hotel – Monivong Blvd (☎ 722951); rooms at US$30; larger doubles at US$36

Hotel Ripole – opposite Dusit Hotel at western end of 118 St (☎ 722713); not bad rooms though slightly noisy; US$15

Hotel Shinwa – 48 Preah Sihanouk Blvd (☎ 018-810787), good location close to Victory Monument, but slightly seedy atmosphere; rooms at US$25/30

La Paillote – opposite the New Market on 130 St (☎ 722151); clean, well-run place with good location and rooms at US$20-30

Lucky Inn – near corner of 51 St and 254 St (☎ 427044); potential to be a good place, with swimming pool (murky) and restaurant on quiet residential street; US$20 rooms poor value, but US$30 doubles not bad; plus 10% tax

Orchidee Hotel – 262 Monivong Blvd (☎ 722576) noisy place with attached karaoke club; rooms at US$15/20/25

Pailin Hotel – 219 Monivong Blvd (☎ 426697); rooms at US$30/45 for singles/doubles; deluxe rooms available at US$50; plus 20% tax

Singapore Hotel – corner of Kampuchea Krom Blvd and Monivong Blvd (☎ 725552); average kind of place with rooms priced at US$17/20 for singles/doubles

Places to Stay – top end

Currently the top hotel in town is the *Sofitel Cambodiana Hotel* (☎ 426288; fax 426290). For a long time it was the only place around that even got close to international standards, but other top-end hotels are starting to spring up and give it a run for its money.

The huge riverside complex took almost a quarter of a century to complete. Begun around 1967, when Prince Sihanouk was chief of state, the unfinished structure and its spacious grounds were used as a military base by the Lon Nol government. Refugees from the fighting in the countryside sheltered under its concrete roof between 1970 and 1975. Work was resumed in 1987 after a Cambodian expatriate living in Hong Kong and two Singaporeans decided to invest at least US$20 million in the project.

The Sofitel Cambodiana has restaurants, bars, a swimming pool, health centre, business centre, shops and all the other amenities you would expect of a hotel that touts itself as five-star. Singles start at US$170, doubles at US$200 and executive suites are priced at US$400.

Le Royal Hotel, next to the National Library on the corner of Monivong Blvd and 92 St, is another hotel with a history. It is being renovated by the Raffles Group and when it opens will probably be the top place in town. Between 1970 and 1975 most journalists working in Phnom Penh stayed here, and part of the film *The Killing Fields* was set in the hotel (though filmed in Hua Hin, Thailand) and when foreign-aid workers set up shop in the country after the Vietnamese takeover, this is where they stayed.

For slightly less expensive upmarket accommodation in the heart of town, there are a couple of possibilities on Monivong Blvd. The *Diamond Hotel* (☎ 427325; fax 426635), at 172-184 Monivong Blvd, is somewhat overpriced given that it offers little more than some of the better mid-range hotels around town, but it is popular with tour groups all the same. Singles start at US$90 and doubles at US$120 plus taxes. The nearby *Allson Hotel* (☎ 362008; fax 362018), near the corner of Monivong Blvd and Kampuchea Krom Blvd, is more of a class act and also has a very good ground-floor restaurant. Rates are US$80/90 for singles/twins; US$105/117 for superior rooms; and US$115/127 for executive suites plus taxes.

Just south of the Russian Embassy on Samdech Sothearos Blvd is the highly rated *Royal Phnom Penh Hotel* (☎ 360026; fax 360036). This Thai-managed hotel has a pleasant garden setting, offers Thai and Chinese dining, a nightclub, bar and coffee shop. Room rates are a flat US$150 for deluxe singles/doubles. Bookings can be made in Bangkok (☎ 589-2021).

The *Juliana Hotel* (tel/fax 366070), at 152 St, northeast of O Russei Market, is another Thai-managed concern. Again it features a garden setting. An expansion project to create more rooms and a swimming pool is under way at the time of writing. Other amenities include a fitness centre and sauna, barber, bar, restaurants and so on. Singles are US$120, twins US$140 and deluxe rooms US$160 plus taxes.

The *Landmark Boulevard Hotel* (☎ 428323; fax 428465) on Norodom Blvd is a new addition to the Phnom Penh hotel scene and is as yet rather undistinguished. There is a rooftop garden restaurant and bar here, and the 2 pm checkout time may be a drawcard for some business travellers. Budget singles/twins are US$90/100, standard rooms US$100/110, and the senior suites come in at US$190/200.

Popular with the Chinese business set is the *Holiday International Hotel* (☎ 427402; fax 427401), at 84 St (just off Monivong Blvd), and the *Sharaton Cambodia Hotel* (no, not *Sheraton*; ☎ ; fax 361199), at 47 St (just north of Wat Phonm). Both these places come complete with Chinese restaurants, karaoke entertainment, and the Holiday even has a casino – if you've never gambled with the Chinese before, enter at your own risk. Rates start at US$100 at the Holiday and US$110 at the Sharaton.

Places to Eat

The increasing affluence of at least some urban Phnom Penhois and the large foreign NGO population of the city has led to an explosion of restaurants. Visitors to Phnom Penh are quite literally spoilt for choice nowadays.

Most of the foreign restaurants around town (and there are a lot of them) are expensive by local standards, but it's worth splashing out at least once on a good French or Italian meal, or at least a pizza.

Cambodian Scattered around town are numerous Khmer restaurants that set up outside tables and chairs in the evenings. These places rarely have English signs and are as much about drinking beer as about eating, but they're lively places for an inexpensive meal. On the corner of 214 St and Monivong Blvd is a popular restaurant with a US$2.50 all-you-can-eat soup deal. The southern end of 51 St, just down from Baggio's Pizza also has a couple of similar restaurants – watch out for the beer girls.

It's a bit of a trek out of town, but on Norodom Blvd, south of the Monivong (Vietnam) Bridge are a string of restaurants dealing in 'crusty rice' dishes served with meat and vegetable stews. The food in these places is inexpensive and very tasty.

The reconstruction of the Japanese Bridge over the Tonlé Sap River has blessed Phnom Penh with a multitude of new Khmer restaurants. Heading west, the restaurants start to appear about a km over the bridge, and they range from small family-run places to enormous complexes with fountains, neon and festooned fairy lights. The *Hang Neak* is probably the most popular with resident foreigners, but it is also one of the more opulent places on this stretch of road. Other popular places worth trying out include: *Kompong Cham, Continental Restaurant* (big, all mod cons), *Som Tam Restaurant*, *Neak Samot* (favoured by affluent Phnom Penhois) and the *Ta Ta Restaurant* (Chinese-style Khmer cuisine). There are dozens more.

For upmarket Khmer cuisine, one of the best places around is the *Pon Lok*, on Sisowath Quay just a few doors up from the FCC. This place has good views of the river from its upstairs dining area, and the English menu takes you on a guided tour of the local cuisine. The house speciality is hot pot. This restaurant is popular with the Khmer cellular-phone set – prices are not cheap (figure on a minimum of US$5 per head).

Not far from the Pon Lok, downstairs from the FCC, is the *Apsara Restaurant*. Again, this is Khmer haute cuisine – not the place for a budget meal – but the food is highly rated and the decor is tasteful.

Beside the Boeng Kak Lake are a couple of long-runners that are still going strong. The *Restaurant Raksmey Boeng Kak*, the southernmost of the two, is built out over the lake and can turn out a delicious meal for less than US$5. Try the excellent duck soup or other traditional Cambodian dishes. The other lakeside restaurant is the *Buong Thong Restaurant*.

For inexpensive Khmer food with a Gallic touch, head down to the *Phnom Kiev Restaurant* on Preah Sihanouk Blvd. The restaurant has a popular garden area out front, and it does good salads and some excellent beef dishes.

American There are a few places around town that do steaks, French fries and so on. *California I* is on Sisowath Quay, just north of the FCC. *California II* is at 55 Sihanouk Blvd. Both are popular with the local expat community. *Wagon Wheel* is close to California I and celebrated for its inexpensive breakfasts of fried eggs and hash browns; its lunchtime and evening meals are good too.

Australian No-frills Aussie pub grub is available at the *Ettamogah Pub* on Preah Sihanouk Blvd, next door to the Lucky Supermarket. The Ettamogah is open from very early in the morning until around midnight. The fish & chips and hamburgers are among the best in town. It's easy to miss this place, as the English sign is not very prominent – look for the open-fronted place with a large Khmer sign outside.

Chinese While there are numerous Chinese restaurants around Phnom Penh, few of them are particularly authentic. The *King of Kings Restaurant* on Preah Sihanouk Blvd, opposite the Phnom Kiev Restaurant, is a shabby place with outside seating but it has cheap dim sum from morning until mid-afternoon.

Probably the best affordable Chinese cuisine in town is at the *Ly Lay Restaurant* on Kampuchea Krom Blvd near the intersection of Sivutha Blvd. The *Hua Nam Restaurant*, at 753 Monivong Blvd (near the intersection of Mao Tse Toung Blvd) is another contender, but meals here are very expensive by local standards.

Continental The FCC, on Sisowath Quay, has a restaurant and bar on its 3rd floor with fabulous views of the Tonlé Sap on one side and the National Museum on the other. The food here has improved immensely since the management of Déja Vu Restaurant (alas no more) took over the catering. With great views, good music and a friendly crowd of regulars, the FCC is an essential stop on the Phnom Penh restaurant circuit.

There are a number of pizzerias around town; opinion is divided as to which is the best. Odds-on favourite, however, is *Baggio's Pizza*, on 51 St near the intersection of Preah Sihanouk Blvd. Small size pizzas (a meal for one) start at around US$5, and if there's

anything to complain about it's the eggplant, which seems to be in every dish unless you request otherwise.

Happy Herb's, on Sisowath Quay, is as close as you get to a Phnom Penh institution. The story goes that Herb taught the local chefs to do the pizzas, and he was always happy – hence the name. If you want your pizza to leave you with a grin for the rest of the day (or evening), tell the waiter you want it 'happy' – those in pursuit of oblivion should request 'very happy'.

The *Seven Seven Cafe*, at the Seven Seven Supermarket on 90 St, also does good pizzas and has an excellent range of other western dishes. It's popular with Phnom Penh expats. *Happy Neth Pizza*, on 110 St, is another good pizza place.

For a splash-out meal, *Red*, on Preah Sihanouk Blvd not far from the Victory Monument, is a restaurant with real ambience. It's upstairs, over Perfumerie Jolie Madame, in a converted French villa. The menu is eclectic and changes periodically, but the friendly staff are happy to make recommendations. Most main courses are around US$7. The *Tropicana Cafe Bar*, on 184 St next to the French Cultural Centre, is another restaurant with class. Again, it's not cheap.

The French owners of *Le Cuistot*, on 108 St, describe their food as Mediterranean. The pastas here are all home-made, and locals rate the lasagne as the best in town. Le Cuistot is a popular place for lunch, with pasta specials from US$3.50.

Out of town, over the Monivong (Vietnam) Bridge, on Highway 1 to Vietnam, are a couple of continental restaurants that are popular with residents of Phnom Penh, particularly on the weekends. Around 4.5 km from Phnom Penh is the *River View Restaurant*. It overlooks the Mekong River and has Khmer/French meals starting at around US$5 for a main course. *L'Imprevu* is 2.5 km farther on, on the other side of the road. It offers French cuisine, steaks and so on in a delightful garden setting with a swimming pool. There are also bungalows for rent here.

Fast Food The good news at the time of

writing is that none of the big fast-food chains grace Phnom Penh. *Mc Sam's*, on 13 St just south of the GPO, is a burger/fried chicken joint that looks very much like it's about to fold. The Sofitel Cambodiana Hotel has dipped it's toe into the fast food market with its *Burger Mania* restaurant. All Laminex, bright lights and squeaky clean surfaces, it's generally deserted. Rumour has it that *McDonald's* are on their way.

French *La Pacha*, on 208 St near the corner of Monivong Blvd, is considered by many to offer the best French cuisine in Phnom Penh. It's an expensive place to dine, however. *La Paillote*, on 130 St, near the New Market, is a good hotel with an excellent French restaurant.

La Casa is a bit of a distance out of town, just off Kampuchea Krom Blvd, on 261 St, but the drive is for a worthy cause. Established by a French NGO, the restaurant trains teenage Khmer orphans in the catering industry. Along with traditional French cuisine, La Casa also does very good pizzas.

On Preah Sihanouk Blvd there are a couple of less formal and less expensive French restaurants. *Cactus*, at 94 Preah Sihanouk Blvd, is a bar/bistro with a good salad buffet at lunch times. In the evenings there is a tapas bar and meals. *L'Atmosphère* is nearby, on the corner of Preah Sihanouk Blvd and Norodom Blvd, and is a classier version of Cactus. *Cordon Bleue* is back down Preah Sihanouk Blvd in the direction of Monivong Blvd. It has good lunch-time deals and is well regarded by French residents of Phnom Penh.

Indian There are some surprisingly good Indian restaurants in Phnom Penh. *Kababeesh*, on 126 St, just around the corner from the Singapore Hotel, is one of the best. Check out the US$2.50 all-you-can-eat lunch buffet. Vegetarian and northern-style tandoori dishes are also available at very reasonable prices.

The *Indian Restaurant*, on Monivong Blvd near the railway station, is another very popular option. *Royal India Restaurant*, on

the corner of 240 St and Monivong Blvd has perhaps the best tandoori in town but service can be haphazard – check your order before it goes in and check the bill afterwards. *King's Bar* is a popular Indian restaurant down the road from the Capital Guesthouse.

Italian *Il Padrino* is on the Wat Phnom circle road, north of the wat, and is a spacious bar/restaurant with good pastas, sandwiches and wines. It's an inexpensive place for a light lunch or for evening drinks.

Japanese As is the case almost everywhere, Japanese food in Phnom Penh is expensive. *Nagasaki*, on the corner of Preah Sihanouk Blvd and 55 St, is reasonably authentic and has pleasant *tatami* rooms if there is a group of you. There's something galling about paying Tokyo prices for a meal in Phnom Penh, however. Another good Japanese restaurant is *Heisei*, on Sisowath Quay. *Midori*, just south of the Victory Monument on Norodom Blvd, is probably the most authentic Japanese restaurant in town – naturally you pay for the privilege.

Malaysian *Mamak's Corner* is on 126 St, next door to Kababeesh and just around the corner from the Singapore Hotel. It's a good place for an early-morning roti chanai and a kopi susu. The decor is minimal, but the food is authentic. It's possible to eat well here for about US$3. Another good Malaysian place is *Singapore Chicken Rice*, on Preah Sihanouk Blvd next door to the Standard Chartered Bank.

Mexican Yes, it's possible to get Mexican fast food in Phnom Penh. *The Mex*, on the corner of Preah Sihanouk Blvd and Norodom Blvd, has both takeaways and inexpensive sit-down meals. You can fill yourself up with a massive burrito for US$2.50.

Pub Grub See the Australian entry for the Ettamogah Pub, which has some of the best pub grub around. *Cathouse Tavern*, on the corner of 118 St and 51 St is a Filipino bar with mock tropical décor and good counter lunches. It only opens in the late afternoons and evenings, however. The meals are not cheap. Jim of the *Irish Rover*, on the corner of 51 St and Preah Sihanouk Blvd, is planning to start providing meals – call in and see if he's got around to it.

Russian Phnom Penh's only Russian restaurant (as far as we know) is *Troika*, down on the corner of Norodom Blvd and 310 St. It's not exactly cheap but then there are not many Russian restaurants in this part of the world.

Thai There are some excellent Thai restaurants in Phnom Penh. A good starting place is the area east of the Victory Monument on Samdech Sothearos Blvd. Here you will find *Chiang Mai* and *EID* (generally pronounced 'eed'). EID has a very loyal following. It's a small place and very basic, but it has arguably the best Thai food in town. Most dishes range from US$2 to US$4. Chiang Mai is just two doors away. Prices are slightly higher but the restaurant is more of a dining experience, and there is more seating – the sit-down area at the back with cushions is good if there is a group of you.

Chao Praya, at 67 Norodom Blvd, is the place to go on a special occasion. The seafood buffets in the evening are lavish but pricey (by Phnom Penh standards) at US$12 per head. *Ban Thai*, south of the Victory Monument on Norodom Blvd, is a Thai/Khmer restaurant in a beautiful garden setting. It's a good alternative to Chiang Mai and EID, where the traffic noise and beggars can be overwhelming.

Vietnamese Nestled between the Thai restaurants EID and Chiang Mai on Samdech Sothearos Blvd is *Saigon House*. It's a small friendly place with prices that won't break the budget. There are also numerous Vietnamese soup places selling pho (noodle soup) on Monivong Blvd.

Self-Catering Baguettes are widely available around town, and usually cost from 200r to 500r. For something to eat with them, Phnom Penh's supermarkets are remarkably well stocked with goodies. Naturally, imported items tend to be expensive. For around US$3-4 you can pick up treats such as salami, Camembert and Brie.

The best of the Phnom Penh supermarkets is the Lucky Supermarket, at 160 Preah Sihanouk Blvd, and the Seven Seven Supermarket at 13, 90 St. Other good stores are the Sunrise Superstore, opposite the north-east corner of the New Market, the Suntan Foodmart at 477 Monivong Blvd, and the Bayon Market at 133 Monivong Blvd.

For fresh bread and cakes, the *French Bakery* opposite the Lucky Supermarket on Preah Sihanouk Blvd is a good place. The *Chef's Deli*, in the Sofitel Cambodiana Hotel foyer, is another bakery outlet, but prices are higher here than at the French Bakery.

Entertainment
All kinds of events take place in Phnom Penh that are impossible to predict. For news of what's going on where while you are in town check with the latest issue of the *Phnom Penh Post* or with the Friday edition of the *Cambodia Daily*.

Cinemas Even if you understand Khmer, Phnom Penh's cinemas are probably best avoided. The patrons are crowded into poorly ventilated halls with no fire escapes.

The Foreign Correspondents' Club (FCC) has movie screenings every Tuesday and Sunday evening. Entry is free for members, US$2 for non-members. The movies being shown are advertised at the FCC from around a week in advance.

The French Cultural Centre has frequent movie screenings – generally several times a week at 6 pm. Check at the centre, where a monthly programme should be available.

Discos Phnom Penh is not exactly the club capital of Asia. The few discos that there are around town are largely the domain of the expat community. Ask around at some of the bars (see below) for the latest hot spots. The most popular place at the time of writing is *Le Saint Tropez* on 214 St opposite the

Chinatown Hotel. Entry is free but drinks start at US$3. It's open from 9 pm to 3 am.

Sharky's, on 130 St, near the corner of 15 St, is a new arrival. Again, entry is free. Most drinks are US$2. It's essentially a disco with a chill-out veranda area. Opinion is divided as to whether it will take off – check it out. *Firecat Club* is a slick disco that is popular with the Chinese set, though you see the occasional westerner in there. It's on the corner of Preah Sihanouk Blvd and 55 St.

Last but not least, *Martini* has been around since the UNTAC days and is about the only place in town that can be counted on to be packed at 1 am on a Thursday, Friday or Saturday night. Martini is both a beer garden (with movies) and a dark dance space. The innumerable women who populate the place do not work for the bar; they are freelance. Much maligned by some, Martini deserves a good word in that, unlike similar places in Bangkok and Manila, there are no women in bikinis dancing on the bar, and there is no hard sell – even single men are left alone providing they assume a look of world-weary disdain and chat with other clients.

Traditional Dance Check the latest on the *Chatomuk Theatre*, just north of the Cambodiana Hotel. At the time of writing it was closed for repairs, but when it reopens it should hold performances of traditional dance by the *National Royal Dance Group* every Friday and Saturday night.

The *Sofitel Cambodiana Hotel* has a Khmer buffet dinner and traditional dance every Friday night from 7.30 pm. During the dry season the performances are held outside. The US$17 per head for the performance and for the meal is steep but worth it if you have the money. Bookings can be made in the foyer of the hotel.

The *Magic Circus Cafe-Theatre*, at 111, 360 St, has traditional song and dance on Saturday night at 8 pm. Performances are more folk-oriented than at the Sofitel Cambodiana or the Chatomuk Theatre. On Sunday at 5 pm, circus performances are held. Tickets are US$2, and drinks and food are available.

Private performances by the National Royal Dance Group can be organised through the Ministry of Tourism or the Ministry of Culture and Fine Arts (both on Monivong Blvd). The going rate for a show (normally held at the Institute of Science) is US$350, so you'll need a big group of you to make it affordable.

Live Music There's little in the way of live music in Phnom Penh. The *Ettamogah Pub*, on Preah Sihanouk Blvd, has a live band every Friday night, a popular night at the Ettamogah. The *Irish Rover*, just down the street, also has regular folk nights.

Bars Undoubtedly the most popular early evening drinking spot is the *FCC*, on Sisowath Quay. Draft Angkor beer costs just US$1, and other drinks are reasonably inexpensive. The *Irish Rover*, on the corner of 51 St and Preah Sihanouk Blvd, is another good spot for an early evening drink. Jim and his charming Khmer wife oversee business and make sure that guests are comfortable. It rarely gets crowded and is a good place to meet people. Just up the road is *Cactus*, a French bar, and *Ettamogah*, an Australian bar – both are popular and serve meals too.

The *Cathouse Tavern* has been around since the UNTAC days. It's on the corner of 51 St and 118 St. It looks a little tired these days, and the music is frequently dire, but it still attracts a crowd. Locals maintain it has the best pool tables in town, and it's relatively easy to get a game. Darts are also available. Beers cost US$2 and the bar is open until about midnight or later.

Probably the most popular late-night haunt in town (apart from Martini – see the Discos entry above) is *Heart of Darkness*. It's on 51 St, south of the New Market. The Heart, as locals call it, is generally deserted before 9.30 pm but often packed after midnight. It's a hole-in-the-wall place with a pool table at the back – forget about getting a game here late at night if you're not a regular. Most drinks are US$1 or not much more, and the music is probably the best in town. It's open late.

If you're up in the Boeng Kak Lake area (or staying at Cloud Nine Guesthouse), you might want to pop into the French-run M-D Bar. It's a funky little place with good sounds and it stays open until the last guest leaves.

Casinos There are two casinos in Phnom Penh. The Naga Floating Casino is near the Sofitel Cambodiana Hotel. Its future is uncertain at the time of writing. The Holiday International Hotel has a casino that is very popular with the Chinese business set.

Spectator Sport
It's worth checking the Friday edition of the *Cambodia Daily* or asking locals about events at the Olympic Stadium, occasionally the venue for kick boxing or football.

Things to Buy
Souvenirs The best place for an overview of antiques, silver items, jewellery, silks and clothes is the Tuol Tom Pong Market. Most of the 'antiques' here are fake and bargaining is required, but it's still a worthwhile place for a browse. The New Market is also worth checking out.

For really tasteful souvenirs of Cambodia consider calling into one of the workshops that have been set up by NGOs and local disabled people and mine victims. The National Centre of Disabled Persons (NCDP) has a shop called NCDP Handicrafts at 3 Norodom Blvd. Articles on sale include silk and leather bags, slippers, *kramas*(scraves), shirts, wallets and purses, and notebooks. The standard of craftwork is very high. Prices for some of the items tend to be high but there is also a lot of reasonably priced items too.

Along similar lines is the handicraft shop at Wat Than. The emphasis here is on products made from Khmer silk. Khemara is a similar operation run by a local NGO and women's self-help groups. It is at 18, 302 St and has a great garden setting. Downstairs is a cafe, while the shop upstairs is a relaxing place for some hassle-free browsing.

Postcards Postcards are widely available in Phnom Penh, some of them of excellent quality. Pick them up at bookshops such as Bert's Books and the bookshop at the Sofitel Cambodiana Hotel, and at the FCC office.

Photographic Monivong Blvd is the best place to pick up photographic supplies and get film processed. The Konika shops are the cheapest places for developing and printing. Print film is widely available, but only Ektachrome 100 is available in slide format.

Daily Needs See the Self-Catering entry of the Places to Eat section above for a rundown of supermarkets around town. Most of them stock essentials such as shampoo, suntan lotion, toothbrushes and the like.

Getting There & Away
Air For information on air services to/from Phnom Penh, see the Getting There & Away and Getting Around chapters.

The Royal Air Cambodge booking office (☎ 428055) is at 206 Norodom Blvd. Opening hours are 7 to 11 am and 2 to 5 pm Monday to Saturday. You can get flights at short notice to Siem Reap, but for other destinations like Ratanikiri and Battambang it's wise to book well in advance.

Lao Aviation (☎ 426563) has two flights a week to Vientiane and can also organise Lao visas for US$25. The office is at 58 Preah Sihanouk Blvd, and is open from 8 to 11.30 am and from 2 to 5 pm Monday to Saturday.

Vietnam Airlines (☎ 364460) has daily flights to Saigon, and can also issue Vietnam visas (US$50 for a five-day service). The office is on Preah Sihanouk Blvd, near the corner of 51 St. Opening hours are from 8 to 11.30 am and 2 to 5 pm Monday to Saturday.

Bangkok Airways (☎ 426707), at 61, 214 St, is only good for booking flights from Bangkok to Koh Samui, but flights between Bangkok and Phnom Penh may be re-established.

Other airlines around town are:

Air France
  Office 11, Sofitel Cambodiana Hotel (☎ 426426)

Dragonair
  19, 106 St (☎ 427652)
Malaysian Air Services (MAS)
  Diamond Hotel, 182 Monivong Blvd (☎ 426588)
Silk Air
  Pailin Hotel, Monivong Blvd (☎ 364747)
Thai Airways
  19, 106 St (☎ 427429)

Bus It is not recommended that foreigners travel around Cambodia by bus. Check with your embassy or with Phnom Penh-based NGOs for the latest situation on security.

The GTS bus service from Phnom Penh to Sihanoukville uses air-con Daewoo buses for the four to five-hour run. At the time of writing, most embassies recommend that travellers fly to Sihanoukville, but the bus service (and others are planned) was popular all the same. Again, check with local authorities for the latest information on this road. Tickets cost US$5 and buses leave at 7 am and 1 pm from the Local (City) bus station.

To Ho Chi Minh City (Saigon) There is a daily air-con bus service to Ho Chi Minh City (Saigon) which leaves at 6 am from the Ho Chi Minh bus station on the corner of 211 St and 182 St. The office is open from 5 to 10 am, and tickets cost US$12. There may also be a pack-'em-in service for US$5. Again, this is a service that most embassies will tell you not to use but it is nevertheless popular.

Train The Phnom Penh Railway Station is close to the corner of Pochentong Blvd and Monivong Blvd. Foreigners should not travel by train in Cambodia. Trains are frequently the target of Khmer Rouge attacks, and in July 1994 three foreigners travelling by train were kidnapped and later killed. Staff at the railway station have been forbidden to sell tickets to foreigners.

Taxi Taxis to Sihanoukville and Kompong Chhnang leave from the Local (City) bus station just south of the New Market. They charge US$4 a head and cram six passengers into their vehicles. It's not a pleasant way to travel, and most embassies advise against it.

Share taxis to Battambang and Siem Reap leave from next to the Dusit Hotel, near the New Market. Travellers should not use these taxis.

Taxis to Ho Chi Minh City (Saigon) cost US$25 from the east side of the Monivong (Vietnam) Bridge in the south of town.

It is also possible to hire taxis on a per-day basis. Rates start at US$25 for around Phnom Penh and for nearby destinations, and then go up according to distance. A return trip to Kompong Cham for example costs US$50. Taxis are easy to find. The area around the Asie Hotel on Monivong Blvd has a number of them, as does the Sofitel Cambodiana Hotel (more expensive) and La Paillote Hotel near the New Market.

The Capital Guesthouse on 182 St can also arrange share taxis to popular destinations around Phnom Penh at reasonable rates.

Boat There are numerous ferry operators north of the Japanese Bridge. Boats go to Kompong Cham, Kratie, Stung Treng, Kompong Chhnang and Siem Reap.

To Siem Reap The most popular boat services are those to Siem Reap. There is much debate as to the safety of the boats. Some travellers swear by the slow boats, which take around 24 hours. In a recent incident, however, one of these boats was shot at and a crew member wounded when the boat accidently strayed into local fishing waters. The express services take around five hours to reach Siem Reap. These boats are subject to dangerous overcrowding, and often have nothing in the way of safety gear. Do not sit inside the express boats, which are mostly Malaysian vessels superannuated from the Rejang River in Sarawak; if the boat overturned the passengers inside would likely have little chance of survival.

Slow boats to Siem Reap leave on an irregular basis, so you will need to ask ahead for the next departure. The cost is US$6. Buy a hammock at the New Market and stock up on food and drinks for the trip.

Express boats to Siem Reap cost US$25. Heiwa Shipping and Golden Sea Express both have daily services at 7 am, arriving at 1 pm. There are a number of other operators using smaller boats to do the trip.

Up the Mekong Possible stops on the Mekong are Kompong Cham, Kratie and Stung Treng. Again, there is argument as to how safe boat travel is along the upper Mekong; embassies advise against it. Slow boats to Kratie leave every four or five days and take two days and one night to complete the trip. Tickets cost US$6. It is possible to stop in Kompong Cham, but you would then have to continue by express boat or wait a long time before the next slow boat happened along. Heiwa Shipping has daily express boats from Phnom Penh to Kompong Cham (US$6) and Kratie (US$14). Boats leave at 7 am and arrive in Kratie at noon. Golden Sea Express runs an identical service every second day.

From Kratie to Stung Treng you will probably have to travel by slow boat. There are sometimes slow boat services from Phnom Penh to Stung Treng, but they are very infrequent. There are no express services from Phnom Penh to Stung Treng.

Getting Around

The Airport Pochentong international airport is seven km west of the centre of Phnom Penh along Pochentong Blvd. Taxis between Phnom Penh and the airport cost US$5 to US$8. The official airport taxi service costs US$10. If you don't have much luggage it is possible to take a moto to or from the airport for US$1. Some of the upmarket hotels have airport minibus and limousine services.

Bus Phnom Penh has a fledgling bus network, but figuring out where and when the buses go is a matter of fearful difficulty. The Local (City) bus station is just south of the New Market, at the northeast end of Charles de Gaulle Blvd. The green-and-white buses were donated by the Paris metropolitan government. You will need the help of someone who speaks Khmer to figure out where any bus goes. Alternatively you might just hop on one and see where you end up. Ticket prices are very reasonable.

Moto Motos are usually 100 cc Hondas. They are easily recognised by the blue-peaked caps worn by the drivers. In areas frequented by foreigners (the Sofitel Cambodiana, the FCC, the Capital Guesthouse), moto drivers generally speak English or a little French. Theoretically a short trip costs 500r, but most drivers demand a flat 1000r for destinations around town. Prices are rarely negotiated in advance – hop on and give the driver 1000r at the end of the trip.

Motorcycle There are numerous motorbike hire places around town. Bear in mind that motorbike theft is a big problem in Phnom Penh, and if yours gets stolen you will be liable. One of the best places for motorbike hire is Lucky! Lucky! on Monivong Blvd next to the Hong Kong Hotel. A 100 cc Honda costs US$4 per day or US$25 per week; 250 cc bikes cost US$7 per day, and they've even got a couple of 800 cc jobs for US$25 per day. The Capital Guesthouse has some beaten-up 100 cc Hondas for US$5 per day.

Petrol is sold all over town in one-litre glass bottles (Johhny Walker black label bottles are favoured, but most vendors make do with Coke and Sprite bottles).

Bicycle You can hire bicycles at the Capital Guesthouse, but take a look at the traffic conditions before venturing forth on one.

Cyclo Cyclos are still common on the streets of Phnom Penh but have lost a lot of business to the moto drivers. Few cyclo drivers speak much English or French, but early in the morning (before the traffic gets heavy) a cyclo can be a pleasant way to see some parts of town. Costs are generally 500r for short trips, 1000r for longer ones.

Boat The Lotus D'Or cruise boat can take up to 30 passengers and can be chartered from Phnom Penh Tourism or directly at the landing place just across from the tourism office. For one to six people the boat costs US$18 per hour, for seven to 10 people US$3 each and for 11 to 30 people it's US$2 each.

Around Phnom Penh

North of Phnom Penh

PREK KDAM FERRY

Until Phnom Penh's Japanese Bridge was completed in 1993, the Prek Kdam Ferry, 32 km north of central Phnom Penh, connected National Route 5 with National Route 6. Ferry services are less frequent these days, though they still operate. There are several restaurants and numerous refreshment stands on the Phnom Penh side of the river next to the ferry landing.

PHNOM UDONG

Udong ('the Victorious') served as the capital of Cambodia under several sovereigns between 1618 and 1866. A number of kings, including King Norodom, were crowned here. The main attraction these days are the two humps of Phnom Udong, which have several stupas on them. Both ends of the ridge have good views of the Cambodian countryside dotted with innumerable sugar palm trees. From Phnom Penh's taller buildings, weather permitting, the bluffs of Udong appear as two symmetrical hills – one of which is topped with spires – in the middle of the plains stretching northward from the city.

Udong is not a major attraction, but for those with the time it's worth seeing. It's generally very quiet, though picnickers tend to arrive from Phnom Penh on the weekends. An armed guard will probably accompany you as you explore the place. The payment for this 'service' is US$1.

The smaller ridge has two structures – both heavily damaged – and several stupas on top. Ta San Mosque faces westward towards Mecca. Only the bullet and shrapnel-pocked walls survived the years of Khmer Rouge rule. There are said to be plans to rebuild it. From the mosque you can see, across the plains to the south, Phnom Vihear Leu, a small hill on which a *vihara* (sanctuary)

stands between two white poles. To the right of the vihara is a building used as a prison under Pol Pot. To the left of the vihara and below it is a pagoda known as Arey Ka Sap.

The larger ridge, Phnom Preah Reach Throap ('Hill of the Royal Fortune'), is so named because a 16th-century Khmer king is said to have hidden the national treasury here during a war with the Thais. The most impressive structure on Phnom Preah Reach Throap is Vihear Preah Ath Roes, 'Vihara of the 18-Cubit Buddha'. The vihara and the Buddha, dedicated in 1911 by King Sisowath, were blown up by the Khmer Rouge in 1977; only sections of the walls, the bases of eight enormous columns and the right arm and part of the right side of the Buddha remain.

About 120m north-west of Vihear Preah Ath Roes is a line of small viharas. The first is Vihear Preah Ko, a brick-roofed structure inside of which is a statue of Preah Ko, the sacred bull; the original of this statue was carried away by the Thais long ago. The second structure, which has a seated Buddha inside, is Vihear Preah Keo. The third is Vihear Prak Neak, its cracked laterite (clay soil) walls topped with a temporary thatch roof. Inside is a seated Buddha guarded by a *naga*, or snake (*prak neak* means 'protected by a naga').

At the north-west extremity of the ridge stand three large stupas. The first one you come to is the cement Chet Dey Mak Proum, the final resting place of King Monivong (ruled 1927 to 1941). Decorated with garudas (half-bird, half-human), floral designs and elephants, it has four Bayon-style faces on top. The middle stupa, Tray Troeng, is decorated with coloured tiles; it was built in 1891 by King Norodom for the ashes of his father, King Ang Duong (ruled 1845 to 1859). But some say King Ang Duong was buried next to the Silver Pagoda in Phnom Penh. The third stupa, Damrei Sam Poan, was built by King Chey Chethar II (ruled 1618 to 1626) for the ashes of his predecessor, King Soriyopor.

An eastward-oriented laterite staircase leads

down the hillside from the stupa of King Monivong. Just north of its base is a pavilion decorated with graphic murals depicting Khmer Rouge atrocities.

At the base of the ridge, close to the path, is a memorial to the victims of Pol Pot containing the bones of some of the people who were buried in approximately 100 mass graves, each containing about a dozen bodies. Instruments of torture were unearthed along with the bones when a number of the two-by-2.5m pits were disinterred in 1981 and 1982.

Getting There & Away
Udong is 40 km from the capital. To get there, head north out of Phnom Penh on National Route 5. Continue past Prek Kdam Ferry for 4.5 km and turn left (southward) at the roadblock and bunker. Udong is 3.5 km south of the turn-off; the access road goes through the village of Psar Dek Krom and passes by a memorial to Pol Pot's victims and a structure known as the Blue Stupa before arriving at a short staircase. Stick to the paths – there may be mines around here.

A taxi out to Phnom Udong and back will cost around US$20. It might be a good idea to hire the car for the day and include another destination such as Kompong Chhnang. The Capital Guesthouse in Phnom Penh can arrange share taxis at US$5 per head for the return trip to Udong.

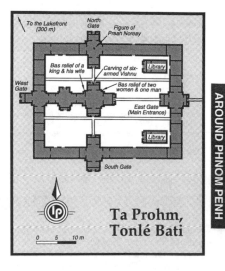

South of Phnom Penh

There are several historical sites of interest in Takeo Province. Most of them can be visited on a day trip from Phnom Penh. A taxi for the day costs US$25 to US$30.

TONLÉ BATI
Ta Prohm Temple
The laterite Temple of Ta Prohm was built by King Jayavarman VII (ruled 1181 to 1201) on the site of a 6th-century Khmer shrine. A stele found here dates from 1574. The site is open all day every day.

The main sanctuary consists of five chambers; in each is a statue, or *lingam* (all of which show signs of the destruction wrought by the Khmer Rouge).

A few metres to the right of the main (eastward-facing) entrance to the sanctuary building, about three metres above the ground, is a bas-relief carving of a woman carrying an object on her head and a man bowing to another, larger woman. The smaller woman has just given birth and failed to show proper respect for the midwife (the larger woman). The new mother has been condemned to carry the afterbirth on her head in a box for the rest of her life. The husband is asking that his be wife forgiven.

Around the corner to the right from the northern entrance of the sanctuary building, about 3.5m above the ground, is a bas-relief scene in which a king sits to the right of his wife. Because she has been unfaithful, a servant is shown in the scene below putting her to death by trampling her with a horse.

Inside the north gate is a badly damaged statue of the Hindu god Preah Noreay. Women come here to pray that they be granted a child.

Yeay Peau Temple
Yeay Peau Temple, named after King Ta

The Legend of Yeay Peau Temple

During the time of the building of Angkor Wat (the early 12th century), King Preah Ket Mealea travelled through Tonlé Bati, where he fell in love with Peau, the beautiful daughter of a rich fish merchant. When Peau fell pregnant to the king, he gave her his royal seal ring and a sacred dagger and requested that the child visit him one day.

Peau gave birth to a boy, who she called Prohm. When Peau later informed her son of his parentage, he took the ring and sacred dagger and set out for Angkor Wat, where he was to live with the king.

After a few years, Prohm was allowed to visit Tonlé Bati. But when he arrived, he did not recognise his mother and, taken by her beauty, he asked her to become his wife. Peau explained that she was his mother, but he refused to believe her.

To settle the matter, Peau suggested that she and Prohm construct a temple; whoever finished first would get their way. Prohm agreed, sure that he could win. On Peau's suggestion, the contest was to be held at night. Two teams formed: all the men of the area to help Prohm and all the women to help Peau. After many hours, Peau sent aloft an artificial morning star lit with candles. The men, thinking it was dawn and that the women could not have finished, went to sleep. Meanwhile, Peau's temple was completed. Defeated, Prohm prostrated himself before Peau and recognised her as his mother. ■

Prohm's mother, is a small structure 150m north of Ta Prohm Temple. Inside, there is a statue of Madame Peau beside a seated Buddha.

Nearby is Wat Tonlé Bati, a modern cement structure heavily damaged by the Khmer Rouge. The only remnant of the pagoda's pre-1975 complement of statues is an 80-cm-high Buddha's head made of metal.

The Lakefront

About 300m north-west of Ta Prohm Temple, a long, narrow peninsula juts into the Bati River. On Sundays, it is packed with picnickers and vendors selling food, drink and fruit. During the rest of the week, however, it's deserted.

Getting There & Away

The access road to Ta Prohm Temple, which is in the Tonlé Bati district of Takeo Province, intersects National Route 2 at a point 33 km south of central Phnom Penh, 21 km north of the access road to Phnom Chisor and 44 km north of Takeo (the capital of Takeo Province). The temple is 2.5 km from the highway. Any bus linking Phnom Penh with the town of Takeo by way of National Route 2 will pass by the access road. Taxis from the Capital Guesthouse in Phnom Penh charge US$5 per head.

PHNOM CHISOR

Try to get to Phnom Chisor early in the day if possible. It's a very uncomfortable climb

in the heat of the midday sun. An enterprising Khmer family has set up a drink stand at the top with a wooden bench.

The main temple stands at the eastern side of the hilltop. Constructed of laterite and brick with carved lintels of sandstone, the complex is surrounded by the partially ruined walls of a 2.5-metre-wide gallery with inward-facing windows.

Inscriptions found here date from the 11th century, when this site was known as Suryagiri. The wooden doors to the sanctuary in the centre of the complex, which open to the east, are decorated with carvings of figures standing on pigs. Inside the sanctuary there are statues of the Buddha.

On the plain to the east of Phnom Chisor is: Sen Thmol (at the bottom of Phnom Chisor); Sen Ravang (farther east); and the former sacred pond of Tonlé Om. All three form a straight line from Phnom Chisor. During rituals held here 900 years ago, the Brahmans and their entourage would climb up to Suryagiri from this direction on a monumental stairway of 400 steps.

There is a spectacular view of the temples and plains from the roofless gallery opposite the wooden doors to the central shrine. Near the main temple is a modern Buddhist vihara used by resident monks.

Getting There & Away

The intersection of National Route 2 and the

eastward-bound access road to Phnom Chisor is marked by the two brick towers of Prasat Neang Khmau (the Temple of the Black Virgin), which may have once served as a sanctuary to Kali, the dark goddess of destruction.

Prasat Neang Khmau is on National Route 2 at a point 55 km south of central Phnom Penh, 21 km south of the turn-off to Tonlé Bati and 23 km north of Takeo town. It's a bit over four km from the highway to the base of the hill.

There are two paths up the 100m-high ridge, which takes about 15 minutes to climb. The northern path, which has a mild gradient, begins at a cement pavilion with windows shaped like the squared-off silhouette of a bell. The building is topped with a miniature replica of an Angkor-style tower. The steeper southern route, which begins 600m south of the northern path, consists of a long stairway. A good way to see the view in all directions is to go up the northern path and come down the southern stairway.

TAKEO TOWN

Takeo, capital of a province of the same name, is best used as a base to explore sites such as Tonlé Bati, Phnom Chisor and Phnom Da (Angkor Borei).

Places to Stay

The *Sam Long Guesthouse* is around the corner from the Restaurant Stung Takeo, near the river. It's a basic outfit with fan-cooled doubles for US$5. There is an English sign outside – it simply says 'Guesthouse'.

Places to Eat

Restaurant Stung Takeo, overlooking the Takeo River, is on the road that demarcates the eastern extremity of town. It's one of the most popular restaurants in town and a good place for lunch during a Takeo Province tour.

Getting There & Away

National Route 2, which links Phnom Penh with Takeo town(77 km), is being upgraded. By the time you have this book in your hands it should be a relatively smooth run. A Taxi is a safer option than the bus.

ANGKOR BOREI & PHNOM DA

Angkor Borei was known as Vyadhapura when it served as the capital of 'water Chenla' in the 8th century. Four artificial caves, built as shrines, are carved into the north-east wall of Phnom Da, a hill south of Angkor Borei. On top of Phnom Da is a square laterite tower open to the north.

Angkor Borei and Phnom Da are about 20 km east of Takeo town along Canal Number 15.

East of Phnom Penh

KOKI

Koki is generally referred to as Koki Beach, which is rather misleading, unless your idea of a beach is a mudflat on the Mekong covered in 'picnic restaurants' on stilts.

Koki is a peculiarly Cambodian institution, a mixture of the universal love of picnicking by the water with the unique Khmer fondness for lounging about on mats. It works like this: for 1500r or so an hour, picnickers rent an area about 2.5m square on a raised pier covered with reed mats. Be sure to agree on the price *before* you rent a space. On Sunday, these piers are jam-packed.

Places to Eat

All sorts of food is sold at Koki Beach on Sunday, though at prices higher than in Phnom Penh. The beach is deserted during the week, but food is available at restaurants along National Route 1 between the Koki turn-off and the capital.

Getting There & Away

Koki Beach is in Kandal Province in the Koki sub-district of Kien Svay district. To get there from the capital, turn left off National Route 1, which links Phnom Penh with Ho Chi Minh City (Saigon) at a point 12 km east of the Monivong (Vietnam) Bridge. There are taxis to Koki from the Chbam Pao share-taxi station, which is just east of the Monivong (Vietnam) Bridge. A moto will take you out there and back for a few US dollars.

AROUND PHNOM PENH

Angkor

The temples of Angkor were built between seven and 11 centuries ago when Khmer civilisation was at the height of its extraordinary creativity. Unparalleled in South-East Asia – though the temples of Bagan in Myanmar (Burma) are a close runner-up – Angkor rates among the architectural wonders of the world.

From Angkor, the kings of the mighty Khmer Empire ruled over a vast territory that extended from the tip of what is now southern Vietnam northward to Yunnan in China and from Vietnam westward to the Bay of Bengal. Angkor's 100 or so temples constitute the sacred skeleton of a spectacular administrative and religious centre. Its houses, public buildings and palaces were constructed of wood – now long decayed – because the right to dwell in structures of brick or stone was reserved for the gods.

It is easy to spend a week or more at Angkor seeing the temples at a leisurely pace, perhaps returning to the main attractions several times to see them in different light conditions. Many travellers feel that about four or five days is the optimum length of time to spend before saturation starts to set in. Even with only two days at your disposal, however, you can get a lot of sightseeing done providing you get an early start in the mornings. If your time is limited and you only have one day to tour the Angkor complex, it would probably be best to organise a tour to get the most out of the day.

SIEM REAP

Siem Reap (pronounced see-EM ree-EP) is a fast-developing town just north of the western extent of the Tonlé Sap Lake. The name Siem Reap means 'Siamese Defeated' *(Siem* means 'Siamese' (Thais); *Reap* means 'defeated').

Even if Siem Reap were not the nearest town to Angkor, it would probably still be worth a short visit. There's a sleepy, rural quality to the place, and this coupled with a good range of accommodation and some good restaurants makes it a good place to unwind for a few days. If there was a local arts and crafts industry it would be easy to draw parallels with Ubud, in Bali, before the advent of mass tourism...for the moment at least, anyway. Siem Reap is obviously destined for big things, and major changes can be expected over the next few years.

On the drawing board is the redevelopment of the Grand Hotel by the Singapore Raffles Group and a US$100-million tourist development project by Malaysian investors who will be constructing two more five-star hotels close to town. Sound and light shows are planned for Angkor itself, while commercial and parkland residential areas are also in the planning stages. It sounds very depressing.

Orientation

It is possible to walk around Siem Reap in an hour or so; there is no risk of getting lost. Route 6 cuts through the north of town past the Grand Hotel and the central market. The Siem Reap River flows north to south through the centre of town, and has enough bridges that you don't have to worry too much about being on the wrong side.

There is no central accommodation area in Siem Reap. The most popular budget guesthouse areas are just off Route 6, to the east of the Grand Hotel, and on Route 6 to the west of the Grand. There are also some popular mid-range hotels in the south of town, near the new market.

Angkor Wat and Angkor Thom are around six km north of town, while the Roluos Group of temples is 12 km east of town along Route 6.

Information

Tourist Office The Angkor office of Cambodia Tourism is in a new white structure opposite the Grand Hotel. There's a sign saying 'Tourist Information' but you will be very lucky to find the staff here awake unless you come in on a prepaid tour and they know you're coming.

For the most part, budget and mid-range travellers in Angkor get their travel information from other travellers or from their guesthouses.

Angkor Conservation Angkor Conservation is responsible for the study, preservation and upkeep of the Angkor monuments. It has its headquarters in a large compound between Siem Reap and Angkor Wat. Over 5000 statues, lingas and inscribed steles are stored here because of the danger of theft from the hundreds of nearby sites where these artefacts were found. As a result, Angkor's finest statuary is inside Angkor Conservation's warehouses, meticulously numbered and catalogued. Unfortunately, without the right contacts, getting a peek at the statues is a lost cause. Hopefully, some of the statuary will eventually go on public display.

Money There are two banks where you can change money in Siem Reap. The Cambodian Commercial Bank is open from 8 am to 3.30 pm Monday to Friday, and changes travellers cheques at 2% commission. Cash advances (with a limit of US$2000) are available for MasterCard, JCB and Visa. No commission is charged for cash advances.

The Foreign Trade Bank is open from 7.30 am to 4 pm Monday to Friday, and from 7.30 to 11.30 am on Saturday. It also charges a 2% commission for changing travellers' cheques. It cannot provide advances on credit cards.

Post & Communications The post office is along the river 400m south of the Grand Hotel d'Angkor. It would probably be best to save your post for Phnom Penh or Bangkok.

Making international calls from Siem Reap is as simple as from Phnom Penh nowadays. There are several Telstar public phone booths around town, including one outside the Cambodia Tourism office. You can buy phone cards at the tourism office if there's anyone there; otherwise try one of the hotels around town.

Country calls within Cambodia are still difficult to make and should be avoided if possible. This situation may have improved, however, by the time you have this book in your hands. If you do get through, calls to Phnom Penh are almost as expensive as international calls.

If you need to send or receive faxes and you're not based in a hotel that has this service, try Angkor International, a business centre just south of the Greenhouse Restaurant on Sivutha St.

The Siem Reap area code is 23.

Dangers & Annoyances Siem Reap itself is perfectly safe to stroll around, even by night. Out at the temples, however, stick to clearly marked trails. There are still mines lurking out there. It is also not recommended that you visit remote sites alone – indeed the local authorities forbid it. There is a serious risk of armed robbery in remote areas.

Things to See
The sights are all out at Angkor. There's precious little to do in Siem Reap itself. The **Central Market**, 1.6 km east of the Siem Reap River (towards Roluos), on the south side of National Route 6, is probably the major attraction. It's a sprawling affair and covered like the Russian Market in Phnom Penh.

There are a couple of medium-sized wats around town, but with the monuments of Angkor so close very few foreign visitors bother with them. **Wat Prohm Reat** is opposite the Bayon Hotel, on the west side of the Siem Reap River. **Wat Dam Nak** is close by on the eastern side of the river.

An increasingly popular and very worthwhile side trip from Siem Reap is to the **Vietnamese Fishing Village** on the Tonlé Sap Lake. The 'village' is actually a straggling collection of moored boats and shacks on stilts over the water at Phnom Krom, where the Phnom Penh ferries pull in. If you come in by ferry, you will pass the village. Boats are available for hire at highly negotiable rates of between US$7 and US$10 for a couple of hours of floating around and picture taking.

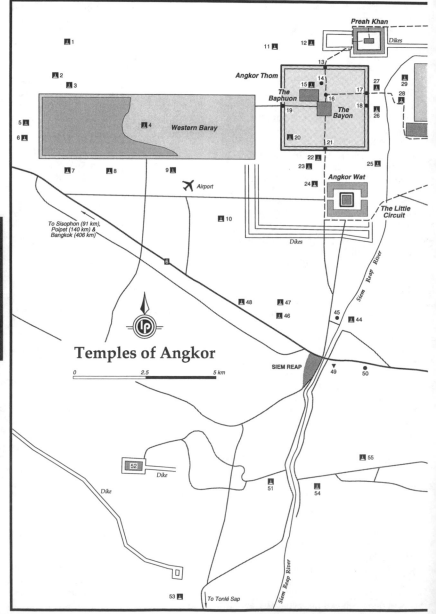

Temples of Angkor

0   2.5   5 km

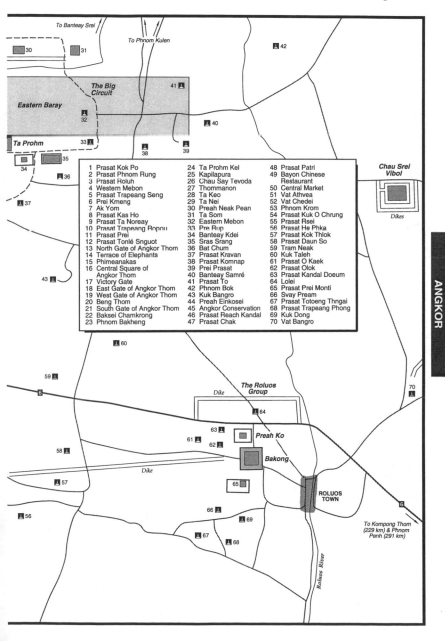

To Banteay Srei

To Phnom Kulen

30

31

42

The Big Circuit

41

Eastern Baray

32

40

Ta Prohm

33

38

39

34

35

36

37

Chau Srei Vibol

Dikes

1 Prasat Kok Po
2 Prasat Phnom Rung
3 Prasat Roluh
4 Western Mebon
5 Prasat Trapeang Seng
6 Prei Kmeng
7 Ak Yom
8 Prasat Kas Ho
9 Prasat Ta Noreay
10 Prasat Trapeang Ropou
11 Prasat Prei
12 Prasat Tonlé Snguot
13 North Gate of Angkor Thom
14 Terrace of Elephants
15 Phimeanakas
16 Central Square of Angkor Thom
17 Victory Gate
18 East Gate of Angkor Thom
19 West Gate of Angkor Thom
20 Beng Thom
21 South Gate of Angkor Thom
22 Baksei Chamkrong
23 Phnom Bakheng

24 Ta Prohm Kel
25 Kapilapura
26 Chau Say Tevoda
27 Thommanon
28 Ta Keo
29 Ta Nei
30 Preah Neak Pean
31 Ta Som
32 Eastern Mebon
33 Pre Rup
34 Banteay Kdei
35 Sras Srang
36 Bat Chum
37 Prasat Kravan
38 Prasat Komnap
39 Prei Prasat
40 Banteay Samré
41 Prasat To
42 Phnom Bok
43 Kuk Bangro
44 Preah Einkosei
45 Angkor Conservation
46 Prasat Reach Kandal
47 Prasat Chak

48 Prasat Patri
49 Bayon Chinese Restaurant
50 Central Market
51 Vat Athvea
52 Vat Chedei
53 Phnom Krom
54 Prasat Kuk O Chrung
55 Prasat Rsei
56 Prasat He Phka
57 Prasat Kok Thlok
58 Prasat Daun So
59 Tram Neak
60 Kuk Taleh
61 Prasat O Kaek
62 Prasat Olok
63 Prasat Kandal Doeum
64 Lolei
65 Prasat Prei Monti
66 Svay Pream
67 Prasat Totoeng Thngai
68 Prasat Trapeang Phong
69 Kuk Dong
70 Vat Bangro

43

60

59

6

The Roluos Group

Dike

64

63

61

62

Preah Ko

58

Dike

57

65

Bakong

56

66

69

ROLUOS TOWN

6

70

To Kompong Thom (229 km) & Phnom Penh (291 km)

67

68

Roluos River

ANGKOR

Places to Stay

The hotel scene in Siem Reap has changed immensely from the early days of Angkor tourism, when travellers were essentially restricted to the venerable Grand and its Villa Apsara annex. A large number of family-run guesthouse have sprung up for budget travellers, while those on mid-range budgets can choose from *pension*-style villas at around US$10 to US$15 or hotels which range from around US$15. There are even a few mid to top-end hotels around town, and these will soon be supplemented by other big-name arrivals.

Places to Stay – bottom end Touts for the budget guesthouses wait at the airport and at the ferry dock. You are not obligated to stay at their guesthouse if you don't like the look of the place. Apart from the guesthouses listed here, there are many other places around town with rooms ranging from US$3 to US$5. Most of the less popular places are known simply by numbers – Guesthouse 258, and so on.

The cheapest guesthouse in town is the *Naga Guesthouse*, near the Hotel de la Paix. Rooms cost as little as US$1, and doubles are available from US$2 to US$3. It's a surprisingly big place, and between the early-morning Angkor tour crowd and the late-night drinking crowd it tends to be rowdy at all times of day. The Naga is much maligned by other guesthouse operators around town, who speculate that the rooms are subsidised by some kind of shady cut the owners have wangled on tickets for Angkor, or even perhaps the boat tickets. This does nothing, of course, to dent the popularity of the place with travellers.

East of the Siem Reap River, just off Route 6, is a cluster of long-running guesthouses that are more intimate and relaxed places to be than the Naga. *Mom's Guesthouse*, next door to the Bayon Restaurant, has been around for quite a while and is overseen by the ever-fussing 'Mom' herself. Singles are US$5 and doubles are US$6. There is one large room with bathroom for US$8. Mom's has a pleasant balcony and does a good coffee, baguette and egg breakfast.

Mahogany Guesthouse, just a couple of doors from Mom's, is the most popular place in this part of town. It's a large two-storey building with a veranda area for socialising. Singles cost US$4, while doubles are US$5-6 depending on the room. Across the road is the *Garden Guesthouse*, which also has singles/doubles at US$5/6. There are a couple of rooms with bathrooms for US$8. The Garden is popular with French travellers.

The other budget section of town is the area just west of the Greenhouse Restaurant on Route 6. Pick of the pack is probably the *Apsara Guesthouse*, a big hotel-style operation. The rooms are spacious and there's a leafy restaurant area in the garden. Singles cost US$3, while doubles cost US$5 or US$7 with bathroom.

The *Takeo Guesthouse* is popular with Japanese travellers and has rooms for US$4, US$6 with bathroom. Next door is the *Chenla Guesthouse*, a clean family-run place with kitchen facilities. It charges US$2 per bed or US$5 for doubles with attached bathroom.

Places to Stay – middle As is the case in Phnom Penh, there has been a mid-range hotel boom in Siem Reap, and there are some very good deals around.

The *Golden Apsara International House* (☎ 57537) is highly recommended. It's a wonderfully hospitable villa with verandas and a pleasant family atmosphere. Fan rooms with attached bathroom start at US$10, while air-con singles/doubles cost US$15/20. Doubles with hot-water showers cost US$25. It is wise to make a reservation, as the Golden Apsara is often full.

Across the road from the Golden Apsara are a couple more villa-style hotels. The *Villa Phkay Proeuk* (☎ 015-919548) has fan singles/doubles for US$5/10 and air-con doubles at US$15. There are a couple of air-con triples, and these are a good deal at US$20. The *Vimean Thmei Hotel* (☎ 57494) is a similar kind of outfit, with fan rooms at US$10 and air-con singles/doubles at US$15/20. Both these places lack the ambience of the Golden Apsara but are friendly and clean.

The *Stung Siem Reap Hotel* (☎ 015-913074)

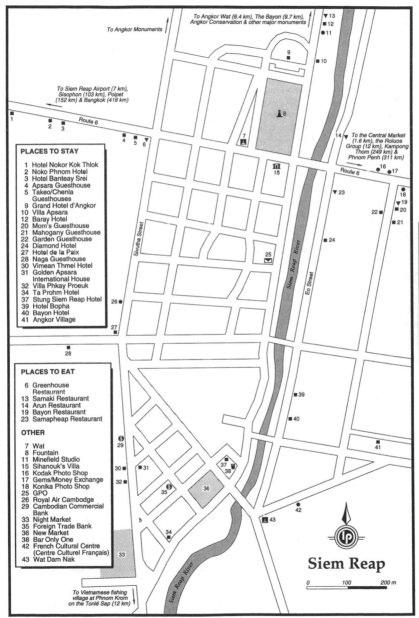

To Angkor Monuments

To Angkor Wat (6.4 km), The Bayon (9.7 km), Angkor Conservation & other major monuments

To Siem Reap Airport (7 km), Sisophon (103 km), Poipet (152 km) & Bangkok (418 km)

Route 6

To the Central Market (1.6 km), the Roluos Group (12 km), Kampong Thom (249 km) & Phnom Penh (311 km)

Route 6

Sivutha Street

Eo Street

Siem Reap River

ANGKOR

PLACES TO STAY

1 Hotel Nokor Kok Thlok
2 Noko Phnom Hotel
3 Hotel Banteay Srei
4 Apsara Guesthouse
5 Takeo/Chenla Guesthouses
9 Grand Hotel d'Angkor
10 Villa Apsara
12 Baray Hotel
20 Mom's Guesthouse
21 Mahogany Guesthouse
22 Garden Guesthouse
24 Diamond Hotel
27 Hotel de la Paix
28 Naga Guesthouse
30 Vimean Thmei Hotel
31 Golden Apsara International House
32 Villa Phkay Proeuk
34 Ta Prohm Hotel
37 Stung Siem Reap Hotel
39 Hotel Bopha
40 Bayon Hotel
41 Angkor Village

PLACES TO EAT

6 Greenhouse Restaurant
13 Samaki Restaurant
14 Arun Restaurant
19 Bayon Restaurant
23 Samapheap Restaurant

OTHER

7 Wat
8 Fountain
11 Minefield Studio
15 Sihanouk's Villa
16 Kodak Photo Shop
17 Gems/Money Exchange
18 Konika Photo Shop
25 GPO
26 Royal Air Cambodge
29 Cambodian Commercial Bank
33 Night Market
35 Foreign Trade Bank
36 New Market
38 Bar Only One
42 French Cultural Centre (Centre Culturel Français)
43 Wat Dam Nak

Siem Reap

0   100   200 m

To Vietnamese fishing village at Phnom Krom on the Tonlé Sap (12 km)

is a good alternative to the family-run villas. The extremely friendly management of this place plans to set up a garden area in front of the hotel. Rooms come with air-con, satellite TV and fridges, and cost from US$30 to US$40.

The *Freedom Hotel* is a new place out near the Central Market. A restaurant and bar is under construction at the time of writing, and when finished this should be a good mid-range place to be based. Fan rooms with attached bathroom are US$10, basic air-con rooms US$15, air-con rooms with hot water US$20, and rooms with satellite TV US$25. The friendly Khmer manager speaks excellent English and is a good source of information about Siem Reap and Angkor.

Hotel de la Paix (☎ 015-911131) is an average mid-range place with a good Chinese restaurant. Singles cost US$20, while doubles/triples are US$25/35. Plans are afoot to renovate this place – expect prices to rise accordingly.

Undoubtedly the classiest act in town is *Angkor Village* (☎ 015-916048). Designed by its owner, a French architect, this all-timber collection of bungalow units set around a recessed restaurant area is excellent value at US$35 for fan rooms or US$55 with air-con. Angkor Village only has 20 rooms, so it is advisable to book ahead.

On the eastern bank of the Siem Reap River is a string of mid-range hotels. None of them stand out, but they can be relied on for basic comforts and decent service. They all sport air-con rooms, satellite TV and hot and cold water. The *Diamond Hotel* (☎ 57995) has a popular Thai restaurant and slightly musty rooms at US$35/45 for singles/doubles. The *Hotel Bopha* (☎ 015-917176) is better value with spacious rooms at US$30/35 for singles/doubles. The *Bayon Hotel* (☎ 015-911769) has some pleasant rooms overlooking the river and costs US$35/40.

A final possibility is the *Baray Hotel* (☎ 015-910814), just north of town on the road out to Angkor. This place has a low-key bar and restaurant and 12 air-con rooms with hot water at US$25. It tends to be quiet and deserves more business than it gets.

Places to Stay – top end In March 1996, the doors of the *Grand Hotel d'Angkor* swung shut in preparation for a head-to-tail over-haul by the Singapore Raffles Group. It's tempting to lament the passing of another decaying colonial institution, but given that the renovators have got their hands on virtu-ally every other hotel in Asia with a colonial pedigree it was inevitable that the Grand would go the same way. The fate of the *Villa Apsara* is uncertain at the time of writing, but until something is done to brush the place up it's best avoided.

Most of the best hotels in town are on Route 6 on the way out to the airport. There's little to choose between them. In terms of value for money, the *Hotel Banteay Srey* (☎ 015-913839), a Thai-managed hotel, is the best. It has tasteful decor and it offers everything (including IDD international calls) that the other top-end hotels in town offer at a flat US$55. As is the case with other top-end hotels there is a 10% government tax and a 10% service tax. The *Hotel Nokor Kok Thlok* (☎ 57488; fax 57991) is rated as the best hotel in Siem Reap. Apart from the fact that virtually none of its foreign guests are able to pronounce its name, this hotel lacks character and it's hard to justify the room rates of US$85/95 for singles/doubles; suites are also available for US$110.

The last top-end hotel in this part of town is the *Noko Phnom Hotel* (☎ 57463). It's a step down from the Banteay Srey Hotel, but better value than the Nokor Kok Thlok, with rooms at US$55/65.

The *Ta Phrom Hotel* (☎ 57409) has a good location down in the south of town next to the Siem Reap River. It's popular with Euro-pean tour groups, and has rates of US$80/90 for singles/doubles, US$120/130 for suites.

Places to Eat

The restaurant scene in Siem Reap is not developing as fast as the hotel scene is, but there are still some very good restaurants around.

The most popular place in town is the *Bayon Restaurant*, next door to Mom's Guesthouse, just off Route 6. It has a pleasant garden setting and the food is consistently excellent – try the curry chicken in baby coconut.

The *Samapheap Restaurant* is close by, next to the river. It has a Thai atmosphere – complete with twinkling fairy lights at night – and the food is a mixture of Khmer, Thai and generic western. It is one of the longest-running restaurants in town. The *Thai Restaurant* at the Diamond Hotel, just down the road from here, has the best Thai food in town, though it helps if you tell the staff you want it 'Thai-style' when you order.

North of Samapheap and beside the river is the *Arun Restaurant*, an inexpensive Khmer restaurant. There's nothing cheap and nasty about it and the meals here are tasty.

The *Greenhouse* is on the corner of Sivutha St and Route 6. It has a good atmosphere and is the only restaurant in town that sells red and white wine by the glass. But the food doesn't quite equal that of the Bayon Restaurant. It has a good mix of Thai and Khmer standards on the menu.

The *Samaki Restaurant* is run by a sprightly elderly Chinese gentleman. His steaks are regarded as the best in Siem Reap by foreign residents, and the Chinese-Khmer dishes are recommended too. The best Chinese food in town can be had at the *Restaurant de la Paix*, at the hotel of the same name on Sivutha St. It's slightly more expensive than most of the other places around town. The Khmer restaurants opposite the main entrance to Angkor Wat are good places for lunch.

Entertainment

Check at the Ta Phrom Hotel for information on classical Khmer dancing. At the time of writing, performances are held on Wednesday and Saturday from 7 to 8 pm in the *Riverside Beer Garden* opposite the hotel. Tickets cost US$3 or US$5 for the front row.

Things tend to wind down fairly early in Siem Reap. Most visitors are up at the crack of dawn sightseeing anyway. The *Bar Only One* is just what it claims to be, and can be found around the corner from the Stung Siem Reap Hotel. It's French-run, and is generally fairly quiet.

There are a couple of dance clubs along Sivutha St. Single men will find themselves being hustled by the dancers at these places and the music is dreadful – an interesting cultural experience perhaps.

Things to Buy

There is no shortage of gift shops around town, though the items on sale are rarely of much interest. Look out for the Bayon coffee mugs. The Minefield Studio is just north of the tourist office on the road to Angkor and has the best T-shirts in town. They're all hand-painted, and while more expensive than they would be in many other parts of Asia, they're the best you'll get in Cambodia.

You can get your Angkor photos printed in Siem Reap quickly and cheaply. Most of the photo shops are on Route 6 just east of the river. The Konika shops are the cheapest, processing roles of 36 for just US$4. If you're using slide film, leave the processing until after you leave Cambodia.

At Angkor itself, you will end up spending a lot of your time fighting off hordes of souvenir sellers. Items being touted include temple bas-relief rubbings, curious musical instruments, ornamental knives, T-shirts and other local crafts.

Getting There & Away

The frequency of flights between Phnom Penh and Siem Reap has increased dramatically over the last few years, and it is now possible to do the trip by boat too. Train connections from Phnom Penh to Sisophon are off-limits to foreigners and justly so – it's a dangerous trip. Do not consider travelling from Siem Reap to Battambang or to Phnom Penh by taxi. It's simply not worth the risk.

Air The only way to fly to Siem Reap is from Phnom Penh with Royal Air Cambodge. At the time of writing there are seven flights a day either way. The earliest flight from Phnom Penh leaves at 6.45 am and the latest at 4 pm. From Siem Reap the earliest flight is at 7.55 am and the latest at 5.15 pm. Flights are serviced by ATR 72s.

Flights between Phnom Penh and Siem

ANGKOR

Angkor Wat Tourism Zone

One of the remarkable things about Angkor is that it is so untouristed. Unlike Thailand and Vietnam, Cambodia's security worries have made it a backwater. Not for much longer.

Among the many schemes hatched to add some zip to South-East Asia's most venerable and awesome historical site is a massive sound and light show. The show is not without its detractors. With three walk-through shows a night, each with a capacity of 500 participants, there are concerns of damage to Angkor Wat, where the show will be held. Prince Ranariddh, Cambodia's prime minister, on the other hand, is exited by the idea and claims to be inspired by the colours of Disney's *Pocahontas*.

The show will be of epic dimensions, and may well be fascinating. According to plans announced in late 1995, it will commence with the French 'discovery' of Angkor Wat.

YTL, The Malaysian company that is financing all this fun, claims it will be 'the greatest show on earth'. One problem, however, is that the show would leave the rest of Siem Reap without power. The company has responded to this by planning to build a US$8.3-million power plant. YTL will probably have two hotels up and running by early 1997: the US$6.7 million Aman Resort; and the US$13.5 million 135-room Chedi Resort. What with the inevitable golf course, conference centres and sports complex (all under planning), poor Siem Reap won't know what's hit it. ■

Reap cost US$55 one way, or US$110 return. There is no need to book your return flight in Phnom Penh as this can be done in Siem Reap. The Royal Air Cambodge office in Siem Reap is south of the Hotel de la Paix on Sivutha St and opening hours are from 6.45 to 11.30 am and 1 to 6 pm daily (yes, no holidays). The office is not computerised so your booking is recorded and confirmed the next day when you pick up your ticket.

Boat Ferries from Siem Reap to Phnom Penh leave from Phnom Krom, 11 km south of Siem Reap. A moto out here costs US$1. Most of the guesthouses in town sell ferry tickets, and there is a bewildering variety of them to choose from. Bear in mind that some of the express boats are probably accidents waiting to happen and get shot at from time to time by Vietnamese fisherpeople armed with AK47s. Breakdowns are frequent, and can be relied on to occur in the middle of the Tonlé Sap Lake at unswimmable distances from the nearest Khmer Rouge-infested mangrove. See the Phnom Penh Getting There & Away section for information about the kinds of ferries running between Siem Reap and Phnom Penh and their costs.

Getting Around

The Airport Many of the hotels and even some of the guesthouses in Siem Reap have a free airport pickup service. The seven-km ride from the airport on the back of a moto costs US$1. Taxis are also usually available at US$3 to US$5.

Car & Motorcycle Most of the hotels and guesthouses can organise taxi hire to see Angkor. The going rate is US$20-25. Minibuses are available from Angkor Tourism or from Cambodia Travel & Tours (☎ 015-918-609) in the south of town. A 12-seat minibus costs US$40 per day, a 22-seat minibus US$80 per day.

Moto Motos are available at daily rates of between US$6 and US$8. Most of the moto drivers are understandably unwilling to carry more than one passenger. It's not fair on the drivers to demand that they do. The average cost for a short trip within town is 500r.

Cyclo You can get around Siem Reap in the town's unique and rather uncomfortable cyclos which are essentially standard bicycles with a two-seat trailer in hitch. You can reach anywhere in town for 500r.

Bicycle Some of the guesthouses around town hire out bicycles. Motorcycles are no longer available for hire. The government now demands that tourists visiting Angkor use a 'qualified guide', which means you are compelled to hire a motorbike or car with a driver.

Temples of Angkor

At its peak in the 12th and 13th centuries, Angkor is estimated to have had a population of about 750,000. This massive labour force enabled a succession of Khmer kings to create entire cities in honour of themselves and their gods, all within the Siem Reap region. The scale and scope of this vast sacred building project has no equal in the history of humankind and the passing of time has only heightened the symbolic power of this, the exquisite stone heart of the Khmer people.

Title Page: Detail of one of the Bayon's massive towers which overlooks Angkor Thom (Photograph by Chris Taylor).

Right: Angkor Wat's galleries feature the largest and finest bas reliefs at Angkor.

CHRIS TAYLOR

HISTORY

Early Years

The Angkor period, in which the temples of Angkor were built and the Khmer Empire consolidated its position as one of the great powers of South-East Asia, covers over 600 years from 802 to 1432. This is quite a sweep of history, encompassing periods of decline and revival, and wars with rival powers in Vietnam, Thailand and Myanmar (Burma). This brief history deals only with the periods that produced the temples that can now be seen at Angkor.

The Angkor period begins with the rule of Jayavarman II (ruled 802-850). Little is known of this king. It is thought that he spent his early years in Java, Indonesia, where he was resident at the Shailendras court. He returned to Cambodia in the late 8th century, and established himself as the head of an independent Khmer kingdom. His court was variously sited in four different locations, notably at Roluos and at Mt Kulen, 40 km north-east of Angkor.

Jayavarman II set a precedent that became a feature of the Angkor period and accounts for the staggering architectural productivity of the Khmers at this time. He established himself as a 'god king' or 'universal king' whose all-reaching power expressed the godlike qualities of Shiva. Shiva's dwelling place is the mythical Mt Meru, and consequently Jayavarman built a 'temple mountain', which symbolised the holy mountain at the centre of the universe. This cult of the god king is known as *devaraja*.

Indravarman I (ruled 877-899) is believed to have been an usurper, and probably inherited the mantle of god king through conquest. He built a 650-hectare reservoir, or *baray*, at Roluos and established the temple Preah Ko. The baray marked the first stage of a massive irrigation system that eventually was to extensively water the lands around Angkor. But it also had religious significance in that Mt Meru is flanked by lakes according to legend – as is often the case, necessity and symbolism dovetail nicely. Indravarman's final work was the Bakong, a pyramidal representation of Mt Meru.

For some reason, Indravarman I's son Yasovarman I (ruled 889-910) looked farther afield when it came time to celebrate his divinity and glory in a temple mountain of his own. After building Lolei on an artificial island in the baray established by his father, he began work on the Bakheng, siting it on the hill known today as Phnom Bakheng (a favoured spot for sunset photographs of Angkor Wat). A raised highway was constructed to connect Bakheng with Roluos, 16 km to the north-east, and a large baray was formed to the east of Phnom Bakheng – it is now known as the Eastern Baray.

Following the death of Yasovarman I, power briefly shifted away from Angkor region briefly to Koh Ker, around 80 km to the north. In 944 power returned again to Angkor under the leadership of Rajendravarman II (944-968), who built the Eastern Mebon and Pre Rup. The rule of his son, Jayavarman V (ruled 968-1001), produced the temples Ta Keo and Banteay Srei.

Classical Age

The so-called classical age refers to the period that produced the temples that are now the highlights of any tour of Angkor: Angkor Wat itself and the city of Angkor Thom. The classical appellation conjures up

Portrait of Jayavarman VII, now housed in the National Museum in Phnom Penh.

ANGKOR

Angkorian Monarchs

A mind-numbing array of kings ruled the Khmer Empire from the 9th century to the 14th century. The following list includes the dates they reigned and the more significant monuments built during their time.

King	Dates of Reign	Temple
Jayavarman II	802-850	
Jayavarman III	850-877	
Indravarman I	877-889	Preah Ko, Bakong (Roluos)
Yasovarman I	889-910	Lolei (Roluos), Bakheng
Harshavarman I	910-928	
Jayavarman IV	928-942	
Harshavarman II	942-944	
Rajendravarman II	944-968	Eastern Mebon, Pre Rup
		Phimeanakas
Jayavarman V	968-1001	Ta Keo, Banteay Srei
Udayadityavarman I	1001-1002	
Suryavarman I	1002-1049	
Udayadityavarman II	1049-1065	Baphuon, Western Mebon
Harshavarman III	1065-1090	
Jayavarman VI	1090-1108	
Dharanindravarman I	1108-1112	
Suryavarman II	1112-1152	Angkor Wat,
		Banteay Samré
Harshavarman IV	1152	
Dharanindravarman II	1152-1181	
Jayavarman VII	1181-1201	Angkor Thom, Ta Nei
		Preah Khan, Preah Palilay
		Ta Prohm, Banteay Kdei
Indravarman II	1201-1243	
Jayavarman VIII	1243-1295	
Sri-Indravarman	1295-1307	
Sri-Indrajayavarman	1307	
Jayavarman Paramesvara	mid-1300s	

images of a golden age of abundance and leisured temple construction. But while this period is marked by fits of remarkable productivity, it was also a time of much turmoil, of conquests and setbacks. The city of Angkor Thom, for example, owes its existence to the fact that the old city of Angkor that stood on the same spot was destroyed in an invasion.

There is much debate as to the origins of Suryavarman I (ruled 1002-1049) – he may have been of Malay origin, but is more likely to have hailed from a noble family in the north-east of Cambodia. He was a usurper to the throne who won the day through strategic alliances and military conquests. Although he adopted the Hindu cult of the god king, he is thought to have come from a Mahayana Buddhist background and may even have sponsored the growth of Buddhism in Cambodia. Certainly, Buddhist sculpture became more commonplace in the Angkor region during his time.

Little physical evidence of Suryavarman I's reign remains at Angkor, but his military exploits brought much of southern Thailand and southern Laos into the ambit of Angkorean control. His son, Udayadityavarman II (ruled 1049-1065), embarked on further military expeditions, extending the empire still farther. He built the Baphuon and the Western Mebon.

From 1065 until the end of the century, Angkor was again divided by various contenders for the throne. The first important monarch of the new regime, when it came to be founded, was Suryavarman II (ruled 1112-1152). Suryavarman II unified Cambodia and led campaigns against Vietnam, extending Khmer influence to Malaya, Myanmar (Burma) and Thailand. He also set himself apart religiously from earlier kings through his devotion to the Hindu deity Vishnu, to whom he devoted the largest and arguably the most magnificent of all the Angkor temples, Angkor Wat.

The reign of Suryavarman II and the construction of Angkor Wat marks one of the high-water marks of Khmer civilisation. But if decline was not inevitable, there were signs that it was waiting in the wings. It is thought that the hydraulic system of reservoirs and canals that supported the agriculture of Angkor had by this time probably been pushed beyond capacity. The construction of Angkor itself was a major strain on resources, and on top of this Suryavarman II led a disastrous campaign against Vietnam late in his reign.

In 1177, the Chams of southern Vietnam, long annexed by the kingdom of Angkor, rose up and sacked Angkor. They burned the wooden city and carried off its accumulated wealth. Four years later Jayavarman VII (ruled 1181-1201) struck back, driving the Chams out of Cambodia and reclaiming Angkor.

Jayavarman VII's reign has given scholars much to debate. It represents a radical departure from those of his predecessors. For centuries the fount of royal divinity had reposed in the Hindu deity Shiva (occasionally Vishnu). Jayavarman VII, however, adopted Mahayana Buddhism and looked to Avalokiteshvara, the Buddha of Compassion, for sponsorship of his reign. In doing so he may very likely have been converting to a religion that already enjoyed wide popular support among his subjects. It may also be that the destruction of Angkor was such a blow to royal divinity that a new religious foundation was thought to be needed.

In his reign Jayavarman VII embarked on a dizzying catalogue of temple projects centred around the Baphuon, which was the site of the city destroyed by the Chams. Angkor Thom, Jayavarman VII's new city, was surrounded by walls and a moat (which became another component of Angkor's complex irrigation system). The centrepiece of Angkor Thom was the Bayon, the temple mountain studded with faces that, along with Angkor Wat, is the most famous of the temples of Angkor. Other temples built during the reign of Jayavarman VII include Ta Prohm, Banteay Kdei and Preah Khan.

After the death of Jayavarman VII around 1220, the Khmer Empire went into decline. The Thais sacked Angkor in 1351, and in 1431 they sacked it again. The Khmer court moved to Phnom Penh.

Angkor Rediscovered

The French 'discovery' of Angkor in the 1860s made an international splash and created a great deal of interest in Cambodia. But 'discovery', with all the romance it implied, was something of a misnomer. For a start, as historian David Chandler points out, when French explorer Henri Mouhot first stumbled across Angkor Wat it was found to contain a 'prosperous monastery...tended by more than 1000 hereditary slaves'. What is more, Portuguese travellers in the 16th century seem to have come across Angkor, referring to it as the Walled City. A 17th-century Japanese pilgrim even drew a detailed plan of Angkor Wat, though he mistakenly concluded he had seen it in India and not in Cambodia.

Still, it was the publication of *Voyage à Siam et dans le Cambodge* by Mouhot in 1868 that first brought Angkor to the public eye. Although

The Bayon formed the centrepiece of Jayavarman VII's new city of Angkor Thom.

Sketch of Angkor by the French explorer Louis Delaporte, published in 1880 in Paris.

Mouhot himself made no such claims, by the 1870s he was being posthumously celebrated as the discoverer of the lost temple city of Cambodia. In fact, a French missionary known as Charles-Emile Bouillevaux had visited Angkor 10 years before Mouhot and published his own account of his findings. It was roundly ignored. It was Mouhot's account, with its rich descriptions and tantalising pen and ink colour sketches of Angkor that turned the ruins into an international craze.

From the time of Mouhot, Angkor became the target of financed French expeditions. A few individuals, such as John Thomson (a Scottish photographer who made the first photographs of the temples and was the first to posit the idea that the temples were symbolic representations of Mt Meru), managed to make their way to Angkor, but for the most part it was to be the preserve of French archeological teams.

The first of these expedition was led by Ernest Doudart de Lagrée and its principal mission was to determine whether the Mekong was navigable into China. Doudart de Lagrée died upstream in Yunnan, but not before taking his team on a detour to Angkor. The team assembled its findings at Angkor into *Voyage d'exploration en Indo-Chine*, which contained valuable archeological details concerning Angkor.

Louis Delaporte, who had joined Doudart de Lagrée on the first mission, led the second assault on Angkor. The aim was to produce plans of the monuments and return to France with examples of Angkorean art. Delaporte brought some 70 pieces back, and his sketches aroused the interest of some Parisian architects, who saw in the monuments of Angkor a bold clash of form and function. Lucien Fournereau, an architect, travelled to Angkor in 1887 and produced plans and meticulously executed cross-sections that were to stand as the best available until the 1960s.

In 1901 the École Française d'Extrême Orient began a long association with Angkor by funding an expedition to the Bayon. In 1907 Angkor, which had been under Thai control, was returned to Cambodia and École took responsibility for clearing and restoring the whole site. In the same year, the first tourists arrived in Angkor – an unprecedented 200 of them in three months. Angkor had been 'rescued' from the jungle and was assuming its place in the modern world.

ARCHAEOLOGY OF ANGKOR

Angkor Restored

With the exception of Angkor Wat, which was restored for use as a Buddhist shrine in the 16th century by the Khmer royalty, the monuments of Angkor had been left to the jungle for many centuries. A large number of the monuments were made of sandstone, which tends to dissolve in contact with dampness. Bat droppings took their toll, as too did sporadic pilfering of sculptures and cut stones. In the cases of some monuments, such as Ta Prohm, the jungle had stealthily waged an all-out invasion, and could only be removed at great risk to the structures it now supported in its web of roots.

Initial attempts to clear Angkor under the aegis of the École Française d'Extrême Orient were fraught with technical difficulties and theoretical disputes. On the technical front, the jungle tended to grow back as soon as it was cleared, and on a theoretical front scholars debated the extent to which temples should be restored and whether later additions (such as Buddha images in Hindu temples) should be removed.

It was not until the late 1920s that a solution came along. It was the method the Dutch had used to restore Borobudur in Java and it was called anastylosis. Simply, it was a method of reconstructing monuments with the original materials used and in keeping with the original form of the structure. New materials were only permitted where the originals could not be found and were to be used discreetly. An example of this method can be seen on the right side of the causeway leading to the entrance of Angkor Wat – it is largely the result of French restoration work.

The first major restoration job was carried out on Banteay Srei in the 1930s. It was deemed such a success that more extensive restoration work was undertaken elsewhere around Angkor, a project that culminated in a massive restoration job on Angkor Wat in the 1960s. Cranes and earth-moving machines were brought to bear, and the operation was backed by an armoury of surveying equipment.

The Khmer Rouge victory and Cambodia's subsequent slide into civil war resulted in far less damage to Angkor than many had assumed. Nevertheless, turmoil in Cambodia resulted in a long interruption of restoration work, allowing the jungle to grow back and once again resume its assault on the monuments. The illegal trade of *objets d'art* on the world art market has also been a major threat to Angkor, and still remains so to a certain extent. Angkor has been under the jurisdiction of the United Nations Educational Scientific and Cultural Organisation (UNESCO) since 1992 as a World Heritage Site, and international and local efforts continue to preserve and reconstruct the monuments.

ANGKOR

An 1868 engraving by Louis Delaporte showing the encroaching jungle at Angkor Thom.

ARCHITECTURAL STYLES

From the time of the earliest Angkorean monuments at Roluos, Khmer architecture was continually evolving, often from the rule of one king to the next. Archaeologists therefore divide the monuments of Angkor into nine separate periods, each named after the foremost example of the art style in question.

Periods of Angkorean Architecture

Preah Ko style	875-893
Bakheng style	893-925
Koh Ker style	921-945
Pre Rup style	947-965
Banteay Srei style	967-1000
Kleang style	965-1010
Baphuon style	1010-1080
Angkor Wat style	1100-1175
Bayon style	1177-1230

To a certain extent, however, the evolution of Khmer architecture was the elaboration of a central theme: the idea of the temple mountain. The earlier a temple was constructed the closer it adheres to this fundamental idea. Essentially the mountain was represented by a blunt-topped tower mounted on a tiered base. At the summit was the central sanctuary, usually with an open door to the east, and three false doors at the remaining cardinal points of the compass.

By the time of the Bakheng period, this layout was being embellished. The summit of the central tower for example was crowned with five 'peaks', in a quincunx arrangement – four cells at the points of the compass and one in the centre. Even Angkor Wat features this layout, though on a grand scale. Other features that came to be favoured included an entry tower and a causeway lined with *naga* (snake) balustrades or sculpture leading up to the temple.

As the temples grew in ambition, the central tower, although the focus of the temple, became a less prominent feature. Courtyards enclosed by colonnaded galleries, with the galleries themselves richly decorated, came to surround the central tower. Smaller towers were placed on gates and on the corners of walls, their overall number generally having a religious or astrological significance.

These refinements and additions culminate in Angkor Wat, which effectively showcases the evolution of Angkorean architecture. The architecture of the Bayon period breaks with tradition to a certain extent in temples such as Ta Prohm and Preah Khan, in which the horizontal layout of galleries, corridors and courtyards seem to completely eclipse the central tower.

The curious narrowness of the corridors and doorways in these structures can be explained by the fact that Angkorean architects only made arches by laying blocks on top of each other, until they met at a central point. These are known as false arches; they can only support very short spans.

INFORMATION

Visitor Fees

Entrance fees to Angkor have finally settled to affordable levels. Visitors now have a choice of a one-day pass (US$20), a three-day pass (US$40) or a one-week pass (US$60). This gives you access to all the monuments of Angkor besides Banteay Srei, which is subject to separate rules due to security problems.

Passes are organised by the 'guide', which for most travellers is their moto or taxi driver.

Organised Tours

One-day tours to Angkor do not give you very long to explore the ruins. They can be booked by tour agencies in Phnom Penh for around US$250; this includes the return flight, entry fees, guide, transport and lunch. Two-day, one-night tours cost US$350 to US$400; three days and two nights cost US$400 to US$450. The increasing flight frequency between Phnom Penh and Siem Reap makes tours easier to schedule but they are heavily booked.

Itineraries

The chief attractions of Angkor can be summed up in Angkor Wat, the 'city' of Angkor Thom (principally the Bayon) and Ta Prohm, which has famously been left to the jungle. On a short visit to Angkor, you might restrict your sightseeing to these three attractions – attempting too much is likely to reduce the whole experience to a whirl of impressions.

A curious lore of itineraries and times for visiting the monuments has coalesced around Angkor since tourism first got started in the 1920s. It is received wisdom that as Angkor Wat faces west, one should be there for sunset, and in the case of the Bayon, which faces east, at sunrise. Ta Prohm, most people seem to agree, can be visited in the middle of the day because of its umbrella of foliage. This is all well and good: Angkor Wat is indeed stunning at sunset; the Bayon is a good place to be for sunrise if you can get out of bed on time. Reverse the order, however, and the temples will still look good – and you'll miss the crowds.

Back in the early days of tourism, the problem of what to see and in what order was left to two basic temple courses: the Little (petit) Circuit and the Big (grand) Circuit. It's difficult to imagine that anyone follows these to the letter any more, but in their time they were an essential component of the Angkor experience and were often undertaken on the back of an elephant.

Little Circuit The 17-km Little Circuit began at Angkor Wat, headed northward to Phnom Bakheng, Baksei Chamkrong and Angkor Thom (in which one visited the city wall and gates, the Bayon, the Baphuon, the Royal Enclosure, Phimeanakas, Preah Palilay, Tep Pranam, the Preah Pithu group, the Terrace of the Leper King, the Terrace of Elephants, the Central Square, the North Kleang, the South Kleang and the 12 Prasats Suor Prat), exited from Angkor Thom via Victory Gate (in the eastern wall), continued to Chau Say Tevoda, Thommanon, Spean Thma and Ta Keo, went north-east of the road to Ta Nei, turned southward to Ta Prohm, continued east to Banteay Kdei and the Sras Srang, and finally returned to Angkor Wat via Prasat Kravan.

The Giant's Causeway at Angkor Thom, part of the Little Circuit at Angkor.

Big Circuit The 26-km Big Circuit was an extension of the Little Circuit: where the latter exited at the east gate of Angkor Thom, the Big Circuit exited at the north gate and continued to Preah Khan and Preah Neak Pean on its way eastward to Ta Som. From here it headed south via the Eastern Mebon to Pre Rup, whence it went westward and then south-westward back to Angkor Wat.

One Day If you only have one day to visit Angkor a good itinerary would be the Bayon for sunrise (or early morning), and a tour of the other attractions of Angkor Thom, before heading over to Ta Prohm late in the morning or early in the afternoon. From here you might visit Ta Keo and then the gate of Angkor Thom en route to Angkor Wat for the last two or three hours before sunset.

Two Days A two-day itinerary might be very similar to the one above, but with more time to explore the temples. Possible additions would be a late afternoon at Phnom Bakheng, which provides a hilly overview of the sunset at Angkor Wat and Preah Khan, which is in a good state of repair but sees less visitors than many of the other main temples.

Three Days or More If you have three days or more to explore Angkor, you should be able to see most of the important sites described in this chapter. One way to approach a three-day tour of Angkor is to see as much as possible on the first day (as in the One-Day entry above) and then spend the next two days in a combination of visiting other sites such as Roluos and revisiting the places you liked best on the first day.

Maps

Quite a number of excellent maps of the Angkor area have been published over the years. Angkor Tourism sells a good one reproduced from the Henri Parmentier guidebook. The May 1982 issue of *National Geographic* magazine has an excellent map showing Angkor in its prime.

ANGKOR WAT

Angkor Wat is the largest and undoubtedly the most breathtaking of the monuments of Angkor. It is also the best preserved, and never fails to reward repeat visits with previously unnoticed details. It was probably constructed as a funerary temple for Suryavarman II (ruled 1112 to 1152) to honour Vishnu, the Hindu deity who the king identified himself with.

There is much about Angkor Wat that is unique among the temples of Angkor. The most significant point is its westward orientation. West is symbolically the direction of death, which once led many scholars to conclude that Angkor Wat was primarily a tomb. This was supported by the fact that the magnificent bas reliefs of Angkor Wat were designed to be viewed in an anti-clockwise direction, a practice which has antecedents in Hindu funerary rites. Vishnu, however, is often associated with the west, and it is commonly accepted nowadays that Angkor Wat was probably both a temple and a mausoleum for Suryavarman II.

Symbolism

The casual visitor to Angkor Wat is struck by its imposing grandeur, and at close quarters its fascinating decorative flourishes and extensive bas

Print of the galleries of Angkor Wat by H Clerget, published in 1873.

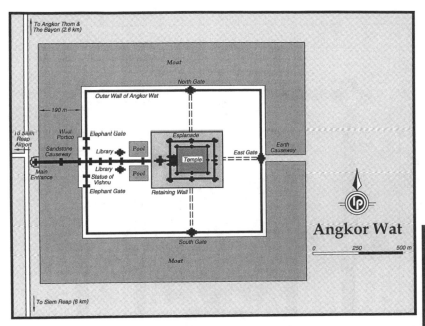

To Angkor Thom &
The Bayon (2.6 km)

Moat

North Gate

Outer Wall of Angkor Wat

— 190 m —

To Siem
Reap
Airport

Wat
Portico

Elephant Gate

Esplanade

Earth
Causeway

Sandstone
Causeway

Library

Pool

East Gate

Temple

Main
Entrance

Library
Statue of
Vishnu

Pool

Elephant Gate

Retaining Wall

South Gate

Moat

To Siem Reap (6 km)

Angkor Wat

0   250   500 m

reliefs. But a scholar at the time of its construction would have revelled at its multilayered levels of meaning in much the same way as a contemporary literary scholar might delight in James Joyce's *Ulysses*.

David Chandler, drawing on the research of Eleanor Moron, points out in his *History of Cambodia* that the spatial dimensions of Angkor Wat parallels the lengths of the four ages, or *yuga*, of classical Hindu thought. Thus the visitor to Angkor who walks the causeway to the main entrance and through this into the courtyards to the final main tower, which once contained a statue of Vishnu, is metaphorically travelling back in time to the first age of the creation of universe.

Of course, like the other temple mountains of Angkor, Angkor Wat also replicates the spatial universe in miniature. The central tower is Mt Meru, with its surrounding smaller peaks, surrounded in turn by continents (the lower courtyards) and the oceans (the surrounding moat). In the central tower, the king prefigures the heaven that awaits him after death, the lofty peak where *apsaras* (heavenly nymphs) frolic with boundless amorous desire.

Architectural Layout

Angkor Wat is surrounded by a moat, 190m wide, that forms a giant rectangle measuring 1.5 by 1.3 km. From the west, a sandstone causeway crosses the moat; the holes in the paving stones held wooden pegs that were used to lift and position the stones during construction, after which the pegs were sawed off. The sandstone blocks from which Angkor Wat was built were apparently quarried many km away (perhaps at Phnom Kulen) and floated down the Siem Reap River on rafts.

ANGKOR

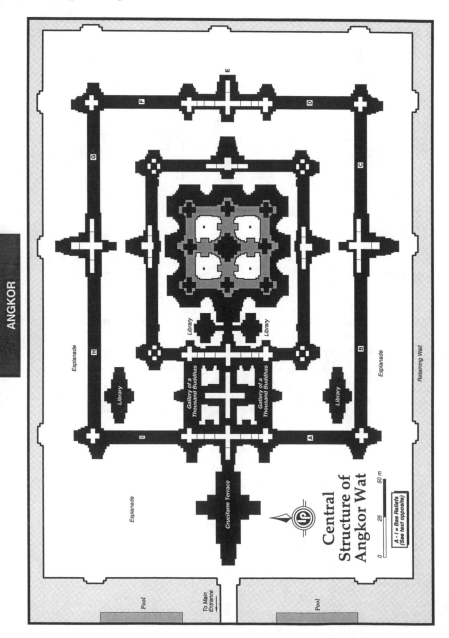

Central
Structure of
Angkor Wat

A - I = Bas Reliefs
(See text opposite)

0   25   50 m

Angkor Bas Reliefs

Stretching around the outside of the central temple complex, which is enclosed by an esplanade framed by a naga balustrade, is an 800m-long series of extraordinary bas reliefs. The carvings were once sheltered by the cloister's wooden roof, which long ago rotted away (except for one original beam in the western half of the northern gallery; the other roofed sections are reconstructions). The following is a brief description of the epic events depicted on the panels in the Gallery of Bas Reliefs. They are described in the order in which you'll come to them if you begin on the west side and keep the bas reliefs to your left.

Detail from the Churning of the Ocean of Milk, the most famous of Angkor Wat's bas reliefs.

A) Battle of Kurukshetra The southern portion of the west gallery depicts a battle scene from the Hindu Mahabarata epic in which the Kauravas (coming from the north) and the Pandavas (coming from the south) advance in serried ranks towards each other, meeting in furious battle. Infantry are shown on the lowest tier, officers on elephant-back and chiefs on the 2nd and 3rd tiers. Among the more interesting details (from left to right): a dead chief lying on a pile of arrows and surrounded by his grieving parents and troops; a warrior on an elephant who has, by putting down his weapon, accepted defeat; and a mortally wounded officer, falling from the conveyance in which he is riding into the arms of his soldiers. Over the centuries, some sections have been polished by millions of hands to look like black marble. The portico at the south-west corner is decorated with sculptures representing subjects taken from the *Ramayana*.

B) Army of Suryavarman II The remarkable western section of the south gallery depicts a triumphal battle march of Suryavarman II's army. In the south-west corner about two metres from the floor is Suryavarman II himself on an elephant, wearing the royal tiara and armed with a battle-axe; he is shaded by 15 umbrellas and fanned by legions of servants. Farther on is a procession of well-armed soldiers and officers on horseback; among them march elephants carrying their chiefs, whose bearing is bold and warlike. Just west of the vestibule is the rather disorderly Thai mercenary army, at that time allied with the Khmers in their conflict with the Chams. The Khmer troops have square breastplates and are armed with spears, the Thais wear headdresses and skirts and carry tridents.

The rectangular holes were created when, long ago, pieces of the scene – reputed to possess magical powers – were removed. Part of this panel was damaged by an artillery shell in 1971.

C) Heaven & Hell The eastern half of the south gallery, the ceiling of which was restored in the 1930s, depicts the punishments and rewards of the 37 heavens and 32 hells. On the left, the upper and middle tiers show fine gentlemen and ladies proceeding towards 18-armed Yama, judge of the dead, seated on a bull; below him are his assistants, Dharma and Sitragupta. On the lower tier is the road to hell, along which wicked people are being dragged by devils. To Yama's right, the tableau is divided into two parts separated by a horizontal line of garudas: above, the elect dwell in beautiful mansions,

ANGKOR

served by women, children and attendants; below, the condemned suffer horrible tortures.

D) Churning of the Ocean of Milk The south section of the east gallery is decorated by the most famous of the bas-relief scenes at Angkor Wat, the Churning of the Ocean of Milk. This brilliantly executed carving depicts 88 *asuras* (devils; on the left) and 92 *devas* (gods) with crested helmets (on the right), churning up the sea to extract the elixir of immortality, which both groups covet. The demons hold the head of the serpent and the gods hold its tail. At the centre of the sea, the serpent is coiled around Mt Mandala, which in the tug of war between the demons and the gods turns and churns up the water. Vishnu, incarnated as a huge turtle, lends his shell to serve as the base and pivot of Mt Mandala. Brahma, Shiva, Hanuman, the monkey god, and Lakshmi, the goddess of beauty, all make appearances, while overhead a host of heavenly female spirits sing and dance in encouragement.

E) Elephant Gate This gate, which has no stairs leading to it, was used by the king and others for mounting and dismounting elephants directly from the gallery. North of the gate is a Khmer inscription recording the erection of a nearby stupa in the 18th century.

F) Vishnu Conquers the Demons The northern section of the east gallery shows a furious and desperate encounter between Vishnu, riding on a garuda, and innumerable *danavas* (demons). Needless to say, he slays all comers. Scholars conjecture that this gallery was executed at a later date, perhaps in the 15th or 16th century.

G) Krishna & the Demon King The eastern section of the north gallery shows Vishnu incarnated as Krishna riding a garuda. He confronts a burning walled city, the residence of Bana the demon king. The Garuda puts out the fire and Bana is captured. In the final scene Krishna kneels before Shiva and asks that Bana's life be spared.

H) Battle of the Gods & the Demons The western section of the north gallery depicts the battle of the 21 gods of the Brahmanic pantheon with various demons. The gods are featured with their traditional attributes and mounts. Vishnu, for example has four arms and is seated on a garuda, while Shiva rides a sacred goose.

I) Battle of Lanka The northern half of the west gallery shows scenes from the *Ramayana*. In the Battle of Lanka, Rama (on the shoulders of the monkey-god Hanuman), along with his army of monkeys, battles 10-headed Havana, seducer of Hama's beautiful wife Sita. Ravana rides on a chariot drawn by monsters and commands an army of giants. ■

Intricate designs and patterns are a feature of Angkor Wat's bas reliefs.

MICK ELMORE

The rectangular wall around the enclosure, which measures 1025 by 800m, has a gate in each side, but the main entrance, a 235m-wide porch richly decorated with carvings and sculptures, is on the western side. In the gate tower to the right as you approach is a statue of Vishnu, 3.25m in height, hewn from a single block of sandstone; its eight arms hold a mace, a spear, a disk, a conch shell and other items. The locks of hair you see lying about have been cut off as an offering either by young women and men preparing to get married or by people who seek to give thanks for their good fortune (such as having recovered from an illness).

An avenue, 475m long and 9.5m wide and lined with naga balustrades, leads from the main entrance to the central temple, passing between two graceful libraries and then two pools.

The central temple complex consists of three storeys, each of laterite which encloses a square surrounded by intricately interlinked galleries. The corners of the 2nd and 3rd storeys are marked by towers topped with pointed cupolas. Rising 31m above the 3rd level and 55m above the ground is the central tower, which gives the whole ensemble its sublime unity. At one time, the central sanctuary of Angkor Wat held a gold statue of Vishnu mounted on a garuda (half-eagle, half-human) that represented the deified god-king Suryavarman II.

Built between 1112-1153, Angkor Wat is considered by many to be one of the most spectacular monuments ever conceived.

ANGKOR

ANGKOR THOM

The fortified city of Angkor Thom, some 10 sq km in extent, was built by Angkor's greatest king, Jayavarman VII (ruled 1181 to 1201), who came to power just after the disastrous sacking by the Chams of the previous Khmer capital. Centred around the Baphuon, Angkor Thom is enclosed by a square wall eight metres high and 12 km in length and encircled by a moat 100m wide, said to have been inhabited by fierce crocodiles.

The city has five monumental gates, one in the north, west and south walls and two in the east wall. The gates, which are 20m in height, are decorated to either side of the passageway with stone elephant trunks and crowned by four gargantuan faces of the bodhisattva Avalokiteshvara facing the cardinal directions. In front of each gate, there stood giant

ANGKOR

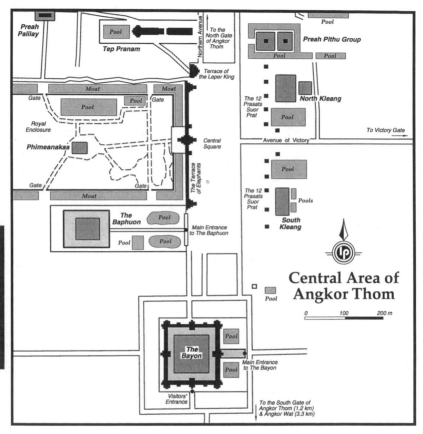

Central Area of Angkor Thom

statues of 54 gods (to the left of the causeway) and 54 demons (to the right of the causeway), a motif taken from the story of the Churning of the Ocean of Milk illustrated in the famous bas relief at Angkor Wat. In the centre of the walled enclosure are the city's most important monuments, including the Bayon, the Baphuon, the Royal Enclosure, Phimeanakas and the Terrace of Elephants.

The Bayon

The Bayon takes an easy second place after Angkor Wat as the most popular of Angkor's many monuments. It's a kind of Buddhism meets Gormenghast, a place of stooped corridors, precipitous flights of stairs, and most of all a collection of 54 gothic towers decorated with over 200 icily smiling, gargantuan faces of Avalokiteshvara. As you walk around, a dozen or more of the visages are visible at any one time – full-face or in profile, almost level with your eyes or peering down from on high.

The Bayon is now known to have been built by Jayavarman VII, though for many years its origins were obscure. Shrouded in dense jungle, it also took researchers some time to realise that it stands in the exact centre of the city of Angkor Thom. There is still much mystery associated with the Bayon – its exact function and symbolism – and this seems only appropriate for a monument whose signature is an enigmatically smiling face.

The eastward orientation of the Bayon leads most people to visit it early in the morning, preferably at sunrise, when the sun inches upwards lighting face after face with warmth. The Bayon, however, looks equally good in the late afternoon, and if you stay for the sunset you get the same effect as at sunrise, in reverse.

Architectural Layout

Unlike Angkor Wat, which looks impressive both close up and from a distance, the Bayon looks like a muddle of rock from a distance. It's only when you get inside the place, and make your way up to the third level that the magic of the temple gets to do its work.

The basic structure of the Bayon is a simple one of three levels, which correspond more or less to three distinct phases of building. The first two levels are square and adorned with bas reliefs. They lead up to a 3rd circular level, which is where you will find the towers and the faces. The central sanctuary of the 3rd level is a cavelike cell in a massive, round upheaval of intricately embellished rock.

ANGKOR

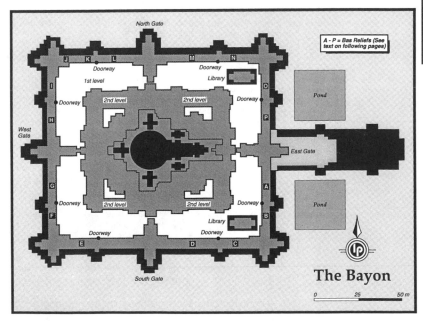

The Bayon

Scene from a bas relief at the Bayon depicting a cockfight in the 12th century.

The Bayon Bas Reliefs

The Bayon is decorated with 1200m of extraordinary bas reliefs incorporating over 11,000 figures. The famous carvings on the outer wall of the 1st level depict vivid scenes of everyday life in 12th century Cambodia. The bas reliefs on the 2nd level do not have the epic proportions of those on the 1st level or the ones at Angkor, and tend to be fragmented. The reliefs described in this section are those on the 1st level. The sequence assumes that you enter the Bayon by the east entrance and view the reliefs in a clockwise direction, with the wall to your right.

A) Just south of the east gate is a three-level panorama. On the 1st tier, Khmer soldiers march off to battle; notice the elephants and the ox carts, which are almost exactly like those still in use. The 2nd tier depicts the coffins being carried from the battlefield. In the centre of the 3rd tier, Jayavarman VII, shaded by parasols, is shown on horseback followed by legions of concubines (to the left).

B) The first panel north of the south-east corner shows Hindus praying to a linga. This image was probably originally a Buddha, later modified by a Hindu king.

C) This panel has some of the best carved reliefs. The scenes are combinations of naval battles between the Khmers and the Chams (with head coverings) and pictures of everyday life by the shores of the Tonlé Sap Lake, where the battle was fought. Look out for images of people picking lice from each other's hair, of hunters hunting, and towards the western end of the panel a woman giving birth.

D) In this panel the scenes from daily life continue and the naval battle shifts to the shore; the Chams are given a thorough thrashing by the Khmers. Scenes include two people playing chess (or a similar board game), a cockfight, women selling fish in the market. The later scenes of meals being prepared and served are in celebration of the Khmer victory over the Chams.

E) The last section of the south gallery is unfinished, depicting a military procession.

F) Again the panel here is unfinished. Elephants are being brought in from the mountains. Brahmans have been chased up two trees by tigers.

G) This panel depicts scenes that some scholars maintain is a civil war. Groups of people, some armed, confront each other, and the violence escalates until elephants and warriors join the melee.

H) The fighting continues on a smaller scale. At the bottom, an antelope is being swallowed by a gargantuan fish. Among the smaller fish is a prawn, under which an inscription says that the king will seek out those in hiding.

I) This panel depicts a procession that includes the king (carrying a bow). Presumably it is a celebration of his victory.

J) At the western corner of the north wall is a Khmer circus. You can see a strong man holding three dwarfs and a man on his back spinning a wheel with his feet; above, there is a group of tightrope walkers. To the right of the circus, the royal court watches the goings-on from a terrace, below which a procession of animals is marching. Some of the reliefs in this section remain unfinished.

K) The two rivers, one next to the doorpost and the other three metres to the right, are teeming with fish.

L) On the lowest level of this unfinished three-tiered scene, the Cham armies are being defeated and expelled from the Khmer kingdom.

M) The Cham armies are shown advancing.

N) This badly deteriorated panel shows the Chams (on the left) chasing the Khmers.

O) This panel shows the war of 1177, when the Khmers were defeated by the Chams and Angkor itself was pillaged. The wounded Khmer king is being lowered from the back of an elephant and a wounded Khmer general is being carried on a hammock suspended from a pole. Directly above, despairing Khmers are getting drunk. The Chams (on the right) are in hot pursuit of their vanquished enemy.

P) Another meeting of the two armies. Notice the flag-bearers among the Cham troops (on the right). The Chams were defeated in the war which ended in 1181, as depicted on panel A. ■

ANGKOR

Built around 1200, the Bayon represents a change in design and construction from the earlier Angkor Wat.

CHRIS TAYLOR

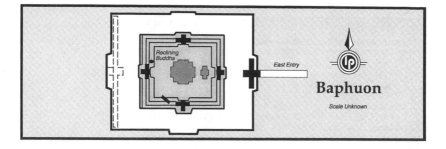

The Baphuon

The Baphuon, a pyramidal representation of the mythical Mt Meru, is 200m north-west of the Bayon. It was constructed by Udayadityavarman II (reigned 1049 to 1065) and marked the centre of the city that existed before the construction of Angkor Thom.

The Baphuon is in pretty poor shape, and at the time of writing restoration work is under way. It is approached by a 200m elevated walkway made of sandstone. The central structure is 43m high, but unfortunately its summit has collapsed (this may be restored).

On the west side of the temple, the retaining wall of the 2nd level was fashioned – apparently in the 15th century – into a reclining Buddha 40m in length. The unfinished figure is a bit difficult to make out, but the head is on the northern side of the wall and the gate is where the hips should be; to the left of the gate protrudes an arm. When it comes to the legs and feet – the latter are entirely gone – imagination must suffice.

The Royal Enclosure & Phimeanakas

1911 cross-section of Phimeanakas published in the Inventaire Descriptif des Monuments du Cambodge.

Phimeanakas stands close to the centre of a walled area that once housed the royal palace, not that there's anything left of it today besides two sandstone pools near the northern wall. Once the site of royal

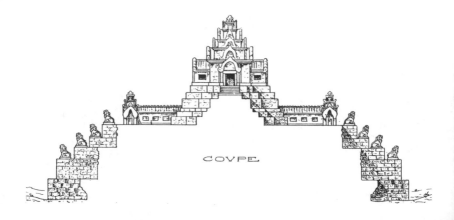

COVPE.

ablutions, these are now used as swimming holes by local children. It is fronted, to the east, by the Terrace of Elephants. The Palace was used by Jayavarman V and Udayadityavarman I.

Phimeanakas means 'Celestial Palace', and an account of it by the Chinese envoy Chou Takuan (Zhou Daguan) has led some scholars to argue that it was once topped by a golden spire. Today it only hints at its former splendour, looking a little the worse for wear.

The temple is another pyramidal representation of Mt Meru with three levels. Most of the decorative features of the temple are broken or have disappeared. Still, it is worth trudging up to the 2nd and 3rd levels (the stairs to the 3rd level are steep) for good views of the Baphuon.

Preah Palilay

Preah Palilay, a rather deteriorated temple 200m north of the northern wall of the Royal Enclosure, was erected during the time of Jayavarman VII (ruled 1181 to 1201). It originally housed a Buddha, which has long since disappeared.

Tep Pranam

Tep Pranam, an 82 by 34m cruciform Buddhist terrace 150m east of Preah Palilay, was once the base of a pagoda of lightweight construction. Nearby is a Buddha 4.5 metres in height – it is a reconstruction of the original. Some Buddhist nuns live in a wooden structure close by.

The Preah Pithu Group

Preah Pithu, which is across the Northern Avenue from Tep Pranam, is a group of five 12th-century Hindu and Buddhist temples enclosed by a wall.

The Terrace of the Leper King

The Terrace of the Leper King, just north of the Terrace of Elephants, is a platform seven metres in height. On top of the platform stands a nude, though sexless, statue. It is another of Angkor's mysteries. The original of the statue is in Phnom Penh's National Museum, and various theories have been advanced to explain its meaning. Legend has it that at least two of the Angkor kings had leprosy, and the statue may represent one of them. A more likely explanation is that the statue is of Yama, the god of death, and that the Terrace of the Leper King housed the royal crematorium.

The front retaining walls of the terrace are decorated with five or more tiers of meticulously executed carvings of seated apsaras; other figures include kings wearing pointed diadems, armed with short double-edged swords and accompanied by the court and princesses, who are adorned with rows of pearls. The terrace, built at the end of the 12th century, between the construction of Angkor Wat and the Bayon, once supported a pavilion made of lightweight materials.

On the south side of the Terrace of the Leper King (facing the Terrace

The Terrace of the Leper King features some exceptional carvings from the 12th century.

of Elephants) there is an entryway to a long, narrow trench, excavated by archaeologists. This passageway follows the front wall of an earlier terrace that was covered up when the present structure was built. The four tiers of apsaras and other figures, including nagas (five, seven, nine or even 11-headed snakes), look as fresh as if they had been carved just yesterday.

The Terrace of Elephants

The 350m-long Terrace of Elephants was used as a giant reviewing stand for public ceremonies and served as a base for the king's grand audience hall. As you stand here, try to imagine the pomp and grandeur of the Khmer Empire at its height, with infantry, cavalry, horse-drawn chariots and elephants parading across the Central Square in a colourful procession, pennants and standards aloft. Looking on is the god-king, crowned with a gold diadem, shaded by multi-tiered parasols and attended by mandarins and handmaidens bearing gold and silver utensils.

The Terrace of Elephants has five outworks extending towards the Central Square, three in the centre and one at each end. The middle section of the retaining wall is decorated with life-size garudas and lions; towards either end are the two parts of the famous parade of elephants.

The Kleangs & the 12 Prasats Suor Prat

Along the east side of the Central Square are two groups of buildings, the North Kleang and the South Kleang, that may at one time have been palaces. The North Kleang dates from the period of Jayavarman V (reigned 968 to 1001).

Along the Central Square in front of the two Kleangs are 12 laterite towers – 10 in a row and two more at right angles facing the Avenue of Victory – known as the Prasats Suor Prat. Archaeologists believe the towers, which form an honour guard of sorts along the Central Square, were constructed by Jayavarman VII (reigned 1181 to 1201). It is likely that each one originally contained either a linga or a statue.

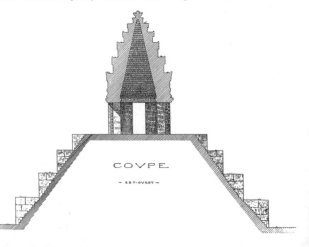

COVPE

– EST-OVEST –

Cross-section of Baksei Chamkrong, published in the 1911 Inventaire Descriptif des Monuments du Cambodge.

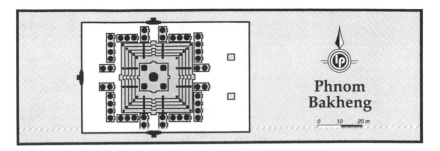

Phnom Bakheng

0   10   20 m

AROUND ANGKOR THOM

Baksei Chamkrong

Located a bit south-west of the south gate of Angkor Thom, Baksei Chamkrong is one of the few brick edifices in the immediate vicinity of Angkor. It was once decorated with a covering of mortar of lime. Like virtually all the structures of Angkor, it opens to the east. In the early 10th century, Harshavarman I erected in this temple five statues: two of Shiva, one of Vishnu and two of Devi.

Phnom Bakheng

Around 400m south of Angkor Thom, the main attraction of Phnom Bakheng is the sunset view of Angkor Wat. Unfortunately (but inevitably) the whole affair has turned into something of a circus, with crowds of tourists gasping up the steep slope of the hill pestered all the way by nimble-footed soft-drink vendors. To get a decent picture of Angkor Wat in the warm glow of the late afternoon sun you will need a 300 mm lens and a tripod, as the temple is 1.3 km away. Still, the sunset over the Tonlé Sap Lake is very impressive from up on the hill.

Phnom Bakheng is also home to the first of the temple mountains built in the near vicinity of Angkor. Yasovarman I (ruled 889 to 910) chose Phnom Bakheng over the Roluos area, where previous temples had been built.

Bakheng is a five-tiered temple mountain with seven levels including the base and the summit. At the base are (or were) 44 towers. Each of the five tiers had 12 towers. The summit of the temple has four towers at the cardinal points of the compass as well as a Central Sanctuary. All these numbers are of symbolic significance. The seven levels, for example, represent the seven Hindu heavens, while the total number of towers, excluding the Central Sanctuary, is 108, a particularly auspicious number and one which correlates to the lunar calendar.

Prasat Kravan

The five brick towers of Prasat Kravan, which are arranged in a north-south line and oriented to the east, were built for Hindu worship in 921. It's unusual in that it was not constructed by royalty and this accounts for its slightly remote location, away from the centre of the capital. Prasat Kravan is just south of the road between Angkor Wat and Banteay Kdei.

The group was partially restored in 1968 and is notable for the bas reliefs cut into the bricks on the interior walls. The images in the largest central tower show eight-armed Vishnu on the back wall, taking the three gigantic steps with which he reclaimed the world on the left wall and riding a garuda on the right wall. The northern-most of the towers has reliefs of Vishnu's consort, Lakshmi.

One of Vishnu's best-loved incarnations was as the dwarf Vamana who reclaimed the world from the demon-king Bali. The dwarf politely asked the demon for a patch of ground upon which to meditate, saying that the patch need only be big enough that he, the dwarf, could walk across it in three paces. The demon agreed, only to see the dwarf swell into a giant who strode across the universe in three mighty steps. From this legend Vishnu is sometimes known as the 'long strider'.

Banteay Kdei & the Sras Srang

Banteay Kdei, a massive Buddhist temple of the second half of the 12th century, is surrounded by four concentric walls. The outer wall measures 500 by 700m. Each of its four entrances is decorated with garudas which hold aloft one of Jayavarman VII's favourite themes, the four visages of Avalokiteshvara. The inside of the central tower was never finished.

Just east of Banteay Kdei is a basin of earlier construction, Sras Srang (Pool of Ablutions), measuring 800 by 400m. A tiny island in the middle once bore a wooden temple, of which only the stone base remains.

There is a mass grave of hundreds of victims of the Khmer Rouge a bit north of Sras Srang on the other side of the road. It is marked by a wooden memorial.

Ta Prohm

Ta Prohm rates with Angkor Wat and the Bayon as one of the most popular attractions of Angkor. Its appeal lies in the fact that, unlike the other monuments of Angkor, it has been left to the jungle, and looks very much the way most of the monuments of Angkor appeared when European explorers first stumbled upon them.

This deliberate neglect has not been without controversy. As long ago as 1942 the French restorer Maurice Glaize lashed out at the sentiments that justify the neglect of Ta Prohm, arguing:

The tourist...who travels in style and comfort to visit ruins where he expects to experience the exhilaration of Mouhot discovering Angkor Wat in 1860...is driven by an outdated individualism, and all that counts for him is a romanticism fuelled by spectacular effects, as symbolised by a section of wall crumbling in the passionate tentacled embrace of voracious trees.

Don't say you weren't warned. But ideological qualms aside, Ta Prohm is a unique other-world experience. The whole temple is cloaked in dappled shadow, its crumbling towers and walls locked in the slow muscular embrace of vast root systems. If Angkor Wat, the Bayon and other temples are testimony to the native genius of the Angkor-period

Lion standing guard near the Sras Srang.

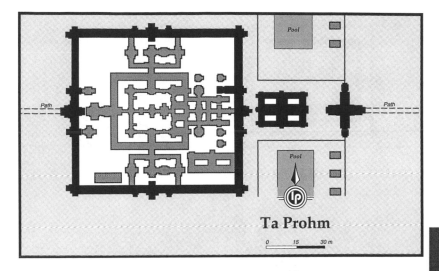

Ta Prohm

Khmers, Ta Prohm reminds us equally of the awesome fecundity and power of the jungle in which the Khmers centred their empire.

Built in approximately 1186, Ta Prohm was a Buddhist temple dedicated to the mother of Jayavarman VII. It is one of the few temples in Angkor where an inscription provides information about its dependents and inhabitants. The numbers are staggering: close on 80,000 people were required to maintain the temple, among them over 2700 officials and 615 dancers.

Ta Prohm is a temple of towers, close courtyards and narrow corridors. Many of the corridors impassable, clogged with jumbled piles of delicately carved stone blocks dislodged by the roots of long-decayed trees. Bas reliefs on bulging walls are carpeted by a dozen different kinds of lichen, moss and creeping plants; and shrubs sprout from the roofs of monumental porches. Trees, hundreds of years old – some supported by flying buttresses – tower overhead, their leaves filtering the sunlight and casting a greenish pall over the whole scene.

There are generally some children at Ta Prohm who, for a small tip, will show you around. This is one temple where it is well worth having a local guide. Most of the children know the best spots for photographs, and will lead you into courtyards you might spend all day trying to find otherwise.

Ta Keo

Ta Keo, built by Jayavarman V (ruled 968 to 1001), was dedicated to Shiva and was the first Angkorian monument built entirely in sandstone. The summit of the central tower, which is surrounded by four lower towers, is more than 50m high. This quincunx arrangement with four towers at the corners of a square and a fifth tower in the centre is typical of many Angkor 'temple mountains'.

The process of decorating Ta Keo's particularly hard sandstone was never completed and the temple has a Spartan feel compared to the lavish decoration of other Angkor monuments.

ANGKOR

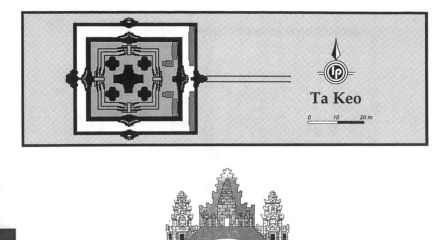

1911 cross-section of Ta Keo, published in the Inventaire Descriptif des Monuments du Cambodge.

Ta Nei

Ta Nei, 800m north of Ta Keo near the north-west corner of the Eastern Baray, was built by Jayavarman VII (ruled 1181 to 1201).

Spean Thma

The bridge of Spean Thma (the name means 'Stone Bridge'), of which an arch and several piers remain, is 200m east of Thommanon. It was one of the final projects for the last great builder of Angkor, Jayavarman VII and is the only large bridge in the vicinity of Angkor of which anything remains. Just north of the bridge is a large and surprisingly elegant water wheel.

Chau Say Tevoda

Just east of the Victory Gate on the east side of Angkor Thom, the Chau Say Tevoda is immediately south of the road. It was probably built during the second quarter of the 12th century and dedicated to Shiva and Vishnu.

Thommanon

The Thommanon Temple is just north of the Chau Say Tevoda and just north of the road. Although unique in itself, it reflects its neighbour as it was built around the same time and has a similar plan. The Thommanon is in much better condition than the rather ruinous Chau Say Tevoda. It was also dedicated to Shiva and Vishnu.

Preah Khan

The temple of Preah Khan ('Sacred Sword') is a good counterpoint to Ta Prohm, though it gets far less visitors. Preah Khan was built by Jayavarman VII (it may have served as his temporary residence while Angkor Thom was being built), and like Ta Prohm it is a place of towered enclosures and shoulder-hugging corridors. Unlike Ta Prohm, however, Preah Khan is in a reasonably good state of preservation, and ongoing restoration efforts should maintain and even improve this situation.

Preah Khan covers a very large area, but the temple itself is within a rectangular enclosing wall of around 700 by 800m. Four processional walkways approach the gates of the temple, and these are bordered by gods carrying a serpent, as in the approach to Angkor Thom. From the central sanctuary, four long vaulted galleries extend in the cardinal directions. Many of the interior walls of Preah Khan were once coated with plaster held in place by holes in the stone.

The main entrance to Preah Khan is, like most other Angkor temples, in the east, but standard practice is to enter at the west gate and walk from here to the north gate (your driver will automatically go to the north gate to wait for you). Be sure to walk the length of the temple to the east entrance before doubling back to the central sanctuary and making your way to the north entrance. The function of the two-storey structure just

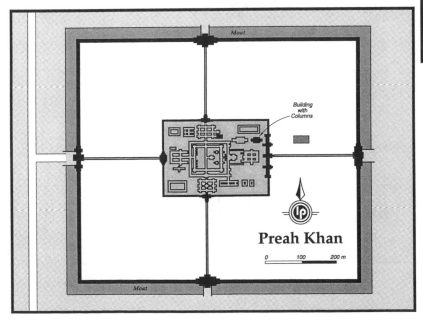

Preah Khan

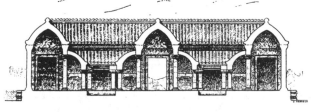

Sketch of Preah Khan's galleries, published in 1911 in the Inventaire Descriptif des Monuments du Cambodge.

inside the east entrance is unknown, but its columns give it an unexpected Mediterranean aspect.

Just north of Preah Khan is Banteay Prei, which dates from the same period.

Preah Neak Pean

The late 12th-century Buddhist temple of Preah Neak Pean (Intertwined Naga), which was built by Jayavarman VII (ruled 1181 to 1201), consists of a square pool with four smaller square pools arranged on each axis. In the centre of the large central pool is a circular 'island' encircled by the two nagas whose intertwined tails give the temple its name. Although it has been many centuries since the pools were last filled with water, it's easy for a modern visitor to envisage the complex as a huge swim-up bar at some fancy hotel.

In the pool around the central island there were once four statues but only one remains, reconstructed from the debris by the French archaeologists who cleared the site. The curious figure has the body of a horse

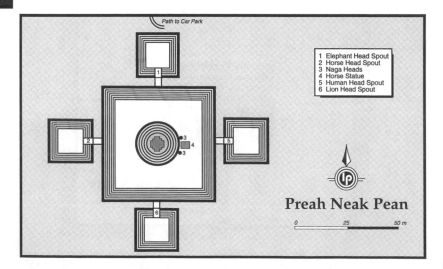

1 Elephant Head Spout
2 Horse Head Spout
3 Naga Heads
4 Horse Statue
5 Human Head Spout
6 Lion Head Spout

Preah Neak Pean

0   25   50 m

supported by a tangle of human legs. It relates to a legend that Avalokiteshvara once saved a group of shipwrecked followers from an island of ghouls by transforming himself into a flying horse.

Water once flowed from the central pool into the four peripheral pools via ornamental spouts which can still be seen in the pavilions at each axis of the pool. The spouts are in the form of an elephant's head, a horse's head, a lion's head and a human head. The pool was used for rites of ritual purification and the complex was originally in the centre of a huge three km by 900m lake, now dried up and overgrown.

Ta Som

Ta Som, which stands to the east of Preah Neak Pean, is yet another of the late 12th-century Buddhist temples of Jayavarman VII. Much of Ta Som is in a ruined state.

The Eastern Baray & the Eastern Mebon

The enormous one-time reservoir known as the Eastern Baray (Baray Oriental) was excavated by Yasovarman I (889 to 910), who marked its four corners with steles. This basin, the most important of the public works of Yasodharapura, Yasovarman I's capital, is seven by 1.8 km. It was fed by the Siem Reap River.

The temple known as the Eastern Mebon, erected by Rajendravarman (ruled 944 to 968), is on an islet in the centre of the Eastern Baray. This Hindu temple is very similar in design though smaller in size to the Pre Rup Temple, which was built 15 to 20 years later and lies immediately to the south. The temple mountain form is surmounted by the usual quincunx of towers. The elaborate brick shrines are dotted with neatly arranged holes which have given some observers the idea that they were once covered in metal plates. In fact, the towers were covered in plaster. The base of the temple is guarded at its corner by stone figures of harnessed elephants, some of which are still in a reasonable state of preservation.

Pre Rup

Pre Rup, built by Rajendravarman II (ruled 944 to 968), is about 1.5 km south of the Eastern Mebon. Like its nearby predecessor, the temple consists of a pyramid-shaped temple mountain with the uppermost of the three tiers carrying five square-shaped shrines arranged as a quincunx.

1911 cross-section of Pre Rup, published in the Inventaire Descriptif des Monuments du Cambodge.

ANGKOR

COUPE SUIVANT XY

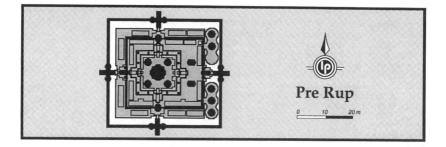

Pre Rup

0   10   20 m

Also like the Eastern Mebon, the brick sanctuaries were once decorated with a plaster coating, fragments of which remain on the south-west tower. There are some fine lintel carvings here.

Pre rup means 'turning the body' and refers to a traditional method of cremation in which the corpse's outline is traced in the cinders, first in one direction and then in the other. A legendary cremation is said to have taken place at this spot.

THE ROLUOS GROUP

The monuments of Roluos, which served as the capital of Indravarman I (reigned 877 to 889), are among the earliest large, permanent temples built by the Khmers and mark the beginning of Khmer classical art. Before the construction of Roluos, only lighter (and non-durable) construction materials had been employed, even for religious structures.

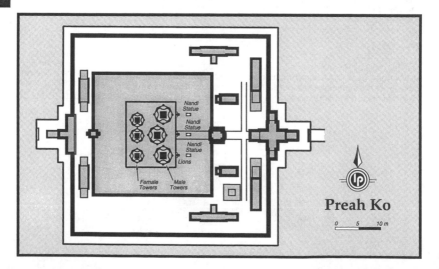

Preah Ko

0   5   10 m

The temples can be found 13 km east of Siem Reap along National Route 6. Preah Ko is 600m south of National Route 6 (to the right as you head away from Siem Reap); Bakong is 1.5 km south of National Route 6.

To get to Lolei from the turn-off to Preah Ko and Bakong, continue eastward for 400m, turn left (north-westward) and continue for half a km. There are modern-day Buddhist monasteries at Bakong and Lolei.

Preah Ko

Preah Ko was erected by Indravarman I in the late 9th century. The six brick towers *(prasats)*, aligned in two rows and decorated with carved sandstone and plaster reliefs, face eastward; the central tower of the front row is larger than the others. There are inscriptions in Sanskrit on the doorposts of each temple.

The temples of Preah Ko ('Sacred Ox') feature three Nandi – or sacred oxen – in front of the first row of temples. It was dedicated by Indravarman I to his deified ancestors in 880. The front towers relate to male ancestors or gods, the rear towers to female ancestors or goddesses. Lions guard the steps up to the temple platform.

Bakong

Bakong is the largest and most interesting of the Roluos Group temples, and has an active Buddhist monastery just to the north of the east entrance. It was built and dedicated to Shiva by Indravarman I, playing

ANGKOR

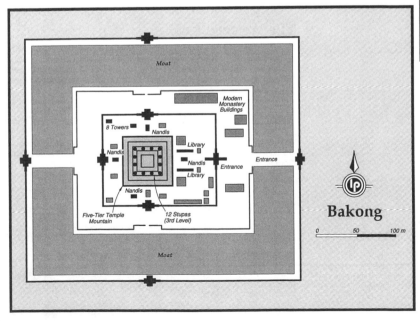

the same role for his capital of Hariharalaya as did Phnom Bakheng for Yasovarman I's Angkor. That is, it was built as a representation of Mt Meru and as such served as the city's central temple. The eastward-facing complex consists of a five-tier central pyramid of sandstone, 60m square at the base, flanked by eight towers (or what's left of them) of brick and sandstone and by other minor sanctuaries. Several of the eight towers down below are still partly covered by their original plasterwork.

The complex is enclosed by three concentric walls and a broad moat. Note the stone elephants on each corner of the first three levels of the central temple. There are 12 stupas – four to a side – on the 3rd tier. The sanctuary on the 5th level was a later addition. There is a modern Buddhist monastery at the north-east corner.

Lolei

The four brick towers of Lolei, an almost exact replica of the towers of Preah Ko although in much worse shape, were built on an islet in the centre of a large reservoir – now rice fields – by Yasovarman I (ruled 889 to 910), the founder of the first city at Angkor. The sandstone carvings in the niches of the temples are worth a look and there are Sanskrit inscriptions on the doorposts. According to one of the inscriptions, the four towers were dedicated by Yasovarman I to his mother, his father and his grandparents on his mother's side on 12 July 893.

OTHER AREAS

The Western Baray

The Western Baray (Baray Occidental), measuring eight by 2.3 km, was excavated to provide water for the intensive cultivation of lands around Angkor. In the centre of the basin is the Western Mebon, where the giant bronze statue of Vishnu, now in the National Museum in Phnom Penh, was found. It is accessible by boat.

Phnom Krom

The temple of Phnom Krom, 12 km south of Siem Reap on a hill overlooking the Tonlé Sap, dates from the 11th century. The three towers, dedicated (from north to south) to Vishnu, Shiva and Brahma, are in a ruined state. The ferry from Phnom Penh and Kompong Chhnang docks near here.

Banteay Samré

Banteay Samré, 400 m east of the south-east corner of the Eastern Baray, was built in the third quarter of the 12th century. It consists of a

Sketch of one of the wings at Banteay Samré, published in the 1911 Inventaire Descriptif des Monuments du Cambodge.

COUPE SUIVANT XY

central temple with four wings preceded by a hall and accompanied by two libraries, the southern one of which is remarkably well preserved. The ensemble is enclosed by two concentric walls.

The road to Banteay Samré should only be attempted in vehicles with high ground clearance.

Banteay Srei

At the time of writing, security problems mean that visitors to Banteay Srei require a special permit plus the protection of armed guards. The risk is very real. In late 1994 an American tourist was shot and killed at Banteay Srei – her armed guards fled.

Banteay Srei features some of the finest examples of Khmer classical art at Angkor.

It's more the pity that Banteay Srei is regarded in many quarters as the jewel in the crown of classical Khmer art. It may not be a particularly extensive temple site, but it is wonderfully well preserved and its relief carvings are among the most accomplished Angkor has to offer.

Banteay Srei was built in the late 10th century and is a Hindu temple dedicated to Shiva. The temple is square in plan, with entrances at the east and west. The east entrance is approached by a causeway. Of chief interest are the three central towers, which are decorated with male and female divinities and beautiful filigree relief work.

Banteay Srei is 21 km north-east of the Bayon and eight km west of Phnom Kulen. Ask in Siem Reap about the security situation before planning a trip out here. Most guesthouses around town can organise a permit, vehicle and guards. The price averages around US$40 per head, depending on numbers and who you organise the trip with.

Phnom Kulen

The sheer walls of Phnom Kulen, which is some 28 km north-east of the Bayon, rise to an elevation of 461m.

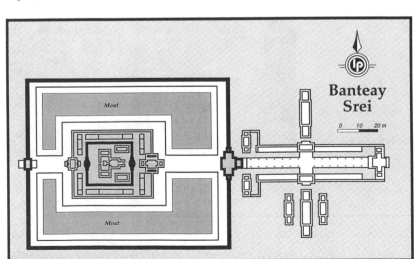

Banteay Srei

0   10   20 m

Beng Mealea

The 12th-century temple of Beng Mealea is about 40 km east of the Bayon (as the crow flies) and 6.5 km southeast of Phnom Kulen. Its ruined state is probably the result of civil strife or wars with the Thais. Beng Mealea is enclosed by a moat measuring 1200 by 900m.

Intricately carved celestial dancers, known as apsaras, are major features of many of the temples of Angkor.

Angkor Wat

Almost every surface within the vast realm of Angkor Wat tells a story, the famed bas-relief sculpture combining scenes of religious ecstasy and mythical beasts with highly detailed military battles. These rich narrative carvings adorn well over one km of the temple's sandstone interior. From the ground, it's difficult to appreciate the fierce symmetry of the 'temple mountain' of Angkor Wat. Laid out as a series of rectangles within rectangles, the monument is anchored by a cruciform courtyard at its centre. The surrounding maze of galleries and outbuildings is home to a lively population of lovingly carved apsaras, who in Hindu mythology are said to bestow sensual favours on kings and heroes who die bravely.

TONY WHEELER

GLENN BEANLAND

Above Right: A statue of Vishnu in one of the galleries at Angkor Wat.

Left: Angkor Wat's central structure dominates the skyline.

Bottom Left: Shadows creeping across the sandstone bas reliefs.

Bottom Right: In Hindu mythology, Angkor Wat's westward aspect symbolises death.

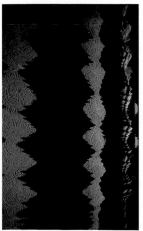

CHRIS TAYLOR

CHRIS TAYLOR

Angkor Thom

A staggering religious monument, a gigantic mystic diagram, an unrivalled architectural masterpiece - Angkor Thom is all of these and more. Designed as a meticulous replica of the Khmer universe, with the intricate Bayon at its heart, the 'Great Royal City' could be regarded as the very spirit of the empire captured in stone. The defiant Jayavarman VII oversaw the creation of this nine-sq km fortified city in the year 1200 as a new capital, and a new beginning, following the devastation wrought by the invading Cham armies. Nearby is the magnificent temple of Ta Prohm, which features central court-yard sanctuaries thought to have been built in honour of the deities Vishnu and Shiva.

Above Left: Bas relief at the Bayon depicting Khmer and Cham soldiers engaged in battle.

Right: The most outstanding features of the Bayon are the 54 towers of smiling faces.

Bottom Left: Ta Prohm bears testament to the awesome power of the jungle.

Bottom Right: A statue at the Terrace of the Leper King.

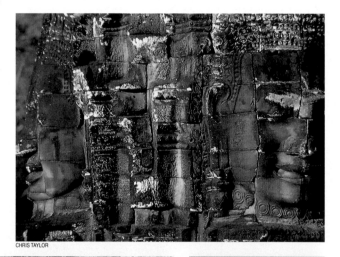

Around Cambodia

The South Coast

KAMPOT
Kampot (population 14,000) is on the Tuk Chhou River, also called the Prek Thom River, five km from the sea. Although many buildings in town were damaged by the Khmer Rouge, Kampot retains much of its charm. Virtually no foreign travellers make it to Kampot, as there are still some security risks involved with getting here.

Durian haters beware: Kampot Province is Cambodia's most important durian producing region.

Information
The GPO is along the river near the Kampot Province Hotel. There is supposed to be a telephone link between Kampot and Phnom Penh.

To Chu Falls
The To Chu Falls are just north of Kampot towards the hills.

Places to Stay & Eat
There are reportedly some hotels and restaurants in Kampot. For accommodation, expect rates of US$5 and upwards.

Getting There & Away
The 148-km drive from Phnom Penh to Kampot along National Route 3 will take around three or four hours, as the section south of Takeo is still in bad shape. The roads around Kampot are in extremely poor condition.

BOKOR HILL STATION
The mountaintop hill station of Bokor (elevation 1080 metres) is famous for its pleasant climate, rushing streams, forested vistas and stunning panoramas of the sea. The best time of year to visit Bokor, which is in the Ele-

phant Mountains, is between November and May.

There's nothing in the way of amenities at Bokor at present. It is possible the area will get redeveloped if Sihanoukville takes off as a tourist destination and lingering security problems associated with the Kampot-Sihanoukville road are solved. Until the area is redeveloped and announced safe, it would be wise to leave it off your itinerary.

Getting There & Away
Bokor is 41 km from Kampot and 190 km from Phnom Penh. The access road is in very bad condition. Although some foreigners have travelled on this road and locals in Sihanoukville claim it is safe, the common consensus among NGOs and embassies in Phnom Penh is that it is dangerous.

POPOKVIL FALLS
The two waterfalls of Popokvil, 14 and 18m high, are not far from the access road to Bokor Hill Station.

KEP
The seaside resort of Kep (Kep-sur-Mer), with its six-km palm-shaded coast road, was once a favourite holiday spot for Cambodia's French-influenced elite, who flocked here to enjoy such pursuits as yachting, gambling, fishing, water skiing and skin diving. Under the Khmer Rouge, the town (founded in 1908) and its many villas were completely destroyed – not neglected and left to decay, but intentionally turned into utter ruins. The Khmer Rouge also turned the underground petrol tank of the old Shell station into a mass grave. By 1979, not a single building remained intact in Kep.

Although there are plans to rebuild Kep and re-establish it as a beach resort, at present it is a bit of a ghost town with just one hotel – the *Kep Hotel*.

Kep is subject to the south-west monsoon.

The best time of year to visit Kep is from the end of October to the end of June.

Getting There & Away
Kep is 24 km south-east of Kampot and 49 km from the Vietnamese town of Ha Tien. The same security risks associated with travel to Kampot apply to Kep. There is a border crossing eight km north of Ha Tien, but it is not presently open for foreigners.

KIRIROM NATIONAL PARK
The hill station of Kirirom, set amid pine forests 675m above sea level, has been established as a national park. It is 112 km south-west of Phnom Penh in the Elephant Mountains to the west of National Route 4.

As yet the area is undeveloped. There are no hotels or restaurants.

SIHANOUKVILLE
Sihanoukville (also known as Kompong Som) is Cambodia's only port. It is gradually being redeveloped as a tourist attraction, but despite the promise of massive Malaysian investment – a casino is planned for Naga Island – tourist numbers are still fairly low.

The kidnapping and murder of three foreigners on National Road 4 between Phnom Penh and Sihanoukville in April 1994 was a tragedy that put the redevelopment of Sihanoukville on hold. Today the area is beginning to bounce back.

At present, the chief attractions of Sihanoukville are the three beaches that ring the headland. None of them are a knockout, but if you can organise a boat trip there is reportedly some great snorkelling and diving around the nearby islands. If it is just beaches and sunbathing you are looking for, however, Sihanoukville may be a disappointment.

Orientation
Sihanoukville is not a small place, and the best way to get around is to hire a motorbike. Sihanoukville itself is east of the main backpackers' beach and close to the more mid-range Ochatial Beach. Due south of town is tiny Ko Pos Beach, which has a solitary mid-range hotel, and the larger Independence Beach, which has the crumbling Independence Hotel – slated for redevelopment.

Information
There are a couple of banks in town, while the post office is near Sam's Guesthouse and the port. The best places for information about things to do in Sihanoukville are the two guesthouses and Claude's Restaurant on Ochatial Beach.

Things to See & Do
The best of the beaches is probably **Ochatial Beach**, though the beach by the guesthouses is not bad either. It's worth taking a bike down to **Independence Beach** and taking a look at the old **Independence Hotel**. Some locals claim the hotel is haunted, and it does indeed have an eerie look about it.

In town there is an average **market** that is worth poking around in for 20 minutes or so. Otherwise the town itself is pretty much devoid of attractions, though it is not an unpleasant place.

Sam's Guesthouse and Claude's Restaurant both have snorkelling gear for hire. Claude's also has a boat and can organise diving trips for experienced divers. The cost for a dive is US$35 with one tank of oxygen. Even if you are not a diver, you might want to call in to Claude's and see if he has any boat trips planned. A day trip to nearby islands costs US$20 per head – for an extra US$7 per head, Claude puts on a seafood lunch with drinks. Sam's Guesthouse also has plans to set up boat trips.

Places to Stay
There is no shortage of places to stay in Sihanoukville, though most of it falls into the mid-range category. The budget accommodation is a couple of km west of town, south of the port area. *Sam's Guesthouse* is the closest outfit to the beach. Victor and his wife Sam are still working on the place at the time of writing. It has a pleasant restaurant with excellent food and six basic rooms in a longhouse setup. Costs are US$5 for one person, US$6 for two.

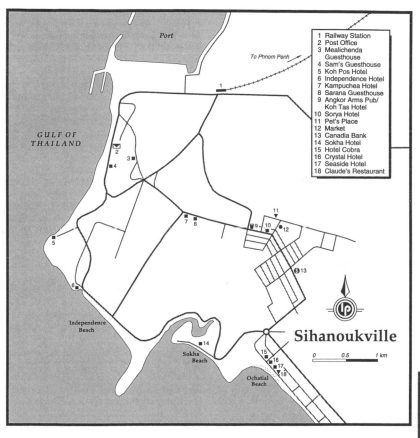

1 Railway Station
2 Post Office
3 Mealichenda
   Guesthouse
4 Sam's Guesthouse
5 Koh Pos Hotel
6 Independence Hotel
7 Kampuchea Hotel
8 Sarana Guesthouse
9 Angkor Arms Pub/
   Koh Tas Hotel
10 Sorya Hotel
11 Pet's Place
12 Market
13 Canadia Bank
14 Sokha Hotel
15 Hotel Cobra
16 Crystal Hotel
17 Seaside Hotel
18 Claude's Restaurant

GULF OF THAILAND

Port

To Phnom Penh

Independence Beach

Sokha Beach

Ochatial Beach

Sihanoukville

0   0.5   1 km

The *Mealichenda Guesthouse* is up on the hill above Sam's. It's a friendly place with an inexpensive restaurant and is very popular with backpackers. Singles cost US$3, doubles US$5.

If you're looking for some peace and quiet, and slightly higher levels of comfort, the *Koh Pos Hotel* is a good option. It has its own small stretch of beach and a beachfront restaurant with great sunset views. Rates are posted at US$15 for a big air-con double with attached bathroom, but mid-week it's usually possible to haggle them down to US$10.

The *Independence Hotel* might shut down at any time for renovations, but at the time of writing it is still hiring out decrepit rooms for US$5. Some travellers love the place, but it's a little isolated and you may be the only person staying in the hotel.

About a km west of town is the *Kampuchea Hotel*, a good value mid-range hotel. All rooms come with satellite TV, air-con and bathrooms and go for a standard US$15. Close by is the *Sarana Guesthouse*, a small family-run place that sees very few foreign guests. Basic fan-cooled doubles with communal bathing facilities cost US$6.

There are a number of mid-range hotels in town. Most of them have rates from US$10 to US$15 for doubles. The *Koh Tas Hotel* (☎ 015-918755) is next door to the Angkor Arms pub and has rooms for US$10. The nearby *Colap Hotel* (☎ 015-913004) is a similar deal with singles/doubles for US$10/13. Other mid-range hotels in town include the *Sorya Hotel* and the *Kompong Som Hotel*.

Sokha Beach was the site of the old French beach resort. The resort still lingers on as the *Sokha Hotel* – the sign outside says *Sopheak Mongkol Motel*. It's basically a sprawl of poorly maintained and overpriced concrete bungalows these days. Costs are US$20/25. Given the alternatives, it's not worth it.

Ochatial Beach is where most Phnom Penh based expats head for a break. It has a good stretch of beach and a string of waterfront hotels. Most of them cost around US$20. The cheapest is the *Eagle's Nest*, which has functional air-con rooms with attached bathrooms at US$10 for a single and US$15 for a double. The *Hotel Cobra* is essentially a knocking shop with an attached karaoke bar – this is a pity because the A-frame air-con bungalows out front are a great deal at US$10. It's doubtful you'd get any sleep here, however.

The best Ochatial hotels are the *Seaside Hotel* (☎ 015-914435) and the *Crystal Hotel* (☎ 015-915523). The Seaside is expanding its operations and it's likely that prices will increase. At the time of writing it has singles on the 1st floor at US$20, doubles at US$25, 'special' doubles at US$40 and one triple room at US$30. All rooms have air-con and come with satellite TV and hot water. The Crystal Hotel is an odd-looking building but the rooms are excellent; they cost US$20/25.

Places to Eat

Both Sam's and the Mealichenda guesthouses have good restaurants. Even if you are based in one of these guesthouses, it's worth making the effort to get down to the *Koh Pos Restaurant*, which has a good range of Cambodian, Thai and western dishes in a pleasant waterfront setting. The cheaper dishes cost around US$2-3. This is a good place to enjoy a beer as the sun goes down.

In town, look out for *Pet's Place*, a small Western-style diner run by Pet, formerly a chef at several popular Phnom Penh restaurants. The meals are not particularly cheap, but if you feel like splashing out on an imported Australian T-bone steak (US$9), this is the place to do it; the pork medallions at US$4.50 are very good.

At Ochatial Beach, *Claude's* is the place to eat out. Claude, the French-Vietnamese owner, is a friendly chap and very knowledgeable about the area. The restaurant has a pleasant garden setting and the food is excellent. Again, budget travellers will find the meals expensive, but it's a good place for a splash-out meal.

Getting There & Away

The official embassy position on Sihanoukville is that travellers should fly here. It would be worth checking as to whether this is still the case. Comfortable bus services are already up and running at the time of writing, and many travellers are disregarding embassy advice and travelling down this way. This doesn't necessarily mean that the road is safe.

Air Flights from Phnom Penh are scheduled four times a week and cost US$40 one way, US$70 return. There is a Royal Air Cambodge office in Sihanoukville close to the CST bus office.

Bus Buses from Phnom Penh to Sihanoukville cost US$5 and leave from the New Market area twice daily at 7 am and 1 pm. The buses are air-con Korean numbers, and fairly comfortable. If you do decide to use this service, take the early-morning service. Buses back to Phnom Penh leave at the same times and depart from the CST office in the centre of town. Other bus services are expected to start up in the near future. Buses take around three to four hours.

Taxi Taxis from Phnom Penh to Sihanoukville leave from the area just to the east of the

Dusit Hotel near the New Market. They cost US$25, or US$4 per head. Those paying US$4 for a ride will find themselves doing the trip at terrifying speeds in very crowded conditions. It's a good idea to get a group of people together and hire a whole taxi – this way you can ask the driver to slow down, and enjoy a bit more room. As already noted, embassies request that their nationals avoid Sihanoukville taxi services until National Route 4 is deemed fully secure. The 232-km trip takes around 2½ hours.

Taxis from Sihanoukville to Phnom Penh can be found opposite the market in town.

Getting Around
The Airport The airport is around 10 km out of town on National Route 4. A moto into town will probably cost around US$2, while taxis (if there are any) will probably cost US$5. Some haggling may be required.

Moto Apart from hiring your own bike, the only way to get around Sihanoukville is by moto. There aren't that many of them around, and in the evenings you may end up waiting by the roadside for quite a long time before one happens along. Most long-distance trips (from Sam's Guesthouse to Claude's Restaurant, for example) cost US$1, while short hops cost 1000r.

Motorbike Hire Ask around at the guesthouses about hiring a motorbike. Sam's Guesthouse can generally organise something for around US$5 per day.

KOH KONG
The beautiful island of Koh Kong, in the Gulf of Thailand, just off the western coast of Koh Kong Province, is only a few dozen km from Thailand and has become a centre for smuggling Thai and Singaporean consumer goods into Cambodia. Although Koh Kong probably has considerable tourist potential, there's unlikely to be much happening here in the foreseeable future.

Koh Kong is just 80 km southeast of Thailand's island of Ko Chang. Some travellers have used it as a border crossing

between Cambodia and Thailand. This is not recommended, for a number of reasons. For one, while it is possible to take boats from Sihanoukville to Koh Kong, and from there to Trat in Thailand, you will be travelling through territory that is mostly the domain of armed smugglers. Female travellers could be at considerable risk, and if anyone out here takes a fancy to your camera (or wallet) you can basically kiss it goodbye. Secondly, you will be arriving in Thailand with an unstamped passport. This can lead to all kinds of complications, including heavy fines.

Getting There & Away Boats leave for Koh Kong on an irregular basis from an area north of the port in Sihanoukville. If you are dead set on making this trip, consult with the guesthouse operators and perhaps the local police before heading off. It's not recommended.

Flights from Phnom Penh to Koh Kong operate four times a week. They cost US$50/100 one-way/return.

Central Cambodia

KOMPONG CHHNANG
Kompong Chhnang is a laid-back town with a certain charm. Just south-east of the Tonlé Sap Lake, it's an important fishing centre with a lively market area, a few guesthouses and hotels and a handful of decent restaurants. Very, very few travellers stop here even though boats to Siem Reap call in to pick up and off-load passengers.

Kompong Chhnang is by no means an important attraction, but if you want to take a look at a provincial Cambodian town that sees nothing in the way of tourism it's worth an overnight stop.

Places to Stay & Eat
The *Rithisen Hotel* is opposite the pier and has singles for US$5 and doubles for US$8. There are also some air-con rooms available at US$8/10. There is also one air-con triple

with a veranda and fridge for US$12 – it's not a bad deal.

There's nothing much in the way of decent food in the waterfront area. Around two km south-east of the pier, around the Victory Monument, are several restaurants that are popular with NGO workers. The *Samaki Restaurant* faces the monument and is not a bad place for a meal. Most dishes are around US$2 and there's an English menu.

Getting There & Away
National Route 5 goes from Phnom Penh to Kompong Chhnang, and the 90-km trip takes around two hours by taxi. You can visit the town as a day trip from Phnom Penh for around US$30.

All the boats connecting Siem Reap and Phnom Penh stop off at Kompong Chhnang. Express boats onward from Kompong Chhnang to Siem Reap cost US$15 and leave at around 9 am. Express boats to Phnom Penh depart at around 11 am and should cost US$4. The slow boats depart irregularly but are very cheap at just 5000r to Phnom Penh and 15,000r to Siem Reap.

PURSAT
The provincial capital of Pursat is a grungy roadstop en route to Battambang. Given that foreign travellers are strongly advised against travelling by road to Battambang, unless you are travelling with a UN convoy you shouldn't be here.

KOMPONG CHAM
Kompong Cham was an important trading post on the Mekong River during the French colonial period. Today it's a medium-sized town with some notable nearby attractions. There's some interesting colonial architecture around town, and the riverside area is a good place for a stroll. Travellers making their way up the Mekong should consider spending a night in Kompong Cham before heading on to Kratie.

Wat Nokor Bayon
Around two km from the river area, Wat Nokor Bayon is an 11th-century Mahayana

Buddhist shrine of sandstone and laterite. It was reconsecrated for Hinayana worship in the 15th century. It's a fascinating place to explore, and chances are in mid-week you will be the only person here. There are numerous alcoves with tucked-away Buddha images, and in one of the rooms is a large reclining Buddha. In certain parts, the laterite walls really do resemble the Bayon at Angkor.

Phnom Pros & Phnom Srei
This two-humped ridge looks a little like Phnom Udong. The names of the two hills translate as 'man hill' and 'woman hill' respectively. Legend has it that two teams, one of men and the other of women, laboured by night to be the first to construct a stupa on their peak by daybreak. The women built a big fire, which the men took to be the rising sun, and thus tricked them into giving up the job unfinished. This, at least, is what locals will tell you if you visit the hills.

The hills, each with a temple, are around 13 km to the west of town, just off National Route 7. Negotiate a taxi to take you out there at the market in town if you don't have your own transport.

Prey Nokor
Prey Nokor, around 38 km south-east of town, was the Khmer capital during the 6th or 7th centuries. It is likely to be only of interest to the archaeologically minded, but those with time may like to head out here and check it out. The outer wall encloses a vast area at the centre with two square sanctuaries.

Places to Stay
There is no shortage of places to stay in Kompong Cham. If you can stretch the budget a bit, stay at the *Mekong Hotel*. It's the only hotel in town and is right on the waterfront, near where the boats and ferries pull in. A cavernous place with a coffee shop and bar, the Mekong Hotel has huge fan-cooled doubles with attached bathroom for US$7 and air-con rooms for US$15. The veranda areas overlooking the Mekong

River are great places to sip a drink late in the afternoon.

The other accommodation options around town are all guesthouses. They all charge a flat US$5 for a room. There's a nameless guesthouse (look for the English sign) directly opposite the ferry pier. Turn right here, walk past the Mekong Hotel and turn left and you will come across the *Monorom Guesthouse*. It's one of the better guesthouses in town, and has a couple of clean air-con doubles for US$10, as well as the usual US$5 fan-cooled rooms.

Back in the other direction (following the waterfront) is a collection of family-run guesthouses. They are all fairly basic and will probably be fairly noisy. Look out for the *Ly Seng Guesthouse*, the *Lucky Guesthouse* and the *Bopear Guesthouse*.

Places to Eat

Opposite the Monorom Guesthouse is the *Mehong II Restaurant*. It's a basic Khmer-Chinese place, but amazingly it has an English menu. Dishes cost US$2-3. The best restaurants in town are a km or so out from the waterfront area. The *Hoa An Restaurant* is probably the pick of the pack, and is popular with NGO workers. Close by is the *Kompong Cham Restaurant*, another popular spot.

Getting There & Away

By road, Kompong Cham is 144 km from Phnom Penh via National Route 7. Kompong Cham and its attractions can be visited as a day trip providing you set off early in the morning. Most taxi drivers will charge US$50 for the return journey. Taxis in Kompong Cham gather in the market area not far from the waterfront. It is impossible to travel on to Kratie by road from Kompong Cham.

Share taxis cost US$4 per head to and from Phnom Penh. In Phnom Penh they leave from near the Dusit Hotel and the New Market. Be warned: they really pack the passengers in and it won't be a pleasant trip.

Express boats between Phnom Penh and Kompong Cham take around two hours and cost US$8. Slow-boat services tend to be fairly infrequent, though it may be worth asking around to see if one is expected.

Express boats to Kratie leave daily at around 9.30 am, cost US$8 and take a couple of hours. There are no scheduled boat services to Stung Treng. You will have to travel to Kratie and attempt to hitch up with a slow boat there, if Stung Treng is your destination. Slow boats to Kratie are infrequent, cost US$4 and take six hours.

KOMPONG THOM

Kompong Thom, north-east of Kompong Cham on National Route 6, is not safe to visit. There are some important archaeological sites north and north-west of Kompong Thom, but until the civil war ends you will have to do your sightseeing elsewhere.

Sambor Prei Kuk

Sambor Prei Kuk (also known as Isanapura) is 35 km north of Kompong Thom. It was the capital of Chenla during the reign of the early 7th-century king Isanavarman. It is said to be the most impressive group of pre-9th century monuments in Cambodia. The site consists of three groups of edifices, most of which are made of brick, whose design prefigures a number of later developments in Khmer art. Sambor Prei Kuk continued to be an important centre of scholarship during the Angkorian period.

Preah Khan

The vast laterite and sandstone temple of Preah Khan, originally dedicated to Hindu deities, was reconsecrated to Buddhist worship in the early 11th century. Nearby monuments include: Preah Damrei, guarded by massive elephants; Preah Thkol, a cruciform shrine two km east of the central group; and Preah Stung, two km south-east of the main group, which includes a tower with four faces.

Koh Ker

Koh Ker (also known as Chok Gargyar) served as the capital of Jayavarman IV (ruled 928 to 942) who, having seized the throne, left Angkor and transferred his capital here, where it remained throughout his reign. The principal monument of this large group of interesting ruins is Prasat Thom (also known as Prasat Kompeng), which includes a 40m-high sandstone-faced pyramid of seven levels. Some 40 inscriptions, dating from 932 to 1010, have been found at Prasat Thom.

PREAH VIHEAR
The important group of Preah Vihear, built on a crest of the Dangkrek Mountains at an altitude of 730m, dates from the reign of Suryavarman I (ruled 1002 to 1049). The complex faces south. There has been talk for some time now of opening up the Preah Vihear area to overland tourists from Thailand.

SIEM REAP
For information on Siem Reap and the temples of Angkor, see the Angkor chapter.

Western Cambodia

BATTAMBANG
It's a sad reflection of the state of Cambodia that the country's second largest city is so difficult to get to. The road to Battambang is a mess, littered with potholes and rapacious checkpoints. UN vehicles do the trip in convoys. Travellers are advised to give the place a miss unless they are able to fly.

During the annual dry-season offensive, which usually kicks off in February and lasts through May, travellers should forget Battambang altogether. The city is frequently under curfew, and getting in and out of the place can become difficult even for journalists with the right contacts.

This is a pity because travellers who have made it to Battambang report that it is an interesting city to explore on foot. It has a bustling market area, and the Sangker River, which cuts through the centre of town is a pleasant feature. There are several wats around town, and 20 km north of the city is

Wat Phnom Sampeou, a hilltop temple approached by a flight of 700 stairs – it provides good views of the area.

Places to Stay & Eat
Battambang was an important UNTAC base, and this has left the city with a number of pretty good mid-range hotels. Prices for an air-con double range from US$10 to US$20. None of the hotels have restaurants.

Cheaper hotels around town include the *Khemara Hotel*, where air-con rooms with satellite TV and in-house adult-movie channels cost just US$10. The *Teo Hotel* is similar and has the same rates. Close to the Khemara is the *Paris Hotel*, which has rooms from US$15 to US$20. The *ODA Hotel* is one of the best in town; rooms cost from US$20 to US$30.

One of the most popular restaurants in Battambang is the *Reak Smey Restaurant*, which is just south of the ODA Hotel.

Getting There & Away
Even if the trains were running regularly it is too dangerous to travel by rail. The road from Battambang to Phnom Penh is in bad condition and subject to security problems, and onward travel from Battambang to Angkor is presently out of the question. It is recommended that anyone who desperately wants to go Battambang fly. Flights from Phnom Penh depart five times a week and cost US$45/90 one-way/return.

PAILIN
Pailin (elevation 257m), 83 km south-west of Battambang near the Thai border, is another place that foreigners won't be visiting for the foreseeable future. It is the Khmer Rouge gem-mining area, and unless you look like a rich Thai gem trader, you have a very good chance of being shot if you turn up unannounced.

SISOPHON
Around 80 km north-west of Battambang, Sisophon is an off-limits destination. Khmer Rouge activity makes it too dangerous to visit.

AROUND CAMBODIA

BANTEAY CHHMAR

At present inaccessible for security reasons, Banteay Chhmar ('Narrow Fortress'), 71 km north of Sisophon, was one of the capitals of Jayavarman II (ruled 802 to 850). The city, enclosed by a nine-km-long wall, had in its centre one of the largest and most impressive Buddhist monasteries of the Angkor period. The sandstone structure, built in the 11th century and dedicated to the deity Avalo-kiteshvara, suffered significant damage during repeated Thai invasions, although many of its huge bas reliefs, which are said to be comparable to those of the Bayon and Angkor Wat, are extant.

POIPET (POAY PET)

Both the rail line and the main road linking Bangkok with Angkor and Phnom Penh pass through the Thai-Cambodian border town of Poipet (Poay Pet). The town is 463 km from Phnom Penh and 265 km from Bangkok. When the civil war finally ends, this will become an overland route between Thailand and Cambodia. The Thai town adjacent to Poipet is Aranyaprathet. There are plans to establish an 'Orient Express' between Bangkok and Phnom Penh via this border crossing, but given the current state of affairs this seems somewhat optimistic.

The North-East

The provinces along Cambodia's northern border see very few foreign visitors. The main problem is access. Ratanakiri, which is probably the foremost attraction of the region, is still fairly difficult to get to. Still, the word seems to be getting around, and it is likely that this part of the country will become increasingly popular as an off-the-beaten-track destination.

KRATIE

It's possible to visit the small riverine town of Kratie by boat from Phnom Penh. There's not a great deal to do here, and care should be taken in mounting expeditions out of town

– some areas around Kratie convert to Khmer Rouge control late in the afternoon. But the town itself is pleasant enough.

Places to Stay

Kratie is not a big place and there are only three hotels. The newly refurbished *Heng Heng Hotel* has clean doubles for US$8, while the *December 30th Hotel* has cavernous but basic rooms for US$5. A third hotel functions largely as a brothel and is best avoided.

Getting There & Away

If National Route 7 was open, Kratie would be a 343-km drive from Phnom Penh and a 141-km ride from Stung Treng. Kratie can be reached from the capital by boat. Express boats do the trip in around five hours and cost US$14. Heiwa Shipping in Phnom Penh has daily boats at 7 am, while Golden Sea Shipping has boats on alternate days, also at 7 am. Slow boats cost US$6 and involve an overnight trip. They only depart every five or six days, however.

STUNG TRENG

Stung Treng is a small town on the upper Mekong. In itself, it has little of interest, but it is emerging as a stop on the overland route to Ratanakiri. The Prek Patang rapids on the Mekong River and Phnom Chi may be worthwhile trips out of town. There is some basic accommodation in Stung Treng, with rates of around US$5.

Getting There & Away

There are three flights a week from Phnom Penh to Stung Treng. Tickets cost US$45/90 one-way/return.

The only other way to get to Stung Treng is by boat. Access may become difficult during the dry season (from February through August), but there should still be some river transport between Kratie and Stung Treng even at this time of year.

RATANAKIRI

Mountainous Ratanakiri Province is generating quite a buzz. The excitement is due to the perennial lure of isolated hill tribes. At present, only a trickle of hardened travellers make it to Ban Lung, the provincial capital, but it is certain that numbers will increase over the next few years.

Ratanakiri is free of both landmines and Khmer Rouge activity, which means it is fairly safe to explore the surrounding countryside and visit some of the hill tribes. On the down side, a considerable amount of illegal logging is said to be going on in the region. The loggers are usually armed and not particularly welcoming to unexpected visitors. It is sensible to explore Ratanakiri with a local moto or jeep driver, but if you have to hire your own bike and do it yourself, take care not to take roads that look like they have been created by loggers.

The best months to visit Ratanakiri are from December to June. In the wet season, the provincial roads become muddy torrents and it will be impossible to get around. Ratanakiri is also a high-risk malaria and dengue-fever area – the mosquitoes come out in force during the rainy season, but the risk is present year-round.

Ban Lung

Ban Lung is a tiny place, and the local airport is just a couple of hundred metres away. It's a good base for visiting the sights around the province but little more.

Places to Stay & Eat There are a couple of guesthouses in Ban Lung with rates of US$5. The *Mountain Guesthouse* is probably the most popular. It's a friendly place with a bakery that does baguettes and coffee. The *Ban Lung Guesthouse* has some rooms with attached bathrooms. There is also a new hotel with air-con rooms from US$10 to US$15 in town. The main travellers' restaurant in town is the *American Restaurant*, famed among other things for its hamburgers. It's a good place to meet young locals who speak English.

Yak Lom Volcanic Lake

Four km east of Ban Lung, this crater lake is one of the main attractions of the region. It forms a near perfect circle and is surrounded by forest. There is a village of the Tumpuon people en route from Ban Lung to the lake.

Waterfalls

It's a good idea to get a local moto driver to take you out to the waterfalls, which are around eight km west of Ban Lung. If you want to drive yourself, there should be information on getting out there at the Mountain Guesthouse.

Bakheo

Bakheo, around 30 km east of town, is a gem-mining area, though the work is being carried out by hand. If you know anything about gems you may be able to pick up some bargains here. Even if you don't, it should still make an interesting trip out of Ban Lung.

Getting There & Away

There are five flights a week from Phnom Penh to Ratanakiri (Ban Lung). Tickets cost US$55/100 one-way/return. Flights are often fully booked for weeks at a time. It may be worth heading out to the airport an hour before scheduled flights to see if a seat becomes available.

The only other way to get to Ratanakiri is via a long haul up the Mekong to Stung Treng (via Kratie), and from there by taxi or on the back of a truck to Ban Lung. The journey from Stung Treng to Ban Lung can take up to 10 hours on very bad roads. Some travellers trying to get to Ban Lung have been turned back by police in Stung Treng, who cited security risks.

Getting Around

Motorbike hire is available in Ban Lung for around US$5 per day. It is best to get a bike with a driver. Jeeps may also be available for hire with a driver at rates of US$30-40 per day.

Health

Your health is at more risk in Cambodia than it is in most other parts of South-East Asia. For a start, health care services are still fairly poor, and in some parts of the country practically non-existent. Still, this is not an invitation to hit the panic button. With some care and an eye to preventive measures, there is no reason why your stay in Cambodia need not be a healthy one. The key to everything lies in your predeparture preparations, your day-to-day health care while travelling and how you handle any medical problem or emergency that does develop.

Travel Health Guides

Probably the best all-round health guide is *Staying Healthy in Asia, Africa & Latin America* by Dirk Schroeder (Moon Publications). This book comes in a compact, easy-to-carry format and also manages to be detailed and well organised. Also recommended is *Travellers' Health* by Dr Richard Dawood (Oxford University Press).

Where There is No Doctor by David Werner (Hesperian Foundation) is a very detailed guide but aimed more at the long-term resident of health risk areas (such as Peace Corps workers) than at the average traveller.

Finally, travellers planning to take the kids along should pick up a copy of *Travel with Children*, by Maureen Wheeler (Lonely Planet). It includes basic advice on travel health for younger children.

Predeparture Preparations

Health Insurance A good travel insurance policy that is strong on medical costs is essential for Cambodia. See the Travel Insurance entry of the Visas & Documents section in this chapter for more details.

Medical Kit A small, straightforward medical kit is a wise thing to carry. A possible kit list includes:

- Aspirin or paracetamol (acetaminophen in the US) – for pain or fever.
- Antihistamine (such as Benadryl) – useful as a decongestant for colds, allergies, to ease the itch from insect bites or stings or to help prevent motion sickness. Antihistamines may cause sedation and interact with alcohol so care should be taken when using them.
- Antibiotics – useful if you're travelling well off the beaten track, but they must be prescribed and you should carry the prescription with you. Some individuals are allergic to commonly prescribed antibiotics such as penicillin or sulpha drugs. If you are, it would be sensible to carry this information when travelling.
- Loperamide (eg Imodium) or Lomotil for diarrhoea; prochlorperazine (eg Stemetil) or metaclopramide (eg Maxalon) for nausea and vomiting. Anti-diarrhoea medication should not be given to children under the age of 12.
- Rehydration mixture – for treatment of severe diarrhoea. This is particularly important if travelling with children, but is recommended for everyone.
- Antiseptic such as povidone-iodine (eg Betadine), which comes as a solution, ointment and impregnated swabs – for cuts and grazes.
- Calamine lotion or Stingose – to ease irritation from bites or stings.
- Bandages and Band-aids – for minor injuries.
- Scissors, tweezers and a thermometer (note that mercury thermometers are prohibited by airlines).
- Insect repellent, sunscreen, suntan lotion, Chapstick and water purification tablets.
- A couple of syringes, in case you need injections in remote parts of Cambodia, where medical hygiene problems can be expected. Ask your doctor for a note explaining why they have been prescribed.

Ideally antibiotics should be administered only under medical supervision and should never be taken indiscriminately. Take only the recommended dose at the prescribed intervals and continue using the antibiotic for the prescribed period, even if the illness seems to be cured earlier. Antibiotics are quite specific to the infections they can treat. Stop immediately if there are any serious reactions and don't use the antibiotic at all if you are unsure that you have the correct one.

In Cambodia, if a medicine is available at all, it is often available over the counter; while it may be cheaper than in the west, you should be careful that the expiry date has not passed. There is also no way of knowing whether correct storage conditions have been followed. Generally, in developing countries, bogus drugs are common and it's possible that drugs which are no longer recommended, or have even been banned, in the west are still being dispensed.

Health Preparations Make sure you're healthy before you start travelling. If you are embarking on a long trip, make sure your teeth are OK. While there is good dental treatment available in Phnom Penh, elsewhere around Cambodia a visit to the dentist would be the last thing you'd want.

If you wear glasses take a spare pair and your prescription. Losing your glasses can be a real problem, although in Phnom Penh it should be possible to get new spectacles made up quickly, cheaply and efficiently.

If you require a particular medication take an adequate supply, as it may not be available locally. Take the prescription or, better still, part of the packaging showing the generic rather than the brand name (which may not be locally available), as it will make getting replacements easier. It's a wise idea to have a legible prescription with you to show you legally use the medication – it's surprising how often over-the-counter drugs from one place are illegal without a prescription, or even banned, in another.

Immunisations Vaccinations provide protection against diseases you might meet along the way. For some countries no immunisations are necessary, but in the case of Cambodia it is recommended that you have certain vaccinations before you go.

You are not legally bound to have any vaccinations before arriving in Cambodia (as is the case in all Asian countries).

Currently yellow fever is the only vaccine subject to international health regulations, and it's impossible to fly directly to Cambodia from an infected area so this is not a problem.

Plan ahead for getting your vaccinations: some of them require an initial shot followed by a booster, while some vaccinations should not be given together. It is recommended you seek medical advice at least six weeks before head off.

Most travellers from western countries will have been immunised against various diseases during childhood but your doctor may still recommend booster shots. The period of protection offered by vaccinations differs widely and some are contraindicated if you are pregnant.

All vaccinations should be recorded on an International Health Certificate, which is available from your physician or government health department.

Vaccinations recommended for Cambodia are:

- Tetanus and Diphtheria – boosters are necessary every 10 years; it is highly recommended you get one.

- Typhoid – available either as an injection or oral capsules. Protection lasts from one to three years. It is highly recommended for Cambodia. You may get some side effects such as pain at the injection site, fever, headache and a general unwell feeling. A new single-dose injectable vaccine, which appears to have few side effects, is now available but is more expensive. Side effects are unusual with the oral form although some people get stomach cramps.

- Hepatitis A – the most common travel-acquired illness, which can be prevented by vaccination. Protection can be provided in two ways – either with the antibody gamma globulin or with a new vaccine called Havrix.

- Tuberculosis – expats living in Cambodia are far more at risk from this disease than short-term visitors, but if you are going to spend some time in the country it is worth considering, as it is prevalent. It is essential for children of 14 years or younger. Known as a BCG immunisation, it should be administered six weeks before arrival.

As you will note, there are two vaccines for hepatitis A (infectious hepatitis). Havrix provides long-term immunity (possibly more than 10 years) after an initial course of two injections and a booster at one year. It may be more expensive than gamma globulin but certainly has many advantages, including length of protection and ease of administration. It is important to know that being a vaccine it will take about three weeks to provide satisfactory protection – hence the need for careful planning prior to travel. Gamma globulin, on the other hand, is not a vaccination but a ready-made antibody which has proven very successful in reducing the chances of hepatitis infection. Because it may interfere with the development of immunity, it should not be given until at least 10 days after administration of the last vaccine needed; it should also be given as close as possible to departure because it is at its most effective in the first few weeks after administration and the effectiveness tapers off gradually between three and six months.

Basic Rules

Care in what you eat and drink is the most important health rule; stomach upsets are the most likely travel health problem (between 30% and 50% of travellers in a two-week stay experience them) but the majority of these upsets will be relatively minor. Don't become paranoid; trying the local food is part of the experience of travel, after all.

Water It is not safe to drink tap water in Cambodia. Theoretically the ice served in restaurants and bars in Phnom Penh and Siem Reap is safe, but if you are new to Asia it would probably be wise to abstain. Bottled water is cheap and widely available in Cambodia; it is safe to drink. Tea or coffee are fine, since the water has been boiled.

Water Purification The simplest way of purifying water is to boil it thoroughly. Vigorous boiling for five minutes should be satisfactory.

Simple filtering will not remove all dangerous organisms, so if you cannot boil water it should be treated chemically. Chlorine tablets (Puritabs, Steritabs or other brand names) will kill many but not all pathogens,

including giardia and amoebic cysts. Iodine is very effective in purifying water and is available in tablet form (such as Potable Aqua), but follow the directions carefully and remember that too much iodine can be harmful.

If you can't find tablets, tincture of iodine (2%) or iodine crystals can be used. Four drops of tincture of iodine per litre or quart of clear water is the recommended dosage; the treated water should be left to stand for 20 to 30 minutes before drinking. Iodine crystals can also be used to purify water but this is a more complicated process, as you have to first prepare a saturated iodine solution. Iodine loses its effectiveness if exposed to air or damp so keep it in a tightly sealed container. Flavoured powder will disguise the taste of treated water and is a good idea if you are travelling with children.

Food There is an old colonial adage which says: 'If you can cook it, boil it or peel it you can eat it...otherwise forget it'. Salads and fruit should be washed with purified water or peeled where possible. Ice cream is usually OK in Phnom Penh, but beware of street vendors and ice cream that has melted and been refrozen. Thoroughly cooked food is safest but not if it has been left to cool or if it has been reheated. Shellfish such as mussels, oysters and clams should be avoided as well as undercooked meat, particularly in the form of mince. Steaming does not make shellfish safe for eating.

If a place looks clean and well run and if the vendor also looks clean and healthy, then the food is probably safe. In general, places that are packed with travellers or locals will be fine, while empty restaurants are questionable. Busy restaurants mean the food is being cooked and eaten quite quickly with little standing around, and it is probably not being reheated.

Nutrition If your diet is poor or limited in variety, if you're travelling hard and fast and therefore missing meals, or if you simply lose your appetite, you can soon start to lose weight and place your health at risk.

HEALTH

Make sure your diet is well balanced. Eggs, beans, and nuts are all safe ways to get protein. Fruit you can peel (bananas, oranges or mandarins for example) is always safe and a good source of vitamins. Try to eat plenty of grains (rice) and bread. Remember that although food is generally safer if it is cooked well, overcooked food loses much of its nutritional value. If your diet isn't well balanced or if your food intake is insufficient, it's a good idea to take vitamin and iron pills.

Finally, make sure you drink enough – don't rely on feeling thirsty to indicate when you should drink. Not needing to urinate or very dark yellow urine is a danger sign. Always carry a water bottle with you on long trips. Excessive sweating can lead to loss of salt and therefore muscle cramping. Salt tablets are not a good idea as a preventative, but in places where salt is not used much adding salt to food can help.

Everyday Health A normal body temperature is 98.6°F or 37°C; more than 2°C higher is a 'high' fever. A normal adult pulse rate is 60 to 80 per minute (children 80 to 100, babies 100 to 140). You should know how to take a temperature and a pulse rate. As a general rule the pulse increases about 20 beats per minute for each °C rise in fever.

Respiration (breathing) rate is also an indicator of illness. Count the number of breaths per minute: between 12 and 20 is normal for adults and older children (up to 30 for younger children, 40 for babies). People with a high fever or serious respiratory illness (like pneumonia) breathe more quickly than normal. More than 40 shallow breaths a minute usually means pneumonia.

In western countries with safe water and excellent human waste disposal systems we often take good health for granted. In years gone by, when public health facilities were not as good as they are today, certain rules attached to eating and drinking were observed – for example, washing your hands before a meal. It is important for people travelling in areas of poor sanitation to be aware of this and adjust their own personal hygiene habits.

Clean your teeth with purified water rather than straight from the tap. Avoid climatic extremes: keep out of the sun when it's hot, dress warmly when it's cold. Avoid potential diseases by dressing sensibly. You can get worm infections through walking barefoot or dangerous coral cuts by walking over coral without shoes. You can avoid insect bites by covering bare skin when insects are around, by screening windows or beds or by using insect repellents. Seek local advice: if you're told the water is unsafe due to jellyfish, crocodiles or bilharzia, don't go in. In situations where there is no information, discretion is the better part of valour.

Medical Problems & Treatment
Potential medical problems can be broken down into several areas. First there are the climatic and geographical considerations – problems caused by extremes of temperature, altitude or motion. Then there are diseases and illnesses caused through poor environmental sanitation, insect bites or stings, and animal or human contact. Simple cuts, bites or scratches can also cause problems.

Self-diagnosis and treatment can be risky, so wherever possible seek qualified help. Although we do give treatment dosages in this section, they are for emergency use only. Medical advice should be sought where possible before administering any drugs.

The best bet in the case of serious illness is to head straight for Phnom Penh, where there are some very good clinics (see the Phnom Penh chapter). There a decision can be made about whether you will need to go to Bangkok or home for further treatment.

Environmental Hazards
Sunburn In Cambodia you can get sunburnt surprisingly quickly, even through cloud. Use a sunscreen and take extra care to cover areas which don't normally see sun – eg, your feet. A hat provides added protection, and you should also use zinc cream or some other barrier cream for your nose and lips. Calamine lotion is good for mild sunburn.

Prickly Heat Prickly heat is an itchy rash caused by excessive perspiration trapped under the skin. It usually strikes people who have just arrived and whose pores have not yet opened sufficiently to cope with greater sweating. Keeping cool but bathing often, using a mild talcum powder or even resorting to air-conditioning may help until you acclimatise.

Heat Exhaustion Dehydration or salt deficiency can cause heat exhaustion. Take time to acclimatise to high temperatures and make sure you get sufficient liquids. Salt deficiency is characterised by fatigue, lethargy, headaches, giddiness and muscle cramps and in this case salt tablets may help. Vomiting or diarrhoea can deplete your liquid and salt levels. Anhidrotic heat exhaustion, caused by an inability to sweat, is quite rare. Unlike the other forms of heat exhaustion it is likely to strike people who have been in Cambodia for some time, rather than newcomers.

Heat Stroke This serious, sometimes fatal, condition can occur if the body's heat-regulating mechanism breaks down and the body temperature rises to dangerous levels. Long, continuous periods of exposure to high temperatures can leave you vulnerable to heat stroke. You should try to avoid excessive alcohol or strenuous activity when you first arrive.

The symptoms include feeling unwell, not sweating very much or at all and a high body temperature (39°C to 41°C). Where sweating has ceased the skin becomes flushed and red. Severe, throbbing headaches and lack of coordination will also occur, and the sufferer may be confused or aggressive. Eventually the victim will become delirious or convulse. Hospitalisation is essential, but meanwhile get victims out of the sun, remove their clothing, cover them with a wet sheet or towel and then fan continually.

Fungal Infections Hot weather fungal infections are most likely to occur on the scalp, between the toes or fingers (athlete's foot), in the groin (jock itch or crotch rot) and on the body (ringworm). You get ringworm (which is a fungal infection, not a worm) from infected animals or by walking on damp areas, like shower floors.

To prevent fungal infections wear loose, comfortable clothes, avoid artificial fibres, wash frequently and dry carefully. If you do get an infection, wash the infected area daily with a disinfectant or medicated soap and water, and rinse and dry well. Apply an anti-fungal powder like the widely available Tinaderm. Try to expose the infected area to air or sunlight as much as possible and wash all towels and underwear in hot water as well as changing them often.

Motion Sickness Eating lightly before and during a trip will reduce the chances of motion sickness. If you are prone to motion sickness try to find a place that minimises disturbance – near the wing on aircraft, close to midships on boats, near the centre on buses. Fresh air usually helps, reading or cigarette smoke doesn't. Commercial anti-motion-sickness preparations, which can cause drowsiness, have to be taken before the trip commences; when you're feeling sick it's too late. Ginger is a natural preventative and is available in capsule form.

Jet Lag Jet lag is experienced when a person travels by air across more than three time zones (each time zone usually represents a one hour time difference). It occurs because many of the functions of the human body (such as temperature, pulse rate and emptying of the bladder and bowels) are regulated by internal 24 hour cycles called circadian rhythms. When we travel long distances rapidly, our bodies take time to adjust to the 'new time' of our destination, and we may experience fatigue, disorientation, insomnia, anxiety, impaired concentration and loss of appetite. These effects will usually be gone within three days of arrival, but there are ways of minimising the impact of jet lag:

- Rest for a couple of days before departure; try to avoid late nights and last-minute dashes for travellers' cheques, passports etc.

HEALTH

- Try to select flight schedules that minimise sleep deprivation; arriving late in the day means you can go to sleep soon after you arrive. For very long flights, try to organise a stopover.
- Avoid excessive eating (which bloats the stomach) and alcohol (which causes dehydration) during the flight. Instead, drink plenty of non-carbonated, nonalcoholic drinks such as fruit juice or water.
- Avoid smoking, as this reduces the amount of oxygen in the aircraft cabin and causes greater fatigue.
- Make yourself comfortable by wearing loose-fitting clothes and perhaps bringing an eye mask and ear plugs to help you sleep.

Infectious Diseases

Diarrhoea A change of water, food or climate can all cause the runs; diarrhoea caused by contaminated food or water is more serious. Despite all your precautions you may still have a bout of mild travellers' diarrhoea but a few rushed toilet trips with no other symptoms is not indicative of a serious problem. Moderate diarrhoea, involving half-a-dozen loose movements in a day, is more of a nuisance. Dehydration is the main danger with any diarrhoea, particularly for children where dehydration can occur quite quickly. Fluid replacement remains the mainstay of management. Weak black tea with a little sugar, soda water, or soft drinks allowed to go flat and diluted 50% with water are all good. With severe diarrhoea a rehydrating solution is necessary to replace minerals and salts. Commercially available ORS (oral rehydration salts) is very useful; add the contents of one sachet to a litre of boiled or bottled water. In an emergency you can make up a solution of eight teaspoons of sugar to a litre of boiled water and provide salted cracker biscuits at the same time. You should stick to a bland diet as you recover.

Lomotil or Imodium can be used to bring relief from the symptoms, although they do not actually cure the problem. Only use these drugs if absolutely necessary – eg, if you *must* travel. For children Imodium is preferable, but under all circumstances fluid replacement is the main message. Do not use these drugs if the person has a high fever or is severely dehydrated.

In certain situations antibiotics may be indicated:

- Watery diarrhoea with blood and mucus. Gut-paralysing drugs like Imodium or Lomotil should be avoided in this situation.
- Watery diarrhoea with fever and lethargy.
- Persistent diarrhoea for more than five days.
- Severe diarrhoea, if it is logistically difficult to stay in one place.

The recommended drugs (adults only) would be either norfloxacin 400 mg twice daily for three days or ciprofloxacin 500 mg twice daily for three days.

The drug bismuth subsalicylate has also been used successfully. It is not available in Australia. The dosage for adults is two tablets or 30 ml and for children it is one tablet or 10 ml. This dose can be repeated every 30 minutes to one hour, with no more than eight doses in a 24 hour period.

The drug of choice in children would be co-trimoxazole (Bactrim, Septrin, Resprim) with dosage dependent on weight. A three day course is also given.

Ampicillin has been recommended in the past and may still be an alternative.

Giardiasis The parasite causing this intestinal disorder is present in contaminated water. The symptoms are stomach cramps, nausea, a bloated stomach, watery foul-smelling diarrhoea and frequent gas. Giardiasis can appear several weeks after you have been exposed to the parasite. The symptoms may disappear for a few days and then return; this can go on for several weeks. Tinidazole, known as Fasigyn, or metronidazole (Flagyl) are the recommended drugs for treatment. Either can be used in a single treatment dose. Antibiotics are of no use.

Dysentery This serious illness is caused by contaminated food or water and is characterised by severe diarrhoea, often with blood or mucus in the stool. There are two kinds of dysentery. Bacillary dysentery is characterised by a high fever and rapid onset; headache, vomiting and stomach pains are also symptoms. It generally does not last longer than a week, but it is highly contagious.

Amoebic dysentery is often more gradual in the onset of symptoms, with cramping abdominal pain and vomiting less likely; fever may not be present. It is not a self-limiting disease: it will persist until treated and can recur and cause long-term health problems.

A stool test is necessary to diagnose which kind of dysentery you have, so you should seek medical help urgently. In case of an emergency the drugs norfloxacin or ciprofloxacin can be used as presumptive treatment for bacillary dysentery, and metronidazole (Flagyl) for amoebic dysentery.

For bacillary dysentery, norfloxacin 400 mg twice daily for seven days or ciprofloxacin 500 mg twice daily for seven days are the recommended dosages.

If you're unable to find either of these drugs then a useful alternative is co-trimoxazole 160/800 mg (Bactrim, Septrin, Resprim) twice daily for seven days. This is a sulpha drug and must not be used by people with sulpha allergies.

In the case of children the drug co-trimoxazole is a reasonable first line treatment. For amoebic dysentery, the recommended adult dosage of metronidazole (Flagyl) is one 750 mg to 800 mg capsule three times daily for five days. Children aged between eight and 12 years should have half the adult dose; the dosage for younger children is one-third the adult dose.

An alternative to Flagyl is Fasigyn, taken as a two gram daily dose for three days. Alcohol must be avoided during treatment and for 48 hours afterwards.

Cholera Cholera vaccination is not very effective. The bacteria responsible for this disease are waterborne, so attention to the rules of eating and drinking should protect the traveller.

Outbreaks of cholera are generally widely reported, so you can avoid such problem areas. The disease is characterised by a sudden onset of acute diarrhoea with 'rice water' stools, vomiting, muscular cramps, and extreme weakness. You need medical help – but treat for dehydration, which can be extreme, and if there is an appreciable delay in getting to hospital then begin taking tetracycline. The adult dose is 250 mg four times daily. It is not recommended in children aged eight years or under nor in pregnant women. An alternative drug would be Ampicillin. Remember that while antibiotics might kill the bacteria, it is a toxin produced by the bacteria which causes the massive fluid loss. Fluid replacement is by far the most important aspect of treatment.

Viral Gastroenteritis This is caused not by bacteria but, as the name suggests, by a virus. It is characterised by stomach cramps, diarrhoea, and sometimes by vomiting and/or a slight fever. All you can do is rest and drink lots of fluids.

Hepatitis Hepatitis is a general term for inflammation of the liver. There are many causes of this condition: drugs, alcohol and infections are but a few.

The discovery of new strains has led to a virtual alphabet soup, with hepatitis A, B, C, D, E, G and others. These letters identify specific agents that cause viral hepatitis. Viral hepatitis is an infection of the liver, which can lead to jaundice (yellow skin), fever, lethargy and digestive problems. It can have no symptoms at all, with the infected person not knowing that they have the disease. Travellers shouldn't be too paranoid about this apparent proliferation of hepatitis strains; hep C, D, E and G are fairly rare (so far) and following the same precautions as for A and B should be all that's necessary to avoid them.

Hepatitis A This is a common disease in most countries, especially those with poor standards of sanitation. Most people in developing countries are infected as children; they often don't develop symptoms, but do develop lifelong immunity. The disease poses a real threat to the traveller, as

HEALTH

people are unlikely to have been exposed to hepatitis A in developed countries.

The symptoms are fever, chills, headache, fatigue, feelings of weakness and aches and pains, followed by loss of appetite, nausea, vomiting, abdominal pain, dark urine, light-coloured faeces, jaundiced skin and the whites of the eyes may turn yellow. You should seek medical advice, but in general there is not much you can do apart from resting, drinking lots of fluids, eating lightly and avoiding fatty foods. People who have had hepatitis must forego alcohol for six months after the illness, as hepatitis attacks the liver and it needs that amount of time to recover.

The routes of transmission are via contaminated water, shellfish contaminated by sewage, or foodstuffs sold by food handlers with poor standards of hygiene.

Taking care with what you eat and drink can go a long way towards preventing this disease. But this is a very infectious virus, so if there is any risk of exposure, additional cover is highly recommended. This cover comes in two forms: gamma globulin and Havrix. Gamma globulin is an injection where you are given the antibodies for hepatitis A, which provide immunity for a limited time. Havrix is a vaccine, meaning that you develop your own antibodies, which gives lasting immunity.

Hepatitis B This is also a common disease, with almost 300 million chronic carriers in the world. Hepatitis B, which used to be called serum hepatitis, is spread through contact with infected blood, blood products or bodily fluids, for example through sexual contact, unsterilised needles and blood transfusions, or via small breaks in the skin. Other risk situations include having a shave or tattoo in a local shop, or having your body pierced.

The symptoms of type B are much the same as type A except that they are more severe and may lead to irreparable liver damage or even liver cancer. Although there is no treatment for hepatitis B, a cheap and effective vaccine is available; the only

problem is that for long-lasting cover you need a six month course. Persons who should receive a hepatitis B vaccination include anyone who anticipates contact with blood or other bodily secretions, either as a health care worker or through sexual contact with the local population, particularly those who intend to stay in the country for a long period of time.

Hepatitis C This is a recently defined virus. It is a concern because it seems to lead to liver disease more rapidly than hepatitis B.

The virus is spread by contact with blood – usually via contaminated transfusions or shared needles. Avoiding these is the only means of prevention, as there is no available vaccine.

Hepatitis D Often referred to as the 'Delta' virus, this infection only occurs in chronic carriers of hepatitis B. It is transmitted by blood and bodily fluids. Again there is no vaccine for this virus, so avoidance is the best prevention. The risk to travellers is certainly limited.

Hepatitis E This is another recently discovered virus, about which little is yet known. It appears to be rather common in developing countries, generally causing mild hepatitis, although it can be very serious in pregnant women.

Care with water supplies is the only current prevention, as there are no specific vaccines for this type of hepatitis. At present it doesn't appear to be too great a risk for travellers.

Typhoid Typhoid fever is another gut infection that travels the faecal-oral route – ie, contaminated water and food are responsible. Vaccination against typhoid is not totally effective and it is one of the most dangerous infections, so medical help must be sought.

In its early stages typhoid resembles many other illnesses: sufferers may feel like they have a bad cold or flu on the way, as early symptoms are a headache, a sore throat, and a fever which rises a little each day until it is around 40°C or more. The victim's pulse is often slow relative to the degree of fever present and gets slower as the fever rises – unlike a normal fever where the pulse increases. There may also be vomiting, diarrhoea or constipation.

In the second week the high fever and slow pulse continue and a few pink spots may appear on the body; trembling, delirium, weakness, weight loss and dehydration are other symptoms. If there are no further complications, the fever and other symptoms will slowly go during the third week. However, you must get medical help before this because pneumonia (acute infection of the lungs) or peritonitis are common complications, and because typhoid is very infectious.

The fever should be treated by keeping the victim cool and dehydration should also be watched for.

The drug of choice is ciprofloxacin at a dose of one gram daily for 14 days. It is quite expensive and may not be available. The alternative, chloramphenicol, has been the mainstay of treatment for many years. In many countries it is still the recommended antibiotic but there are fewer side effects with Ampicillin. The adult dosage is two 250 mg capsules, four times a day. Children aged between eight and 12 years should have half the adult dose; younger children should have one-third the adult dose.

People who are allergic to penicillin should not be given Ampicillin.

Worms These parasites are most common in rural, tropical areas and a stool test when you return home is not a bad idea. They can be present on unwashed vegetables or in undercooked meat and you can pick them up through your skin by walking in bare feet. Infestations may not show up for some time, and although they are generally not serious, if left untreated they can cause severe health problems. A stool test is necessary to pinpoint the problem and medication is often available over the counter.

Tetanus This potentially fatal disease is found in undeveloped tropical areas. It is difficult to treat but is preventable with immunisation. Tetanus occurs when a wound becomes infected by a germ which lives in the faeces of animals or people, so clean all cuts, punctures or animal bites. Tetanus is also known as lockjaw, and the first symptom may be discomfort in swallowing, or stiffening of the jaw and neck; this is followed by painful convulsions of the jaw and whole body.

Rabies Rabies has been reported in Cambodia (and, in one case, in Phnom Penh). It is caused by a bite or scratch by an infected animal. Dogs are noted carriers as are monkeys and cats. Any bite, scratch or even lick from a warm-blooded, furry animal should be cleaned immediately and thoroughly. Scrub with soap and running water, and then clean with an alcohol solution. If there is any possibility that the animal is infected, medical help should be sought immediately. In a person who has not been immunised against rabies this involves having five injections of vaccine and one of immunoglobulin over 28 days starting as soon as possible after the exposure. Even if the animal is not rabid, all bites should be treated seriously as they can become infected or can result in tetanus.

A rabies vaccination is now available and should be considered if you are in a high-risk category – eg, if you intend to explore caves (bat bites could be dangerous) or work with animals.

Tuberculosis (TB) Although this disease is widespread in many developing countries, including Cambodia, it is not a serious risk to travellers. Young children are more susceptible than adults and vaccination is a sensible precaution for children under 12 travelling in endemic areas. TB is commonly spread by coughing or by unpasteurised dairy products from infected cows. Milk that has been boiled is safe to drink; the souring of milk to make yoghurt or cheese also kills the bacilli.

Bilharzia Bilharzia, or blood flukes, are minute waterborne worms. The larvae infect certain varieties of freshwater snails, found in rivers, streams, lakes and particularly behind dams. The worms multiply and are eventually discharged into the water surrounding the snails.

They attach themselves to your intestines or bladder, where they produce large numbers of eggs. The worm enters through the skin, and the first symptom may be a tingling and sometimes a light rash around the area where it entered. Weeks later, when the worm is busy producing eggs, a high fever may develop. A general feeling of being unwell may be the first symptom; once the disease is established abdominal pain and blood in the urine are other signs.

Avoiding swimming or bathing in fresh water where bilharzia are present is the main method of preventing the disease. Even deep water can be infected. If you do get wet, dry off quickly and dry your clothes as well. Seek medical attention if you have been exposed to the disease and tell the doctor your suspicions, as bilharziasis (also known as schistosomiasis) can be confused with malaria or typhoid in the early stages. If you cannot get medical help immediately, praziquantel (Biltricide) is the recommended treatment. The recommended dosage is 40 mg/kg of body weight in divided doses over one day. Niridazole is an alternative drug.

Diphtheria Diphtheria can be a skin infection or a more dangerous throat infection. It is spread by contaminated dust contacting the skin or by the inhalation of infected cough or sneeze droplets. Frequent washing and keeping the skin dry will help prevent skin infection. A vaccination is available to prevent the throat infection.

Sexually Transmitted Diseases Sexual contact with an infected partner spreads these diseases. While abstinence is the only 100% preventative, using condoms is also effective. Gonorrhoea and syphilis are the most common of these diseases; sores, blisters or rashes around the genitals, discharges or pain when urinating are common symptoms. Symptoms may be less marked or not observed at all in women. Syphilis symptoms eventually disappear completely but the disease continues and can cause severe problems in later years. The treatment of gonorrhoea and syphilis is by antibiotics.

There are numerous other sexually transmitted diseases, for most of which effective treatment is available. However, there is no cure for herpes and there is also currently no cure for AIDS.

HIV/AIDS HIV, the Human Immunodeficiency Virus, may develop into AIDS, Acquired Immune Deficiency Syndrome. HIV is a major problem in many countries, and is present in Cambodia's large population of prostitutes. Any exposure to blood, blood products or bodily fluids may put the individual at risk. In Cambodia and many other developing countries, transmission is predominantly through heterosexual sexual activity. This is quite different from industrialised countries, where transmission is mostly through contact between homosexual or bisexual males or contaminated needles in intravenous drug users. Apart from abstinence, the most effective preventative is always to practise safe sex using condoms. It is impossible to detect the HIV-positive status of an otherwise healthy-looking person without a blood test.

HIV/AIDS can also be spread through infected blood transfusions; most developing countries cannot afford to screen blood for transfusions. It can also be spread by dirty needles – vaccinations, acupuncture, tattooing and ear or nose piercing can potentially be as dangerous as intravenous drug use if the equipment is not clean. If you do need an injection, ask to see the syringe unwrapped in front of you, or better still, take a needle and syringe pack with you overseas – it is a cheap insurance package against infection.

Fear of HIV infection by injection should never preclude treatment for serious medical conditions. Although there may be a risk of infection, it is very small indeed.

Insect-Borne Diseases

Malaria This serious disease is spread by mosquito bites. If you are travelling in endemic areas it is extremely important to take malarial prophylactics. Symptoms include headaches, fever, chills and sweating which may subside and recur. Without treatment malaria can develop more serious, potentially fatal effects.

Malaria is very much present in Cambodia, though if your trip includes only Phnom Penh and Siem Reap, there is very little risk of contracting the disease. The high risk areas are the north-east of Cambodia (Ratanakiri, Mondulkiri, Kratie and Stung Treng), areas around Battambang and Pursat, and coastal areas such as Kampot and even Sihanoukville.

There are a number of different types of malaria. The one of greatest concern is *falciparum* malaria, and it is present in Cambodia. It is responsible for the very serious cerebral malaria, and can be fatal. Contrary to popular belief cerebral malaria is not a new strain.

The problem in recent years has been the emergence of increasing resistance to commonly used antimalarials like chloroquine, maloprim and proguanil. Newer drugs such as mefloquine (Lariam) and doxycycline (Vibramycin, Doryx) are often recommended for chloroquine and multidrug-resistant areas. Expert advice should be sought, as there are many factors to consider when deciding on the type of antimalarial medication, including the area to be visited, the risk of exposure to malaria-carrying mosquitoes, your current medical condition, and your age and pregnancy status.

It is also important to discuss the side-effect profile of the medication, so you can work out some level of risk-versus-benefit ratio. It is also very important to be sure of the correct dosage of the medication prescribed to you. Some people inadvertently have taken weekly medication (chloroquine) on a daily basis, with disastrous effects. While discussing dosages for prevention of malaria, it is often advisable to include the dosages required for treatment, especially if

your trip is through a high-risk area that would isolate you from medical care. The main messages are:

- Primary prevention must always be in the form of mosquito avoidance measures. The mosquitoes that transmit malaria bite from dusk to dawn, and during this period travellers are advised to:

  1) wear light-coloured clothing
  2) wear long pants and long-sleeved shirts
  3) use mosquito repellents containing the compound DEET on exposed areas
  4) avoid highly scented perfumes or aftershave
  5) use a mosquito net – it may be worth taking your own

- While no antimalarial is 100% effective, taking the most appropriate drug significantly reduces the risk of contracting the disease.

- No one should ever die from malaria. It can be diagnosed by a simple blood test. Symptoms range from fever, chills and sweating, headache and abdominal pains to a vague feeling of ill-health, so seek examination immediately if there is any suggestion of malaria.

Contrary to popular belief, once a traveller contracts malaria they do not have it for life. One of the parasites may lie dormant in the liver but this can also be eradicated using a specific medication. Malaria is curable, as long as the traveller seeks medical help when symptoms occur.

Dengue Fever There is no prophylactic available for this mosquito-spread disease; the main preventive measure is to avoid mosquito bites. A sudden onset of fever, headaches and severe joint and muscle pains are the first signs before a rash starts on the trunk of the body and spreads to the limbs and face. After a further few days, the fever will subside and recovery will begin. Full recovery can take up to a month or more. Serious complications are not common in adults, but small children suffering from a fever for more than 24 hours should be taken to a doctor.

Dengue is present in Cambodia and reaches its peak incidence in the rainy season, from July to October. Extra care to avoid being bitten by mosquitoes should be taken at this time of year.

Typhus Typhus is spread by ticks, mites or lice. It begins with fever, chills, headache and muscle pains followed a few days later by a body rash. There is often a large painful sore at the site of the bite and nearby lymph nodes are swollen and painful. Uncommon in travellers, typhus can be treated under medical supervision.

Tick typhus is spread by ticks. You should take precautions if walking in rural areas in Cambodia – this only applies in mine-free Ratanakiri. Seek local advice on areas where ticks pose a danger and always check your skin carefully for ticks after walking in a danger area, such as a tropical forest. A strong insect repellent can help, and serious walkers in tick areas should consider having their boots and trousers impregnated with benzyl benzoate and dibutylphthalate.

Cuts, Bites & Stings

Cuts & Scratches Skin punctures can easily become infected in hot climates and may be difficult to heal. Treat any cut with an antiseptic such as Betadine. Where possible avoid bandages and Band-aids, which can keep wounds wet. Coral cuts are notoriously slow to heal, as the coral injects a weak venom into the wound. Avoid coral cuts by wearing shoes when walking on reefs, and clean any cut thoroughly with sodium peroxide if available.

Bites & Stings Bee and wasp stings are usually painful rather than dangerous. Calamine lotion will give relief and ice packs will reduce the pain and swelling. There are some spiders with dangerous bites but antivenins are usually available. Scorpion stings are notoriously painful, but are generally not fatal. Scorpions often shelter in shoes or clothing.

Snakes To minimise your chances of being bitten always wear boots, socks and long trousers when walking through undergrowth where snakes may be present. Don't put your hands into holes and crevices, and be careful when collecting firewood.

Snake bites do not cause instantaneous death and antivenins are usually available, though in remote Ratanakiri getting hold of them will almost certainly require getting back to Phnom Penh.

Keep the victim calm and still, wrap the bitten limb tightly, as you would for a sprained ankle, and then attach a splint to immobilise it. Then seek medical help, if possible with the dead snake for identification. Don't attempt to catch the snake if there is even a remote possibility of being bitten again. Tourniquets and sucking out the poison are now comprehensively discredited.

Jellyfish Taking local advice is the best way of avoiding contact with these sea creatures and their stinging tentacles. Stings from most jellyfish are painful but not often fatal. Dousing in vinegar will de-activate any stingers which have not 'fired'. Calamine lotion, antihistamines and analgesics may reduce the reaction and relieve the pain.

Bedbugs & Lice Bedbugs live in various places, but particularly in dirty mattresses and bedding. Spots of blood on bedclothes or on the wall around the bed can be read as a suggestion to find another hotel. Bedbugs leave itchy bites in neat rows. Calamine lotion may help.

All lice cause itching and discomfort. They make themselves at home in your hair (head lice), your clothing (body lice) or in your pubic hair (crabs). You catch lice through direct contact with infected people or by sharing combs, clothing and the like. Powder or shampoo treatment will kill the lice and infected clothing should then be washed in very hot water.

Leeches & Ticks Leeches may be present in damp rainforest conditions; they attach themselves to your skin to suck your blood. Trekkers often get them on their legs or in their boots. Salt or a lighted cigarette end will make them fall off. Do not pull them off, as the bite is then more likely to become infected. An insect repellent may keep them away.

If a tick is found attached, press down around the tick's head with tweezers, grab the head and gently pull upwards. Avoid pulling the rear of the body. Vaseline, alcohol or oil will persuade a tick to let go. You should always check your body if you have been walking through a tick-infested area, as they can spread typhus.

Women's Health
Gynaecological Problems Poor diet, lowered resistance due to the use of antibiotics for stomach upsets and even contraceptive pills can lead to vaginal infections when travelling in hot climates. Keeping the genital area clean, and wearing skirts or loose-fitting trousers and cotton underwear will help to prevent infections.

Yeast infections, characterised by a rash, itch and discharge, can be treated with a vinegar or even lemon-juice douche or with yoghurt. Nystatin suppositories are the usual medical prescription. Trichomonas is a more serious infection; symptoms are a discharge and a burning sensation when urinating. Male sexual partners must also be treated, and if a vinegar-water douche is not effective medical attention should be sought. Metronidazole (Flagyl) is the prescribed drug.

Pregnancy Most miscarriages occur during the first three months of pregnancy, so this is the most risky time to travel as far as your own health is concerned. Miscarriage is not uncommon, and can occasionally lead to severe bleeding. The last three months should also be spent within reasonable distance of good medical care. A baby born as early as 24 weeks stands a chance of survival, but only in a good modern hospital. Pregnant women should avoid all unnecessary medication, however vaccinations and malarial prophylactics should still be taken where possible. Additional care should be taken to prevent illness and particular attention should be paid to diet and nutrition. Drugs such as alcohol and nicotine, for example, should be avoided.

Women travellers often find that their periods become irregular or even cease while they're on the road. Remember that a missed period in these circumstances doesn't necessarily indicate pregnancy.

Traditional Medicine
Traditional medicine is widely practised in Cambodia, in part because western medical care is largely unavailable (the Khmer Rouge killed almost all of the country's doctors who did not flee abroad). Some traditional treatments (eg the use of some herbs) appear to work, but others, such as that based on the belief that paraplegics can be cured by suspending them over a fire, produce catastrophic results.

The vertical red marks often visible on the necks and torsos of both male and female Cambodians are made by rubbing the skin very hard with coins. This treatment is supposed to dilate the blood vessels and is said to be good for anyone feeling weak or ill.

Headaches are treated by applying suction cups to the forehead and face. These have the same effect on blood circulation as leeches – namely, to draw blood to the point of suction.

Index

MAPS

TEXT

Map references are in **bold** type.

LONELY PLANET JOURNEYS

JOURNEYS is a unique collection of travellers' tales – published by the company that understands travel better than anyone else. It is a series for anyone who has ever experienced – or dreamed of – the magical moment when they encountered a strange culture or saw a place for the first time. They are tales to read while you're planning a trip, while you're on the road or while you're in an armchair, in front of a fire.

JOURNEYS books will catch the spirit of a place, illuminate a culture, recount a crazy adventure, or introduce a fascinating way of life. They will always entertain, and always enrich the experience of travel.

FULL CIRCLE
A South American Journey
Luis Sepúlveda
Translated by Chris Andrews

Full Circle invites us to accompany Chilean writer Luis Sepúlveda on 'a journey without a fixed itinerary'. Extravagant characters and extraordinary situations are memorably evoked: gauchos organising a tournament of lies, a scheming heiress on the lookout for a husband, a pilot with a corpse on board his plane . . . Part autobiography, part travel memoir, *Full Circle* brings us the distinctive voice of one of South America's most compelling writers.

THE GATES OF DAMASCUS
Lieve Joris
Translated by Sam Garrett

This best-selling book is a beautifully drawn portrait of day-to-day life in modern Syria. Through her intimate contact with local people, Lieve Joris draws us into the fascinating world that lies behind the gates of Damascus.

ISLANDS IN THE CLOUDS
Travels in the Highlands of New Guinea
Isabella Tree

This is the fascinating account of a journey to the remote and beautiful Highlands of Papua New Guinea and Irian Jaya. The author travels with a PNG Highlander who introduces her to his intriguing and complex world. *Islands in the Clouds* is a thoughtful, moving book, full of insights into a region that is rarely noticed by the rest of the world.

LOST JAPAN
Alex Kerr

Lost Japan draws on the author's personal experiences of Japan over a period of 30 years. Alex Kerr takes his readers on a backstage tour: friendships with Kabuki actors, buying and selling art, studying calligraphy, exploring rarely visited temples and shrines . . . The Japanese edition of this book was awarded the 1994 Shincho Gakugei Literature Prize for the best work of non-fiction.

SEAN & DAVID'S LONG DRIVE
Sean Condon

Sean and David are young townies who have rarely strayed beyond city limits. One day, for no good reason, they set out to discover their homeland, and what follows is a wildly entertaining adventure that covers half of Australia. Sean Condon has written a hilarious, offbeat road book that mixes sharp insights with deadpan humour and outright lies.

SHOPPING FOR BUDDHAS
Jeff Greenwald

Shopping for Buddhas is Jeff Greenwald's story of his obsessive search for the perfect Buddha statue. In the backstreets of Kathmandu, he discovers more than he bargained for . . . and his souvenir-hunting turns into an ironic metaphor for the clash between spiritual riches and material greed. Politics, religion and serious shopping collide in this witty account of an enlightening visit to Nepal.

LONELY PLANET TRAVEL ATLASES

Lonely Planet has long been famous for the number and quality of its guidebook maps. Now we've gone one step further and in conjunction with Steinhart Katzir Publishers produced a handy companion series: Lonely Planet travel atlases – maps of a country produced in book form.

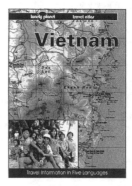

Unlike other maps, which look good but lead travellers astray, our travel atlases have been researched on the road by Lonely Planet's experienced team of writers. All details are carefully checked to ensure the atlas corresponds with the equivalent Lonely Planet guidebook.

The handy atlas format means no holes, wrinkles, torn sections or constant folding and unfolding. These atlases can survive long periods on the road, unlike cumbersome fold-out maps. The comprehensive index ensures easy reference.

- full-colour throughout
- maps researched and checked by Lonely Planet authors
- place names correspond with Lonely Planet guidebooks
  – no confusing spelling differences
- legend and travelling information in English, French, German, Japanese and Spanish
- size: 230 x 160 mm

Available now:
Chile; Egypt; India & Bangladesh; Israel & the Palestinian Territories;
Jordan, Syria & Lebanon; Laos; Thailand; Vietnam; Zimbabwe, Botswana & Namibia

---

LONELY PLANET TV SERIES & VIDEOS

Lonely Planet travel guides have been brought to life on television screens around the world. Like our guides, the programmes are based on the joy of independent travel, and look honestly at some of the most exciting, picturesque and frustrating places in the world. Each show is presented by one of three travellers from Australia, England or the USA and combines an innovative mixture of video, Super-8 film, atmospheric soundscapes and original music.

Videos of each episode – containing additional footage not shown on television – are available from good book and video shops, but the availability of individual videos varies with regional screening schedules.

Video destinations include: Alaska; Australia (Southeast); Brazil; Ecuador & the Galápagos Islands; Indonesia; Israel & the Sinai Desert; Japan; La Ruta Maya (Yucatán, Guatemala & Belize); Morocco; North India (Varanasi to the Himalaya); Pacific Islands; Vietnam; Zimbabwe, Botswana & Namibia.

Coming soon: The Arctic (Norway & Finland); Baja California; Chile & Easter Island; China (Southeast); Costa Rica; East Africa (Tanzania & Zanzibar); Great Barrier Reef (Australia); Jamaica; Papua New Guinea; the Rockies (USA); Syria & Jordan; Turkey.

The Lonely Planet TV series is produced by:
Pilot Productions
Duke of Sussex Studios
44 Uxbridge St
London W8 7TG UK

Lonely Planet videos are distributed by:
IVN Communications Inc
2246 Camino Ramon
California 94583, USA

107 Power Road, Chiswick
London W4 5PL UK

Music from the TV series is available on CD & cassette.
For ordering information contact your nearest Lonely Planet office.

PLANET TALK

Lonely Planet's FREE quarterly newsletter

We love hearing from you and think you'd like to hear from us.

When...is the right time to see reindeer in Finland?
Where...can you hear the best palm-wine music in Ghana?
How...do you get from Asunción to Areguá by steam train?
What...is the best way to see India?

For the answer to these and many other questions read PLANET TALK.

Every issue is packed with up-to-date travel news and advice including:

* a letter from Lonely Planet co-founders Tony and Maureen Wheeler
* go behind the scenes on the road with a Lonely Planet author
* feature article on an important and topical travel issue
* a selection of recent letters from travellers
* details on forthcoming Lonely Planet promotions
* complete list of Lonely Planet products

To join our mailing list contact any Lonely Planet office.

Also available: Lonely Planet T-shirts. 100% heavyweight cotton.

LONELY PLANET ONLINE

Get the latest travel information before you leave or while you're on the road

Whether you've just begun planning your next trip, or you're chasing down specific info on currency regulations or visa requirements, check out the Lonely Planet World Wide Web site for up-to-the-minute travel information.

As well as travel profiles of your favourite destinations (including interactive maps and full-colour photos), you'll find current reports from our army of researchers and other travellers, updates on health and visas, travel advisories, and the ecological and political issues you need to be aware of as you travel.

There's an online travellers' forum (the Thorn Tree) where you can share your experiences of life on the road, meet travel companions and ask other travellers for their recommendations and advice. We also have plenty of links to other Web sites useful to independent travellers.

With tens of thousands of visitors a month, the Lonely Planet Web site is one of the most popular on the Internet and has won a number of awards including GNN's Best of the Net travel award.

http://www.lonelyplanet.com

LONELY PLANET PRODUCTS

Lonely Planet is known worldwide for publishing practical, reliable and no-nonsense travel information in our guides and on our web site. The Lonely Planet list covers just about every accessible part of the world. Currently there are eight series: *travel guides*, *shoestring guides*, *walking guides*, *city guides*, *phrasebooks*, *audio packs*, *travel atlases* and *Journeys* – a unique collection of travellers' tales.

EUROPE

Austria • Baltic States & Kaliningrad • Baltic States phrasebook • Britain • Central Europe on a shoestring • Central Europe phrasebook • Czech & Slovak Republics • Denmark • Dublin city guide • Eastern Europe on a shoestring • Eastern Europe phrasebook • Finland • France • Greece • Greek phrasebook • Hungary • Iceland, Greenland & the Faroe Islands • Ireland • Italy • Mediterranean Europe on a shoestring • Mediterranean Europe phrasebook • Paris city guide • Poland • Prague city guide • Russia, Ukraine & Belarus • Russian phrasebook • Scandinavian & Baltic Europe on a shoestring • Scandinavian Europe phrasebook • Slovenia • St Petersburg city guide • Switzerland • Trekking in Greece • Trekking in Spain • Ukrainian phrasebook • Vienna city guide • Walking in Switzerland • Western Europe on a shoestring • Western Europe phrasebook

NORTH AMERICA

Alaska • Backpacking in Alaska • Baja California• California & Nevada • Canada • Hawaii • Honolulu city guide • Los Angeles city guide • Mexico • Miami city guide • New England • Pacific Northwest USA • Rocky Mountain States • San Francisco city guide • Southwest USA • USA phrasebook

CENTRAL AMERICA & THE CARIBBEAN

Central America on a shoestring • Costa Rica • Eastern Caribbean • Guatemala, Belize & Yucatán: La Ruta Maya • Jamaica

SOUTH AMERICA

Argentina, Uruguay & Paraguay • Bolivia • Brazil • Brazilian phrasebook • Buenos Aires city guide • Chile & Easter Island • Chile travel atlas• Colombia • Ecuador & the Galápagos Islands • Latin American Spanish phrasebook • Peru • Quechua phrasebook • Rio de Janeiro city guide • South America on a shoestring • Trekking in the Patagonian Andes • Venezuela

Travel Literature: Full Circle: A South American Journey

ANTARCTICA

Antarctica

ISLANDS OF THE INDIAN OCEAN

Madagascar & Comoros • Maldives & Islands of the East Indian Ocean • Mauritius, Réunion & Seychelles

AFRICA

Arabic (Moroccan) phrasebook • Africa on a shoestring • Cape Town city guide • Central Africa • East Africa • Egypt• Egypt travel atlas• Ethiopian (Amharic) phrasebook • Kenya • Morocco • North Africa • South Africa, Lesotho & Swaziland • Swahili phrasebook • Trekking in East Africa • West Africa • Zimbabwe, Botswana & Namibia • Zimbabwe, Botswana & Namibia travel atlas

MAIL ORDER

Lonely Planet products are distributed worldwide.They are also available by mail order from Lonely Planet, so if you have difficulty finding a title please write to us. North American and South American residents should write to Embarcadero West, 155 Filbert St, Suite 251, Oakland CA 94607, USA; European and African residents should write to 10 Barley Mow Passage, Chiswick, London W4 4PH; and residents of other countries to PO Box 617, Hawthorn, Victoria 3122, Australia.

NORTH-EAST ASIA

Beijing city guide • Cantonese phrasebook • China • Hong Kong, Macau & Canton • Hong Kong city guide • Japan • Japanese phrasebook • Japanese audio pack • Korea • Korean phrasebook • Mandarin phrasebook • Mongolia • Mongolian phrasebook • North-East Asia on a shoestring • Seoul city guide • Taiwan • Tibet • Tibet phrasebook • Tokyo city guide

Travel Literature: Lost Japan

MIDDLE EAST & CENTRAL ASIA

Arab Gulf States • Arabic (Egyptian) phrasebook • Central Asia • Iran • Israel & the Palestinian Territories • Israel & the Palestinian Territories travel atlas • Jordan & Syria • Jordan, Syria & Lebanon travel atlas • Middle East • Turkey • Turkish phrasebook • Trekking in Turkey • Yemen

Travel Literature: The Gates of Damascus

ALSO AVAILABLE:

Travel with Children • Traveller's Tales

INDIAN SUBCONTINENT

Bangladesh• Bengali phrasebook• Delhi city guide • Hindi/Urdu phrasebook • India • India & Bangladesh travel atlas • Indian Himalaya • Karakoram Highway • Nepal • Nepali phrasebook • Pakistan • Sri Lanka • Sri Lanka phrasebook • Trekking in the Indian Himalaya • Trekking in the Karakoram & Hindukush • Trekking in the Nepal Himalaya

Travel Literature: Shopping for Buddhas

SOUTH-EAST ASIA

Bali & Lombok • Bangkok city guide • Burmese phrasebook • Cambodia • Ho Chi Minh city guide • Indonesia • Indonesian phrasebook • Indonesian audio pack • Jakarta city guide • Java • Laos • Lao phrasebook • Laos travel atlas • Malay phrasebook • Malaysia, Singapore & Brunei • Myanmar (Burma) • Philippines • Pilipino phrasebook • Singapore city guide • South-East Asia on a shoestring • Thailand • Thailand travel atlas • Thai phrasebook • Thai audio pack • Thai Hill Tribes phrasebook • Vietnam • Vietnamese phrasebook • Vietnam travel atlas

AUSTRALIA & THE PACIFIC

Australia • Australian phrasebook • Bushwalking in Australia• Bushwalking in Papua New Guinea • Fiji • Fijian phrasebook • Islands of Australia's Great Barrier Reef • Melbourne city guide • Micronesia • New Caledonia • New South Wales & the ACT • New Zealand • Northern Territory • Outback Australia • Papua New Guinea • Papua New Guinea phrasebook • Queensland • Rarotonga & the Cook Islands • Samoa • Solomon Islands • South Australia • Sydney city guide • Tahiti & French Polynesia • Tasmania • Tonga • Tramping in New Zealand • Vanuatu • Victoria • Western Australia

Travel Literature: Islands in the Clouds • Sean & David's Long Drive

THE LONELY PLANET STORY

Lonely Planet published its first book in 1973 in response to the numerous 'How did you do it?' questions Maureen and Tony Wheeler were asked after driving, bussing, hitching, sailing and railing their way from England to Australia.

Written at a kitchen table and hand collated, trimmed and stapled, *Across Asia on the Cheap* became an instant local bestseller, inspiring thoughts of another book.

Eighteen months in South-East Asia resulted in their second guide, *South-East Asia on a shoestring*, which they put together in a backstreet Chinese hotel in Singapore in 1975. The 'yellow bible', as it quickly became known to backpackers around the world, soon became *the* guide to the region. It has sold well over half a million copies and is now in its 8th edition, still retaining its familiar yellow cover.

Today there are over 180 titles, including travel guides, walking guides, language kits & phrasebooks, travel atlases and travel literature. The company is one of the largest travel publishers in the world. Although Lonely Planet initially specialised in guides to Asia, we now cover most regions of the world, including the Pacific, North America, South America, Africa, the Middle East and Europe.

The emphasis continues to be on travel for independent travellers. Tony and Maureen still travel for several months of each year and play an active part in the writing, updating and quality control of Lonely Planet's guides.

They have been joined by over 70 authors and 170 staff at our offices in Melbourne (Australia), Oakland (USA), London (UK) and Paris (France). Travellers themselves also make a valuable contribution to the guides through the feedback we receive in thousands of letters each year.

The people at Lonely Planet strongly believe that travellers can make a positive contribution to the countries they visit, both through their appreciation of the countries' culture, wildlife and natural features, and through the money they spend. In addition, the company makes a direct contribution to the countries and regions it covers. Since 1986 a percentage of the income from each book has been donated to ventures such as famine relief in Africa; aid projects in India; agricultural projects in Central America; Greenpeace's efforts to halt French nuclear testing in the Pacific; and Amnesty International.

'I hope we send the people out with the right attitude about travel. You realise when you travel that there are so many different perspectives about the world, so we hope these books will make people more interested in what they see. These are guidebooks, but you can't really guide people. All you can do is point them in the right direction.'
– **Tony Wheeler**

LONELY PLANET PUBLICATIONS

Australia
PO Box 617, Hawthorn 3122, Victoria
tel: (03) 9819 1877 fax: (03) 9819 6459
e-mail: talk2us@lonelyplanet.com.au

USA
Embarcadero West, 155 Filbert St, Suite 251,
Oakland, CA 94607
tel: (510) 893 8555 TOLL FREE: 800 275-8555
fax: (510) 893 8563
e-mail: info@lonelyplanet.com

UK
10 Barley Mow Passage, Chiswick,
London W4 4PH
tel: (0181) 742 3161 fax: (0181) 742 2772
e-mail: 100413.3551@compuserve.com

France:
71 bis rue du Cardinal Lemoine, 75005 Paris
tel: 1 44 32 06 20 fax: 1 46 34 72 55
e-mail: 100560.415@compuserve.com

World Wide Web: http://www.lonelyplanet.com